Ireland in International Affairs
Interests, Institutions and Identities

Ireland in International Affairs
Interests, Institutions and Identities

Essays in honour of
Professor N.P. Keatinge FTCD, MRIA

Editors
Ben Tonra
Eilís Ward

INSTITUTE OF PUBLIC
ADMINISTRATION

First published in 2002
by the Institute of Public Administration
57-61 Lansdowne Road
Dublin 4
Ireland

www.ipa.ie

British Library Cataloguing in Publication Data
A catalogue record for this book is available from the British Library

ISBN 1 902448 76 6

Cover design by Butler Claffey Design, Dun Laoghaire
Typeset by the Institute of Public Administration
Printed by Betaprint, Dublin

Contents

Foreword

Ronald J. Hill

It gives me exceptional pleasure to introduce this volume of essays dedicated to my former colleague, Patrick Keatinge, whom I first met in 1969 when I joined the staff of Trinity College's Political Science Department. By then, Patrick was well in place, and he quickly dropped the teaching of French politics in order to pursue an interest that allowed him to make a highly original contribution both to scholarship and to Ireland's understanding of itself and its place in the world.

Patrick graduated from Trinity in 1960 and went to do a Master's in international relations at the London School of Economics, returning to TCD as a junior lecturer in 1963. His Trinity doctoral thesis became the basis of his first book, *The Formulation of Irish Foreign Policy,* published in 1973. His second book, *A Place Among the Nations: Issues of Irish Foreign Policy* (1978), was the first study of Ireland's growing international stature by a scholar with a political scientist's training.

At this remove, it is perhaps difficult to remember how tentative Ireland's approach to international relations was. Despite the nation's long history of missionary work overseas, its countless sons and daughters who had formed core elements of other nations in North America, Australia and elsewhere, its distinguished engagement with the United Nations, its contributions to all the UN peacekeeping missions, to a 'blow-in' in the late 1960s the country still appeared to be absorbed with looking inward for its identity, and to view the world through the prism of its relationship with the nearest neighbour.

That relationship remains perhaps the most important of Ireland's bilateral relations, largely but not solely because of the continuing significance of the 'northern' question; but it has been to a significant extent displaced by the forthright and confident way in which the Irish nation has grasped the opportunities offered by involvement in Europe. Just compare the number of foreign embassies in Dublin and Irish embassies abroad today with the picture thirty years ago!

Through his writings, his teaching and his close involvement with the Institute of European Affairs, Patrick Keatinge chronicled this emergence from the shadow of Great Britain, analysing and helping Irish people to understand the changes that were taking place and how they were affected by the change, and similarly helping the rest of the world to appreciate the changes taking place in this country.

European security, in which Ireland's military neutrality has come to be regarded as part of the country's identity, was the topic of Patrick's book, *A Singular Stance: Irish Neutrality in the 1980s*, published in 1984. With this volume, and other explorations of the theme, Patrick became a well-known expert on the European neutrals, and was in much demand to contribute to conferencnes and symposia here and abroad.

The value of Patrick's contribution to these important debates is indicated by the range of contributors to this collection of essays: not only former colleagues and students, but individuals who have themselves played an important part in the development of Ireland's role in the modern world. Patrick Keatinge's understanding of the international dimension of the past half-century of nation-building is unrivalled – and, indeed, his retirement from TCD in 1999 left a gap that could not be filled by a single individual. His dry humour is also much missed in the corridors and classrooms of College Green.

Outside College, he had an association with the Institute of European Affairs from the very beginning, and spent several fruitful years on secondment to that institution. He was from the start also active on the National Committee for the Study of International Affairs, established under the auspices of the Royal Irish Academy and seen as the forerunner of a fully-fledged Irish Institute of International Affairs when mooted by Foreign Minister Garret FitzGerald at the launching of Patrick's first book in 1973. Alas, a properly resourced institute has not come into being, but the National Committee has provided a valuable forum for the discussion of Ireland and world affairs, and Patrick's regular contributions to its annual journal, *Irish Studies in International Relations*, chronicled developments year by year.

This collection of essays is dedicated to an industrious and conscientious scholar, whose academic achievements established his reputation far beyond these shores. Ireland today is widely admired internationally, and it can truly be said to punch well beyond its weight in international affairs. These essays pay due tribute to a scholar who has done much to explain how and why that has become possible, and they deserve to be widely read.

Introduction

Ben Tonra and Eilís Ward

The purpose of this text is threefold; first it is to honour the contribution of an academic who, more than any other, established the discipline of international relations in Irish academia. Second, it is to make a substantive contribution to the ongoing debate about Ireland's place in the world and the relationships that derive therefrom. Third and finally, it is to celebrate the study of international relations in Ireland and to make the case that the limited profile of international relations and Irish foreign policy in Irish universities substantially weakens our capacity to think strategically about Ireland in the world.

We came to this project with the ambition of honouring Patrick Keatinge's contribution to his field of study but doing so in a way that would go beyond a simple celebration. Patrick's method of teaching and supervision was one that privileged exploration over discovery. He is also a pragmatist and was always ready to pounce gently on unwary graduate students if their theoretical ambitions overwhelmed their factual underpinnings. To that end, this text is an effort to marry the theoretical with the empirical, the academic insight with practical experience and the social sciences with the humanities. We have invited our contributors with those goals in mind – and they comprise an eclectic mix of academics, writers, journalists and foreign policy practitioners.

There was no common rubric applied to the project – no conscious effort to impose an overarching theme or leitmotif. Instead, contributors were asked to reflect on their proposed subject matter and to pay special attention to those issues that might have a special resonance with Patrick Keatinge in mind.

We hope that you will agree that this volume is a worthy testament to a researcher, teacher, colleague, friend and generous mentor who has chosen to hang up his theoretical compass, pack away his conference overnight bag and leave his telephone off the hook.

Patrick Keatinge: charting the unexplored realms of Irish foreign policy

Patrick Keatinge was the pioneer of the study of international relations in Ireland and one of the earliest explorers of Irish foreign policy. As the first to map Irish foreign policy it was he who guided at least two generations of academics through the shoals, reefs and rip-tides of international relations and their application to the study of Ireland's relationship(s) with the rest of the world. This was achieved in the teeth of not little difficulty because he had to compile his own archives of Irish foreign policy documents and press reports, to search out even the most basic relevant statistical data and, with wit and self-deprecating humour, to engage senior foreign policy officials in a dialogue on the tools, purpose and structures of Irish foreign policy.

Apart from his immensely popular undergraduate lectures on Irish foreign policy, Patrick was also to be found behind almost every initiative designed to broaden and deepen our understanding of Irish foreign policy. He engaged directly with policy makers through his lectures at the Department of Foreign Affairs and at the Curragh Camp. He was an early supporter and contributor to proposals for an Irish institute on international affairs and later to the Royal Irish Academy's National Committee for the Study of International Affairs. He was also centrally involved in the creation of the Institute for European Affairs (IEA). Moreover, whether destined for a newspaper, a think-tank report or an academic press, his written work was always accessible to a broad audience of readers.

While never a theoretician, he always demanded that his students engage with the latest academic thinking. In that context he was an invaluable – if often somewhat sceptical – guide to the sometimes self-conscious ebbs and flows of international relations theory. His own overall approach might best be described as being rooted in a liberal (with a small 'l') tradition of international relations scholarship with its focus on internationalism, on the construction and significance of inter-state institutions, on the domestic roots of foreign policy and on the importance of history to an understanding of states and their international role.

In doing all of the above Patrick essentially framed the landscape for the study of international relations and foreign policy studies in Ireland. This he did at a time when there was little enough interest in things international in Ireland, not to mention a lack of international interest in things Irish.

It is every academic's ambition to stake out an uncharted territory and, much as Victorian explorers and scientists did with the natural world, name it and frame how it is viewed by generations to come. Done badly or done well, this first mapping sets the tone of enquiry thereafter. Fortunately for those of us who have come since Patrick first began his work, we can be thankful for a thorough, analytically lively and intellectually incisive inheritance. It is both a testament to him and a criticism of the academic community in Ireland that his established framework has to date never been seriously challenged. The liberal assumptions and world-view established within his first work – *The Formulation of Irish Foreign Policy* – remain the benchmark for scholarship in the field. There has not been any comprehensive attempt by more recent scholars to update this detailed account to reflect new empirical realities in terms of government structures and new policy challenges. While others have challenged Keatinge's approach or substantive conclusions on aspects of Irish foreign policy (for instance, Sharp, 1990; Salmon, 1989) none has offered a cartographical projection to challenge that established by Keatinge in the early 1970s. In the main, scholarship has chosen to focus on different aspects of Irish foreign policy such as the historical excavation of its development, Ireland's relationship with the developing world, neutrality, and Ireland's relationship with Europe.

Patrick's own intellectual journey – as defined by his publications record – is one that faithfully reflects the central academic interests in Irish foreign policy over the last thirty years. His earliest contributions applied liberal and comparative methods towards analysing an Irish case study as an example of a small West European polity (Keatinge, 1973 and 1978). These two texts established him as the central Irish foreign policy expert. Thereafter, his focus shifted somewhat to the twin interests of Irish neutrality and Europe. Here his enquiries centred upon Irish peculiarities as the only 'neutral' in the European Communities and as a neutral firmly identified with the 'West' throughout the Cold War period. His central work on Irish neutrality came in the early 1980s at the time of a vigorous and somewhat vituperative domestic debate (Keatinge, 1984).

On Europe his interests mirrored the development of an emerging research community on Irish membership of the European Communities. His work in this regard sought to explicate Europe to a domestic audience – especially through his early association with the Dublin-based Institute of European Affairs – and also to raise awareness among European scholars of the Irish case study in so far as it reinforced and/or challenged our understanding of small states in Europe.

As foreign and security policy developed as a distinct policy area of the European Union, his focus moved from Ireland and Europe in general terms (Keatinge, 1991) to the study of Irish and European security issues and the ways in which Ireland's unique foreign and security policy might relate to the development of the European Union's emerging security and defence policy (Keatinge, 1996). In this work his aim might be said to have been to identify both synergies and contradictions between the conduct and goals of Irish foreign policy and those of an emerging EU policy. Patrick never saw himself as an advocate or an evangelist but he was always impatient with those he saw deliberately manipulating or falsifying facts in order to buttress their arguments.

Patrick's academic trajectory, from the detailed particularities of Irish foreign policy to the generalities of Ireland in and as part of Europe, reflects a broader shift in academic perspective towards Irish foreign policy. No self-respecting course entitled 'Irish Foreign Policy' could today but foreground the European context within which an 'Irish' foreign policy is formulated. This reflects the overarching influence that EU membership has had on Ireland as an international actor. In turn this relationship prompts the question: does something called 'Irish' foreign policy still exist?

How much of the foreign policy that this state engages in has derived from within an exclusively sovereign framework of policy making and execution? The international environment is certainly characterised by interdependence and collaboration for even the largest and most powerful of states. But Ireland's small size and limited capacity render it particularly sensitive as an international actor. While it is certainly not the case that the requirements of collaborative foreign policy making within the EU (through the Common Foreign and Security Policy of the Union) wholly defines the substance of Irish foreign policy, it is the case that much of 'Irish' foreign policy is fed through the complex policy machinery that is 'Brussels'. Through the treaties, Irish governments have undertaken not to undermine or weaken agreed policies emerging from the CFSP. While British-Irish and US-Irish relations may be seen as *domains reserveés* in national policy making and while Irish development aid has a high and distinctive national profile, the European context to foreign policy making is significant. Indeed, so significant is it that it has led some even to suggest the 'Europeanisation' of Irish foreign policy (Tonra, 2001).

It is therefore perhaps a live issue as to whether or not there is any analytical utility in studying 'Irish' foreign policy – is it something that can be usefully studied on its own terms and outside the context of an emerging EU foreign, security and defence policy? Moreover, in view of some radical analyses of globalisation and its impact upon the national foreign policies of states – especially smaller states – are there other reasons to call Irish foreign policy into question?

Desperately seeking an Irish foreign policy?

There are substantial reasons to explore the idea of a distinctly 'Irish' foreign policy. Below we set out three substantial reasons for conducting a search in the first place.

The first issue is that, while in comparative historical terms there has not been a lot of 'Irish' foreign policy to look at, the Irish experience adds to our understanding of small state foreign policy development. Irish independence in 1921, for example, was an equivocal and contested event with the state's capacity to issue its own passports and to conduct its own bilateral relations outside of the British Empire qualified for more than a decade. Ireland's constitutional development in this period is significant both for what it meant to the creation of the British Commonwealth and the example that it offered to other British colonies and dependant territories. Moreover, it would be wrong in principle to associate foreign policy quantity with quality. The comparative inexperience of Irish policy makers did not forestall their contribution to international politics especially, for example, during the inter-war years within the context of the League of Nations. The choices made by representatives of the

Irish state and their accompanying moves on the international stage offer further case study material to the study of small state foreign policy and the significance of international organisations.

Second, explanations must be offered for the state's failure to promote its international interests and to develop a broader field of bilateral relations. It might seem incredible in the twenty-first century but it is the case that even the establishment of a Department of External Relations was initially contested. The Department of Finance initially proposed that no such department of state was necessary and that any functions arising from the necessity of dealing with external matters might most effectively and parsimoniously be expedited by a few officials attached to the prime minister's office. Moreover, even once the department was established there was a conservative and limited vision of its role, function and organisation. Ireland's diplomatic infrastructure – in terms of personnel, in terms of resources and in terms of overseas representation – was, and remains today, a fraction of the size of that of similarly sized states elsewhere in Europe.

The paucity of official attention to international affairs was, at least in the early years of the state's independence, only very partially compensated for by the calibre and dedication of the handful of individuals that devoted their careers to the representation of the state's interests overseas. For the most part these were men – and they were almost always men – of vision and ability. They engaged with the great issues of the day such as reform of the British Empire, the life and death throes of the League of Nations, disarmament, the rule of international law, post-war European reconstruction, human rights, the United Nations, the Cold War, international justice, on a par with their colleagues from other foreign ministries. They did so without a substantial domestic constituency and very often without specific or substantive instructions from home. Much of the literature established by a small group of specialised Irish diplomatic historians represents 'Irish' foreign policy as being the work of a few men who operated out of a base largely untouched by domestic debates and input, creating an analysis that framed national policy within an extremely narrow, elite perspective. To what extent, then, can we truly say that these individuals, some holding high elected office but most appointed to their diplomatic positions, represented 'Irishness', 'Irish interests' or even 'Ireland'?

The third issue, which arises neatly as a corollary to the previous one, is the fact of domestic disinterest in foreign policy. It is something of a truism that in modern democracies domestic public attention is only rarely engaged in the discussion of high politics and diplomacy. In most states, however, there is an identifiable strata of informed opinion-makers in the universities, the trade unions, the political parties, in business, in voluntary organisations, among artists and writers, philosophers and journalists who keep themselves abreast of international events and to whom, in times of crisis or sudden challenge, the general mass of opinion turns for explanation and alternative analyses. It can persuasively be argued that in Ireland that strata has been exceptionally narrow, weakly constituted and, as a consequence, incapable of generating or sustaining long-standing strategic debates about Ireland's place in the world and its responsibilities therein. Moreover, while public debate has certainly intensified and deepened in recent years, public opinion and indeed Irish elites continue to treat foreign policy issues in a largely superficial manner. This is not the case on issues of aid and international development[1], and, more recently, on human rights policy[2] – in these policy areas a serious and structured dialogue has been created between the formal policy-making apparatus of the state and what has come to be termed civil society. It is perhaps no coincidence that a reputation for human rights protection and support for the developing world have both contributed significantly to Ireland's image abroad.

While the general lacuna may not be unique to Ireland it is further noteworthy in so far as even parliament has struggled to organise itself into a semi-coherent forum for foreign policy debate. Foreign policy traditionally has been deemed the preserve of the Executive, comprising both cabinet government and the civil service elite. The struggle within the Irish parliament to establish the Joint Oireachtas Committee on Foreign Affairs and the decision to stop publishing its proceedings are but two examples of the ongoing internal resistance to opening up debate on the detail and processing of foreign policy.

Given this tradition of corralling off the foreign policy process, it is perhaps no surprise that the public's engagement with Irish foreign policy, in all its dimensions, has been limited. There are signs, however, that this is changing. The national debate held prior to the publication of the White Paper on Foreign Policy, and the fact of the paper's publication in itself, were two indications of an opening, even if limited, of 'high' politics to greater public access. The debate on the Nice Treaty can also be seen as a sign of the strength of opinion-formers outside the formal state framework.

To the extent that the arguments about domestic disinterest contain any truth, some responsibility rests upon the shoulders of the academic community for not having done more to promote and to foster a substantial, robust and informed discussion of international affairs. It cannot, for example, be left to the policy practitioners to generate that substantive discussion. First, there are simply too few of them, too narrowly spread across issues and regions, to devote themselves to the kind of outreach necessary. Second, such policy actors must inevitably be seen as partial to the choices and strategic direction of the government of the day. The academic community has the responsibility not only to promote informed debate but also to do so in a way that engenders diversity and opens up choices in foreign policy. Third, there will always be a need, in any policy arena, for the critical voice which will hold any policy decision or outcome up to scrutiny in the light of domestic concerns and international frameworks such as provided for under international law.

Sadly, Irish academia, and political scientists in particular, have not engaged in a rigorous and continuous manner with matters of Irish foreign policy. The discipline is, in itself, relatively new to the Irish academic landscape and international relations is furthermore, not firmly established as a core teaching and research discipline within third-level institutions. As things stand, contemporary Irish foreign policy as a distinct undergraduate course is not taught anywhere in a third-level institution in the Republic of Ireland.[3] Provision at postgraduate level is little better, with – in 2001 – just one dedicated course on offer. The absence of Irish foreign policy from classrooms and lecture halls has an inevitable and direct impact on the prospects for research in the area from third-level institutions.

Furthermore, the research interests of academic staff is a crucial catalyst for further research in any substantive area. Yet, in the new millennium, the number of full-time, permanent academic staff members in Irish third-level institutes engaging in active research (and teaching) on issues even related to Irish foreign policy, is less than a handful. Moreover, there does not exist, at any Irish university, a department, chair or centre for the study of international relations. What elements that do exist have been constructed from and through other areas of study – development, communications, European Studies or politics. The absence of staff may also reflect hiring patterns and the labour market implications of a truly globalised profession where advanced training/research on a subject as specialised as Irish foreign policy is no great asset when competing with international graduates for jobs either inside or outside Ireland. In such a truly global labour market, the chances of finding experts on Irish foreign policy are few.

This situation is in contrast to the area of European studies (which may or may not include a foreign policy or international relations dimension), which has flourished in the third-level sector in recent decades. Such teaching and research has been supported by modest levels of direct EU funding which has served to initialise postgraduate programmes, individual courses and even university chairs with an interest in things European. Similarly, the discipline of development studies has grown with assistance from a variety of state, semi-state and NGO agencies devoted to raising public awareness of development issues and placing these upon the academic agenda in a number of different disciplines and third-level programmes.

We would argue that this lack of academic consideration for international relations has had a clear impact upon the substance of Irish foreign policy and is reflected in domestic debates on issues related to foreign policy. The launch in 1994 of a consultative process leading to the publication of the first ever White Paper on Irish foreign policy in 1996 generated less than sixty-five written submissions from members of the public – of which fewer than half a dozen came from individuals or academic centres associated with any of the universities. The overwhelming majority – more than 70 percent – came from NGOs and voluntary sector agencies, especially in the area of development aid.

It is remarkable that Ireland still does not have a national centre for the study of international affairs or of Irish foreign policy – a characteristic that marks it out within the member states of the EU. The debates on the 2001-2002 war in Afghanistan were notable for the paucity of home-grown experts on the many international dimensions of the war and Ireland's role within the Security Council. While international expertise should always be brought to bear in such circumstances it is nonetheless striking how the debates revealed the limited competence in Irish public and academic life to address complex international events and to place Ireland, in however limited a function, into the picture of those events.

The need for an expanded dialogue

The nature of Irish foreign policy has changed radically since Patrick Keatinge first sat down to describe and explain institutions, issues and processes in the 1960s and 1970s. But it is important also to consider some other factors and, we suggest, reassert perhaps now more than ever the need for an expanded dialogue and intellectual engagement with the specifically Irish dimensions of foreign policy, be that what emanates from Iveagh House alone or what emerges through policy co-operation in Brussels or what is being discussed over coffee in the more than one hundred NGOs, small and large, that engage with activist politics surrounding issues of global peace, justice, development and human rights.

It is important not to lose the focus on what happens within domestic politics: the deep, and sometimes invisible roots of foreign policy. To do so is to lose sight of the relationships between the broader domestic polity and the policy makers, the embedded nature of foreign policy considerations within a national socio-economic and historical context, and of the issue of identity itself. The challenge is to keep these in focus alongside the institutionalisation that occurs within the EU or the UN and the socialisation of officials and politicians that is part and parcel of international life today and the international system. As policy makers and practitioners, claims on their identity can run in both (and apparently opposite) directions simultaneously

Even as Irish policy makers are part of a process of Europeanisation and respond to what has been called a consultation reflex, this is not the same as arguing that officials and politicians arrive in the meeting rooms of European institutions to create a policy framed exclusively in 'European' interests. Their contribution to collective debates and policy action is constructed from their position as Irish representatives and their sense of what it is that they, as Irish policy makers, can bring to the table. According to the White Paper, 'Ireland's foreign policy is about much more than self-interest... it is a statement of the kind of people that we are' (Government of Ireland: 7).

'Ireland' is a valid unit of analysis within the world stage today. The issue for researchers and academics is perhaps not whether to interrogate the 'Irishness' of our role in international life but how to do so. What are the lessons to be learned? Can our experience be seen in any instance as a universally relevant and/or applicable model for other (small/postcolonial) states? How do the deep structures of community and identity play out in Ireland's international involvement? Finally, how do we proceed to answer these questions in a way that avoids what one of our contributors so wonderfully termed, in a different forum, auto-exoticism?

Patrick Keatinge's work has given a lead. Firstly, as stated earlier, the historical context must be present - both in terms of institutions and issues. Secondly, the evolutionary process of foreign policy must be stressed within that, focusing upon institutional changes and reform of policy processes. Thirdly, analysts must factor in the external context − the constraints, whether real or imaginary, that circumscribe or frame national foreign policy debates. Ireland has never been in a position to play a power game in Realist terms and is unlikely ever to do so. At the same time, inductive empirical observation would suggest that Irish policy makers have room for manoeuvre and Irish foreign policy should therefore not be seen as part of the flotsam and jetsam of international politics. Finally, there are themes particular to Ireland that have resonances elsewhere either because they are distinct or because they reflect something general about small states within the international system.

All of this, of course, has to be contextualised in the framework of a 'new' Ireland that is economically vibrant, comparatively wealthy, a destination of international migration and a place in which traditional sources of authority − the state, church, political parties − have been significantly weakened. In terms of Irish foreign policy, therefore, there are new stories to tell about Ireland in the world that go beyond statist conceptions of interest and which engage with new phenomena − both domestic and international. It is the ambition of the editors that this text will offer some guidance as to where Irish foreign policy has come from and where it is going. We do so as a way of marking Patrick Keatinge's foundational role in understanding both our past and present.

Dublin

October 2001

Notes

1   This is a growing trend which began in the 1970s with the emergence of non-governmental aid organisations, largely linked to religious organisations, and solidarity, human rights and campaigning groups, many of which are part of European and global networks.

2   See for instance the recent publication, Ireland: An audit of compliance with international human rights standards, 2000, Amnesty International Irish Section, Dublin, 2000.

3   The subject remains 'on the books' in some other institutions (i.e. it could be taught at some future date).

Chapter 1

Ireland, Peacekeeping and Defence Policy: Challenges and Opportunities

Ray Murphy

Membership of the United Nations (UN) has been a cornerstone of Irish foreign policy since 1955.[1] Indeed, for the years prior to Irish accession to the European Community, the UN was the primary forum through which Irish policy makers could express their concerns across a wide range of international issues. A strong and effective UN, especially in the area of conflict prevention, was a key policy objective of Irish foreign policy within which peacekeeping operations have come to play a central role.[2] As a small country, Ireland has always had a vested interest in the promotion of multilateral diplomacy and collective security. Despite its deficiencies, the UN offered this small 'middle power' a voice among the states of the world. Eager to participate fully in every aspect of the organisation, Ireland was not hesitant about committing its defence forces to UN command in far flung lands largely unknown to most Irish people at the time.

Today, participation by the defence forces and gardaí in a range of UN sponsored activities is seen as unremarkable.[3] This involvement has become a significant element of Irish foreign policy, and a concrete manifestation of Irish commitment to the UN and the maintenance of world peace.[4] A tradition of active membership of both the League of Nations and the UN has also assisted in establishing this peacekeeping tradition.[5] Furthermore, Ireland's own experience of colonialism, its non-membership of any military alliance and its foreign policy profile in a number of issue-areas such as decolonisation, disarmament and human rights have all combined to make it an acceptable contributor to peacekeeping and related activities.[6]

13

Despite the ongoing involvement in peace support operations, there is surprisingly little debate on this issue in Ireland. There seems to be a general acceptance that Ireland's contribution to peacekeeping operations are good for the defence forces and the international community. While this may be correct, it is not something that should be just assumed. In 1993, Ireland changed the legal basis for troop participation in UN operations so as to allow an Irish contribution to UNOSOM II in Somalia which went beyond the traditional remit of UN policing operations. This brought about a fundamental change in policy, after which participation in peacekeeping forces not specifically of a police nature was permitted.[7] This did generate some debate as to whether or not Ireland should be contributing forces to new kinds of military action by the United Nations.

The most significant political developments in this field in recent years have been the publication of government White Papers on both foreign policy and defence.[8] The White Paper on Foreign Policy was criticised as being strong on ideals, but weak in identifying Irelands interests and the practical implications of foreign policy decisions. Likewise, the White Paper on Defence was seen to be dominated by bland descriptive passages, mixed with cost cutting suggestions disguised as expenditure analysis, and an especially glib assumption regarding the domestic security situation following the Good Friday Agreement.[9] The Paper was widely criticised as lacking policy analysis and vision.[10]

The surprise decision associated with the White Paper on Defence to reduce the size of the defence forces to around 10,500 sparked off a serious public dispute between the Department of Defence and the defence forces.[11] This had the unfortunate consequence of detracting attention from other defence and security issues discussed in the White Paper. Although both the foreign policy and defence forces White Papers were vague in many respects, the chapters dealing with overseas peace support operations did set out the background to Irish involvement, and the factors that will inform the government's consideration of requests for troops. They also spelled out the guiding principles the government should consider in deciding whether or not to participate in more robust military enforcement missions.

While these criteria are clear guiding principles, they leave considerable discretion to the government of the day and underline the government's reluctance to fetter its discretion in foreign policy matters. The publication of the criteria should have facilitated greater democratic accountability and an informed parliamentary debate. This does not seem to have been the case. What is most surprising about the criteria and guidelines is how little reference is actually made to them in the debates seeking approval for participation.[12] Part of the problem may be the need to respond quickly to humanitarian emergencies. The key issue relating to peacekeeping and Irish foreign policy arising from the White Paper on Foreign Policy was the focus on maintaining military neutrality while fostering a security role for Ireland within Europe.[13] The security role within Europe was expanded upon in the White Paper on Defence with a commitment to pledge troops to the European Rapid Reaction Force.[14] While participation in UN operations per se is uncontroversial, the move towards 'subcontracting' peace support operations to regional organisations such as the North Atlantic Treaty Organisation (NATO) or the claim by such organisations in given situations that they are operating within a UN 'mandate' presents difficulties.

The debate stimulated by the publication of the White Paper on Foreign Policy was a welcome attempt to engage the Irish public in the formulation of foreign policy, and it has assisted in identifying and clarifying some key issues. The importance of maintaining a clear distinction between traditional peacekeeping and operations involving some degree of military enforcement action is not just important for the UN, but also for contributing states such as Ireland. Today's intra-state conflicts present complex and dangerous situations for all peacekeepers, and while there is general support from the Irish public for participation in such operations, they are not prepared to accept any significant casualties or unnecessary exposure to risk. Politicians in Ireland are not unlike their counterparts elsewhere; they will respond to public opinion and may even succumb to a media driven agenda. The real risks are not well understood, and although Ireland has contributed to UNIFIL for more than twenty years, there is still a large degree of ignorance among the Irish general public of the prevailing dangers for UN peacekeepers.[15] For this reason it is useful to consider the implications of Irish participation, and how these were perceived historically.

The implications of UN membership for Ireland

In spite of the fact that Ireland was not admitted to membership of the UN until December 1955, the possibility of Irish participation in UN enforcement operations was discussed at length in the Dáil in July 1946 when the first debate regarding UN membership took place. The proposal to join the UN was controversial at the time, but it is evident that it was a decision taken in full knowledge of the fact that the UN Charter, unlike that of the League of Nations, contained coercive military provisions binding on all member states by the decision of the Security Council.[16] Indeed, the origins of the UN in 1945 can be seen as an extension into peacetime of the wartime alliance against the 'Axis powers'. In fact, the term 'United Nations' originally dates from the Allied Atlantic Charter of 1941. In the course of the debate, many deputies present displayed a keen awareness of the commitments involved and, with considerable foresight, drew attention to the inherent weakness in the collective security provisions of the Charter that were intended to be the cornerstone of UN policy in the maintenance of international peace and security.[17]

The then Taoiseach, Eamon de Valera, was initially unenthusiastic about membership. This was not surprising given what he saw as the failure of the major powers to support its predecessor, the League of Nations, and the distribution of power and responsibilities within the new organisation. The UN was premised upon the maintenance of a consensus among the major powers and former wartime allies:

> in all these organisations being projected ... for the maintenance of international peace, there is a tendency to give the great powers an overwhelming influence, which generally means, in the long run, that if they keep together all goes well but, when they want to quarrel, then the whole purpose for which the League (sic) was established goes to pieces.[18]

De Valera's extensive experience with the League of Nations made it obvious to him that the collective security provisions of the UN were not designed to deal with the ideological divisions of the post-war period. What was not evident then, however, was that the military and other commitments under the Charter would not materialise as planned. Consequently, when de Valera did decide that Ireland should apply for membership, he went to great lengths to point out the 'serious obligation contained in Article 25 of the Charter', and the military significance of the Articles contained in Chapter VII.[19] Even at that early stage the problems associated with the veto were apparent.[20] While the implications for Irish neutrality were a source of some confusion in the Dáil, certain deputies did consider that membership would have serious consequences.[21] In contrast to the Swiss position, it is noteworthy that de Valera, the person most identified with Ireland's wartime neutrality, did not consider UN membership as presenting any significant problem for Irish foreign policy. However, he did share the concern of other deputies regarding the military obligations imposed by admission 'as there was no indication whatsoever as to what contribution they might expect from us'.[22]

Not all of the debate was so well informed or incisive in analysis. There were persistent attempts to raise the question of the partition of the island of Ireland, and submissions such as those from W.T. Cosgrave, leader of the opposition, that they consider for a moment the 'grave factor .... that up to the present the Vatican had not been invited to participate in the framing of the Charter'.[23] Another deputy seemed concerned by the absence of any reference to 'the Supreme Being'.[24] Nonetheless, when the motion was passed, those present for the debate would have been well aware of the potential for Irish military involvement in UN enforcement action under the provisions of the Charter. At that time even the most imaginative observers had not considered the concept of preventive diplomacy or peacekeeping.

Despite de Valera's early reservations, it was probably a fear of isolation on the world stage that finally prompted him to opt for UN membership. The decision was thus based on pragmatic considerations rather than any idealistic commitment to the UN itself.[25] There are interesting parallels here with the Irish debate on participation in the NATO-sponsored Partnership for Peace and the Irish contribution to the UN-mandated but NATO-commanded Stabilization Force (SFOR) and Kosovo Force (KFOR) missions in the former Yugoslavia. There were very real fears among officials in the Department of Foreign Affairs and the military that if Ireland did not participate in such initiatives it would be isolated and excluded from international developments in peacekeeping.[26] Those fears echoed similar concerns expressed by de Valera some fifty years earlier in relation to membership of the UN.[27]

When the Dáil approved the motion to apply for UN membership on 26 July 1946, the government did not hesitate to exercise its mandate. It was somewhat ironic then that, after protracted debate and consideration of the issue, the actual application to join was vetoed by the Soviet Union. The prospect of this happening does not appear to have occurred to anyone in Ireland at that time. The reason given for vetoing the application was that Ireland did not have any bilateral diplomatic relations with the Soviet Union.[28] This was a dubious justification for a policy primarily based on Cold War rivalry. At that time the General Assembly was dominated by pro-Western countries. The so-called Afro-Asian group – a product of de-colonisation in the 1950s and 1960s – had yet to develop and begin to dominate debates in the General Assembly. A clue to Soviet reasoning may also lie in the history of the League of Nations, because Ireland was one of only three countries that opposed Soviet admission in 1934.[29] A US-Soviet brokered 'package deal' facilitated Ireland's membership alongside that of other applicant states and managed to increase the size of the General Assembly, without changing significantly the balance of Cold War forces within it.[30] This arrangement was so delicately balanced that Ireland's membership was in doubt almost up to the last moment.[31] It is unlikely that the Soviet Union monitored the Dáil debate on the matter, but had it done so, it would have confirmed its suspicions that Ireland was unambiguously aligned with the pro-Western group of states then dominant within the UN.

Ireland did eventually gain admission in December 1955. By this time the advent of the Cold War had made the potential for collective security and enforcement action under the Charter seem redundant. The UN was turning instead to a policy of 'political-military control of local conflict by politically impartial essentially non-coercive methods'.[32] Thus, when UN membership became a real possibility the Taoiseach, John A. Costello, resisted attempts to debate the issues fully once more, pointing out that in real terms the obligations were now less onerous than they had been in 1946.[33] Once the hurdle of admission was over, the immediate issue confronting the government was the formulation of a coherent foreign policy that would present an individual perspective on international affairs. Because Ireland had been outside the central institutional framework for international affairs over the previous fifteen years, Irish foreign policy was somewhat underdeveloped. Cosgrave, then Minister for External Affairs, was quick to realise that UN policy would require 'nothing less than the basic principle on which our policy towards the outside world and its problems is based'.[34]

Cosgrave led the Irish delegation to its first UN General Assembly session in the autumn of 1956. By this time he had formulated three broad principles upon which Irish participation would be based.[35] These represented as clear and unambivalent a statement of Ireland's pro-Western anti-communist policy as can be found and it appeared to vindicate Soviet reservations about Irish membership. Even the question of partition was relegated to avoid giving the impression that 'we have no interest in matters of international policy save that of partition alone'.[36] There was still no mention of peacekeeping or related activities, but Cosgrave did add a significant rider in acknowledging that Ireland would have certain sympathy with peoples seeking self-determination.[37] Although this may appear as something of an afterthought, it was an important distinguishing feature in Irish foreign policy. It could, if adhered to, provide Ireland with an opportunity to adopt an independent policy in relation to de-colonisation and self-determination in the decade ahead. It was not surprising then that Ireland was expected to vote along similar lines to that of the United States, and in the course of attending its first session of the General Assembly, the Irish delegation did nothing to disappoint these expectations, the thrust of Irish policy being 'unequivocally pro-Western and unremittingly anti-Soviet'.[38]

Although Cosgrave did not get an opportunity to oversee the implementation of his principles, because the coalition government of which he was a member was defeated at a general election within a year, they nevertheless proved to be influential.[39] Cosgrave was succeeded by Frank Aiken,[40] an experienced politician who aspired to playing a similar role in the UN to that played by de Valera in the League of Nations. On account of this, a stronger emphasis was placed on Cosgrave's second principle, that of 'independence'. This was not surprising because Aiken had been critical of the contradictions apparent between the first two principles enunciated by Cosgrave, and the third.[41]

Aiken's period in office spanned a number of significant international developments, some of which did test the mettle of

Ireland's espoused independence in relation to foreign policy issues.[42] In hindsight, these may not seem very significant. However, in the context of the time they did indicate a willingness by Aiken to take an independent stance on certain issues.[43] On account of this, 'the Irish delegation carried rather more weight in the Assembly, during this period, than what might have been expected from the size and importance of the country it represented'.[44]

Ireland and 'middle power' status

Ireland's history as a former colony, and Aiken's reputation for independence at the UN, combined with non-membership of any military alliance, went a long way towards Ireland acquiring 'middle power' status. The term 'middle power' is common in the language of peacekeeping. It has never been defined clearly and can have different connotations depending on the context in which it is used. Hammarskjöld adverted to the term frequently when discussing peacekeeping.[45]

Nevertheless, it would be a mistake to consider Ireland a 'middle power' in terms of voting patterns at the UN. A study of Irish voting there between 1956 and 1970 found it more clearly aligned to the Western block.[46] But, the basic nature of the Irish position was demonstrated by the consistently high degree of similarity with Sweden, according to one commentator.[47] Another commentator similarly concluded that Ireland was a consistent supporter of the United States policies at the UN during the period 1957 to 1961.[48] It was also observed that Ireland headed the list of those states which, because of their voting record, were 'pro-United States'.[49] Ireland, in fact, was found to have voted more often with the United States than did three members of NATO; Denmark, Norway and Greece.

By the time Ireland did gain membership of the UN, the concept of collective security and enforcement action had been made effectively redundant by the Cold War. While Ireland could not claim to have played any significant part in this transformation, the changed situation did offer a new and important role as 'peacekeeper' or 'middle power' policeman. It was against this background that peacekeeping became a central feature of Irish foreign policy in the early nineteen sixties. While it may be argued that this policy has been largely no more than declaratory without consequential action, Ireland, in terms of its size and resources, has made a substantial contribution to peacekeeping operations that continues to the present day.

The establishment of the United Nations Emergency Force (UNEF) in 1956 was the first practical application of Hammarskjöld's concept of preventive diplomacy.[50] The actual contributors to this force were not the so-called great powers, but rather small and middle power intermediaries like Ireland, drawn from sources acceptable to the parties involved. Though Ireland was not called upon to contribute troops to this force, the government had agreed in principle to do so if called upon by the Secretary-General.[51] The success of the force laid down foundations and precedents with regard to future peacekeeping forces and the principle of non-coercive moral authority was also used in the setting up of smaller observation and verification missions.

The defence forces and the peacekeeping tradition

Although peace support operations are generally associated with the UN, in reality Ireland has contributed to operations under the auspices of NATO, the Organisation for Security and Co-operation in Europe (OSCE) and the European Union.[52] While the single most important contribution in recent years was UNIFIL in Lebanon, peace support operations involve nearly one thousand military personnel in a range of countries. In future this will also include the UN Stand By Arrangements System, which the government agreed to support in 1996.[53] The defence forces have been traditionally a small and well-integrated force in Irish society. In recent times, most of the duties performed have been in the role of 'aid to the civil power', or as a stand-by force to maintain essential services during serious industrial disputes. They do not possess any heavy support weapons usually associated with the modern armies of larger states and they are accustomed to operating without such equipment.[54] Despite their conventional structure, the real role of the defence forces has been closer in nature to that of a garrison-based 'gendarmerie' than a modern army.[55] In this way the defence of Ireland was seen by many as requiring little more that a paramilitary force to quell civil disorder.[56] These factors, together with the emphasis on adaptability and an ability to operate independently of large scale supporting forces, combined to make the defence forces especially suitable for traditional UN-type peacekeeping missions. However, these very same factors also contributed to an ambiguity surrounding the role of the defence forces in modern Ireland.

The first indication of Ireland's potential suitability as a UN troop contributor state came in 1958, when officers participated in an observer mission in Lebanon. However, Ireland's first major involvement in peacekeeping came two years later when Irish troops departed for the Congo in July 1960.[57] This was one of the most important decisions made by any Irish government in relation to the UN and foreign policy, and it was certainly the most significant decision taken in the context of defence and security matters since the foundation of the state. It was in a very real sense a baptism of fire for Irish peacekeepers that demonstrated Ireland's commitment to the principles of the UN Charter.[58] It is very much to the credit of the soldiers involved, and the Irish government of the day, that neither wavered in their support for the UN at a time when it was undergoing its most serious crisis to date. In many ways the Congo crisis marked the high point in Irish involvement with the UN.[59] The precedent for Irish participation in peacekeeping was thereby established, and an Irish contingent was still in the Congo when a request was received for another unit to participate in the peacekeeping Force in Cyprus.[60]

In October 1973, the UN decided to send a peacekeeping force to the Sinai desert to monitor the cease-fire between Israel and Egypt following the Yom Kippur War.[61] Almost simultaneously with agreement being reached on the establishment of the United Nations Emergency Force II (UNEF II), the 25 Infantry Group from Ireland was arriving for a tour of duty with the UN force in Cyprus. Following a request by the Secretary-General, and Dáil approval, this unit spent just one week in Cyprus when it was transferred to UNEF II in the Sinai.[62] However, in early 1974 following the Dublin and Monaghan bombings, the government withdrew the Irish contingent.[63] The decision did not come as a surprise to the Irish military authorities.[64] In hindsight, it can be said that the threat to the security of the state was not as great as that perceived by the government at the time. Although the decision may have damaged temporarily Ireland's standing with the UN as a reliable troop contributor to peacekeeping operations, the adverse consequences of the decision have long since faded into insignificance.[65]

The Secretary-General again requested that Ireland contribute a unit to form part of the United Nations Interim

Force in Lebanon (UNIFIL) in 1978.[66] Despite the difficult and quite often dangerous nature of the mission, up to recently the government has generally expressed its continued support for the UN force in the area.[67] This again underscores Ireland's commitment to UN peacekeeping and the high price that participation in such operations entails. It is not surprising then that fulsome tributes to Irish UN personnel are commonplace.[68] Among the disadvantages of participation is the fact that it added to the difficulties of under-strength units at home, and must have prompted the question in some quarters; if all these officers and personnel can be permanently abroad, why do we need them in the first place? It also allowed the Department of Foreign Affairs a significant influence on matters that were essentially military in nature.[69] Although this did not matter at most times, it was significant because the Department of Foreign Affairs was usually very supportive of Irish involvement in UN peacekeeping operations even when civil servants in the Departments of Defence and Finance opposed participation.

Although the Irish commitment to the UN forces in Somalia (UNOSOM II) was quite small and numbered just 180 personnel, the decision to participate had significant political and military implications.[70] It was the first time Irish soldiers participated in a Chapter VII peace enforcement operation of this kind and it set a precedent that helped pave the way for the current participation in the Stabilisation Force in the former Yugoslavia.[71] It marked a watershed in Irish involvement in peacekeeping activities, and a realisation that Ireland could be left behind in the changing nature of the international security environment unless it too adapted to events. Though the UN operation in the Congo (ONUC) in the 1960s did involve a degree of enforcement action to which the Irish contingent was a party, the recent decisions to participate in SFOR, KFOR, UNAMET (East Timor) and UNOSOM II were conscious decisions made in response to the changed international environment. In the case of SFOR, KFOR and UNAMET, the government has also agreed to pay all the expenses associated with Irish participation. More significantly, the participation in the NATO-led, albeit UN-mandated operations, placed Irish troops under the de facto command of NATO for the first time.[72] There are significant legal and constitutional difficulties involved in command and/or control of Irish forces by non-defence force personnel, but successive governments to date have quietly ignored these.[73]   Despite this, Irish military and other personnel have adapted successfully to such missions. However, there remains an ongoing need to keep up to date in training, and to ensure that equipment levels and standards reflect the new demands being made on the defence forces.

In 1994, a leaked confidential report by Price Waterhouse consultants described the defence forces as, inter alia, 'badly structured, too old, poorly trained, and inappropriately equipped'.[74]   Though this was controversial at the time, the Defence Forces Review Implementation Plan later accepted and adopted the report's essential conclusions.[75]   After neglect over many years by successive governments, most of the deficiencies in structures, training and equipment identified were self evident to members of the defence forces.[76]   However, others were not, and the Price Waterhouse analysis offered a serious indictment of the levels of training and of management structures, which they rightly identified as the key to operational capability in the defence forces.[77]   This had important implications for participation on UN operations, because deficiencies in training would also undermine operational capability on the ground. As a result, the government committed itself to reorganise the defence forces as an 'all arms conventional force'.[78]

This raises the question, how have Irish soldiers been so successful at conflict resolution and peacekeeping duties in general, despite the deficiencies identified? While the defence forces were supposedly organised and trained to fulfil a primary role in the defence of the state against aggression, their most important function evolved to being that of providing military assistance to the civil power.[79]   Internal security tasks expanded due primarily to the conflict in Northern Ireland and these became the major operational focus of the defence forces. In this way much of the work of the army over the past twenty-seven years has in fact been the performance of duties of a police nature. This is one of the reasons why Irish troops adapted so successfully to a UN peacekeeping role where the duties performed up to recently have also, for the most part, been of a police character. Other important reasons were evident in a recent analysis of the strengths and weaknesses of the defence forces. These included the 'can do' and professional approach of military personnel at all levels which has meant that the roles assigned by government have been carried out despite impediments to operational effectiveness. This success has also relied upon development and retention of conventional military skills despite the many barriers preventing the implementation of an optimum training programme.[80] The difficulty with the 'can do' work ethos is that in the long run it can be counterproductive if it perpetuates the illusion that all is well, when this in fact is not the case. This was one of the reasons identified as contributing to the debacle of Canadian involvement in the UN operation in Somalia.[81] In this regard the deficiencies identified in the recent review would indicate that matters were anything but satisfactory.

The implications of participation in peacekeeping operations

There has been considerable research into the characteristics of peacekeeping forces and one distinguished sociologist proposed the 'constabulary' concept in relation to conventional military forces participating in peacekeeping operations.[82] The military establishment becomes a 'constabulary' force when it is continuously prepared to act, committed to the minimum use of force, and seeks international relations rather than victory.[83] He suggested that the military would look upon such police-type work as less important and prestigious than traditional military operations. While this may have been true in the past among the armed forces of the larger powers, it was never the case with the defence forces.[84] Later, four characteristics that render a military force suitable for peacekeeping missions were identified.[85] The first is an emphasis on a high degree of adaptability in the military sector, including an ability to operate independently of large scale supporting forces. The second is a major emphasis on the differentiation of skills and the development of initiative in professional training. The third is a distinctly non-political role. The fourth and final characteristic is a high degree of discipline.

The defence forces at present satisfy all of these requirements. The first two requirements are straightforward and could be said to be necessary characteristics of any small viable military force. Furthermore, since the end of the civil war and the establishment of the modern Irish state, the army has avoided any involvement in politics. There has never been a suggestion of partiality by the army made by any deputy in the course of debates about the defence forces.

The success of the army in peacekeeping is evidence that it has a sufficiently high level of discipline. Further evidence is provided by the manner in which the army carries out the many and varied roles that it is called upon to fulfil. The soldiers are drawn from all sections of Irish society. The majority live in homes alongside their civilian counterparts and not in barracks or on military bases, a factor that has assisted the integration of the army in Irish society, as well as helping to foster its democratic ethos.

The defence forces' involvement in UN operations has been considerable. When one considers their small size and the fact that they were generally several thousand personnel below authorised strength, their contribution has been enormous. Even in absolute terms the contribution is impressive – in 1986 the Irish battalion was the second largest in UNIFIL. One of the consequences of the low strength is that it has nearly always proved necessary to establish the units that serve with peacekeeping forces from the defence forces as a whole. Although this has obvious disadvantages, experience shows that any problems that arise in practice are resolved easily and the unit adopts an identity of its own very quickly. The organisation of an infantry battalion serving with UNIFIL is significantly different from that at home. In fact, the so-called infantry battalion in Lebanon comprises infantry, artillery, cavalry, signals, engineering, supply and transport, ordnance and medical corps personnel. For this reason it is self-sufficient, and tailor-made for the tasks it performs.[86]

It is difficult to assess in general terms the impact that this involvement has had on the defence forces. As a matter of policy, military service abroad is voluntary, and for the most part there are more volunteers than places available.[87] It is evident from conversations with serving and former personnel of the army that what is generally referred to in Irish military circles as 'overseas service' has always been viewed as a welcome respite from the day to day barrack routine at home.[88] It has also boosted morale, especially in the early 1960s when the government first agreed to contribute large numbers of troops to the peacekeeping operation in the Congo. UN service has increased the wages and salaries of serving personnel by way of overseas allowances, a factor not to be overlooked when considering the number of volunteers of all ranks for service with the UN. However, it was the new sense of purpose which the army felt in the 1960s that provided the most significant boost to morale. *The Irish Times* in 1963 summed up the effect:

there had been created a better public image of the army. This had been achieved by much mention in the speeches of politicians at home and abroad. The national newspapers have given it much publicity albeit somewhat dramatic and hysterical at times ... there was the enormous benefit in experience that active service gives ... (and) ... Irish troops did at last receive adequate pay in terms of overseas allowances.[89]

More importantly, from a military point of view, peacekeeping operations provide an ideal training ground for an army of Ireland's size and resources. This is especially true in southern Lebanon today, owing to the general operational environment of the UN Force there. The training and exercising of at least two battalions for UN service annually is probably the most obvious non-monetary benefit arising from the present level of commitment to UNIFIL. Contributions to other missions allow officers in particular to hold command and staff appointments in international forces that would otherwise not be open to them.[90] This experience, though difficult to quantify and evaluate, is recognised as being of immeasurable benefit to the training standards and other requirements associated with professional armies.

Despite the current deficiencies in training and equipment, these and other military aspects of Irish involvement with the UN today compare favourably with those of the early 1960s.[91] In keeping with the long-standing tradition of participation in UN activities, and in an effort to harness the extensive experience accumulated to date, the defence forces opened a UN Training School in 1993.[92] The first army battalions that formed up for UN duty in the Congo were not well equipped for the mission ahead, and nor were they well informed politically of the situation there. One retired senior officer recalled how the Irish soldiers arrived to the sweltering heat of Central Africa in heavy 'bulls wool' uniforms and with bolt-action rifles.[93] In military terms, they were responsible for a huge area and they had at their disposal a mere sixteen jeeps, no helicopters and no armoured cars.[94] He compared the strength of the army then at around eight thousand, to the strength during World War II at about fifty thousand, and remarked that most of the men were absorbed doing routine duty. As a result, the standard of basic training was poor and almost non-existent in some instances. It is ironic that the Irish troops' lack of reliance upon heavy support weapons –

thus defining their weakness as a traditional army – has worked so precisely in their favour in defining them as ideal peacekeepers. While the basic infantry soldier is well equipped and supported at that level, on an overall basis the army does not possess expensive military hardware. Because weapons and equipment of this nature are not permitted in a traditional peacekeeping role, the Irish soldier has adapted particularly well to peacekeeping duties, because he or she is unaccustomed to depending upon such equipment anyway. The army's role within the state is also such that few soldiers experience live combat situations and most incidents involving Irish soldiers on UN service are more in the nature of skirmishes than full-scale battles.[95] This generally means that the army is unaccustomed to offensive military operations and resorting to the use of force. As a result of this, army personnel can be very adept at resolving confrontations by negotiation and mediation, qualities useful in any mission that seeks to establish a degree of peace and security in an area by deploying an international UN force. It is, however, noteworthy that the defence forces have not had any difficulty adapting to peace enforcement missions either.

The primary role of the defence forces is to defend the state against aggression. However, the capacity to fulfil this mission is hampered by the lack of adequate resources. In such a situation it may well be asked why the state maintains a standing army at all? The answer probably lies in the historical background to the foundation of the Irish state. The perceived threat to the democratically elected government and the institutions of the state has always been greater from within the state than from any potential foreign aggressor, except for a period during World War II. This may account in part for the disproportionate strength of the army when the defence forces were established. The independent state of Ireland has never been invaded and its soldiers have not participated in any foreign wars. Security and defence matters are seldom topics of public debate, and when they do arise it is usually in the context of European integration and neutrality. Unlike most other European countries, the ministerial portfolio of defence is regarded as a minor cabinet post. Successive Ministers for Defence from different political backgrounds have not been known for their political dynamism or significant contribution to public debate on security or defence.[96] The Department of Defence and the Irish military authorities have been equally reticent over the years. The lack of policy and debate on defence issues reflected a general lack of ideas and interest at all levels. In recent years, the formation of representative associations and the publication of strategy statements, annual reports, and the White Paper has improved this situation, but the overall level of public debate and knowledge remains low.

Since World War II the Irish army has suffered from a lack of purpose and a certain ambiguity regarding its role. Ireland's refusal to join NATO, largely on account of partition, and a policy of non-membership of military alliances meant that the army was denied any international role.[97] This decision had serious implications for national defence.[98] As a result, the defence forces became run down in the 1950s and early 1960s.[99] Participation in UN peace support operations has therefore significantly enhanced the image of the defence forces as a disciplined and well-integrated military force both at home and abroad. Although it is difficult to assess the impact UN service has had in general, soldiers of all ranks are unanimous in their belief that it has improved considerably both training and morale in the defence forces.[100]

Guidelines for future participation

The Irish government has committed itself to supporting the unique role and authority of the UN in the field of conflict resolution and peacekeeping. However, in view of the number, size and complexity of current peace support operations, it was deemed necessary to develop a selective response to future requests from the UN based on certain factors.[101] These factors are so broad and imprecise that it could be said that all peacekeeping forces established will fall foul of at least one or more of them, and they could thus be used to avoid participation in, or even to deny the legitimacy or raison d'être of certain operations. This, however, is too cynical a view, and the factors are just what they are stated to be, i.e. matters relating to an operation which will be taken into account when deciding whether or not it is appropriate to participate. It can also be claimed that if these were rigidly applied in the past, Ireland would not be in Lebanon today, and we would not have participated in any UN peacekeeping mission mounted to date. In this regard they are somewhat unrealistic, and they do not reflect precedent or practice to date. Nonetheless, they are potentially useful guidelines in assessing the nature and extent of what Ireland's support should be for any UN peace support operation.

Some of the factors, if interpreted and applied in a wise and flexible manner, might even provide a yardstick by which to measure the likely success of the operation, with or without Irish participation. Others reflect very subjective considerations, such as consistency with broader foreign policy objectives, and the extent of other similar commitments. These are legitimate factors for any sovereign state to take into account, and each request must be considered on its own merits. What should not be ignored though, is that the very complexity and evolving nature of peacekeeping may diminish the role of the defence forces, and the White Paper on Foreign Policy is somewhat unrealistic in this regard. It appeared to assume that Ireland would always be in demand as a contributor to peacekeeping operations. This is not necessarily the case. If Ireland wants to stay in what has been described as the 'premier league' of peacekeepers, then it must ensure that it is in a position to do so.[102]

There will always be a need for traditional peacekeeping, but there may not always be need for Irish personnel to form part of such operations. The support from Ireland for the inclusion of the so called Petersburg tasks of peacekeeping and similar humanitarian tasks into the Amsterdam Treaty on Europe indicated a growing awareness of the need to respond to the changing international security environment.[103] The White Paper on Defence also recognised the changing trends in international peace support operations, while at the same time the government has consistently stressed that participation in UN approved European peace support initiatives does not change Ireland's traditional policy on military neutrality.[104] This may well be official government policy, but it is hard to reconcile it with the fact of participation with other European states in military operations of whatever nature, and the increasing co-operation envisaged for European Union states under the common foreign and security provisions of the Amsterdam and Nice treaties.[105]

Although Ireland was not tarnished by the policies pursued by other contributors to the UN operation in Somalia, participation in any enforcement mission is risky. Apart from the obvious physical danger, there are other more fundamental issues to be considered. The real agenda of the larger powers may not be apparent at first, and small or middle powers run the risk of being dragged unwittingly into an intervention that owes little to the noble aspirations of the UN Charter. Humanitarian intervention and international law are not always high on the priorities of those states whose motives and policies are determined by the *realpolitik* of international relations and domestic concerns.

Taking into account the experience of Somalia, the Irish government's approach to participation in future enforcement operations will be guided by certain criteria.[106] There is nothing radical or innovative about the criteria, and they are broadly similar to those adopted by Canada.[107] However, the level of public knowledge and debate has been increased by their publication. They set down the factors to be taken into account before a decision is made to participate, and they allow for the political and military implications of individual missions to be assessed and evaluated on an ongoing basis. Then, an informed decision can be taken on the basis of all the facts. This may lead to accusations of naiveté, especially because we must now compete with other states to participate in such operations.[108] The end of the Cold War has witnessed the industrial-military complex of both camps searching for a new identity and raison d'être. The recent UN sponsored military operations have provided a means for armed forces to resist pressure to rationalise and reduce their capacity. Proposals from smaller states indicate that this is not simply a concern of the larger powers.[109] Nonetheless, Ireland should not be afraid to decline to participate in any UN operation when this is the right course of action to take.

The guidelines were applied for the first time in 1996, when the Irish government decided to contribute troops to the proposed Canadian-led UN intervention force planned for Central Africa.[110] In the event, the troops were not required. When the matter of contributing troops to the NATO-led SFOR and KFOR was being considered, the guidelines were applied again. There was general support for the proposal from the main political parties.[111] The defence forces and the Department of Foreign Affairs were strong advocates of the proposal.[112] In July 1999, Ireland agreed to send a transport company to Kosovo as part of KFOR. There was nothing radical or new in this decision, and its role is very similar to that performed by the Irish contingent with UNOSOM II.[113] Nonetheless, Irish involvement in SFOR and KFOR sets the scene for a longer-term re-orientation of Irish participation in international peace support operations. If the defence forces are to retain the skills and reputation acquired to date in the new context of European security, then it may be necessary to participate in the organisations where best contemporary practice is developed. This is all the more so with the UN move from traditional peacekeeping to more complex peace support operations conducted by regional organisations with UN approval. This was a significant development for Ireland that should assist in ensuring that the prominent role played by the defence forces to date in peacekeeping operations is not diminished in the future. This is an important consideration because some of Ireland's attributes for traditional peacekeeping, namely the non-membership of NATO and the lightly armed nature of Irish armed forces, could be barriers to participation in future UN but NATO-led regional operations.

There is, however, a positive dimension to Ireland's situation. Peacekeeping was confined usually to small and middle powers, whereas enforcement operations are dominated by the larger powers. With the UN in financial crisis, there may be little alternative but to hand over enforcement operations to regional bodies such as NATO. This has serious implications not just for the UN, but for smaller states like Ireland that are not part of any formal military or regional alliance. Nonetheless, Ireland's military neutrality and history, the very factors that excluded it from such alliances, make Irish soldiers especially acceptable as traditional peacekeepers. The need for contributors to such operations will continue, and Ireland is well placed to support and contribute to the myriad of tasks that such missions involve.

Conclusion

The decision to allow Irish troops to participate in the UN enforcement mission in Somalia was one of the most significant developments in Irish defence and foreign policy in recent years. The need to pass enabling legislation in Ireland arose from the dualist nature of Ireland's legal system, rather than any new obligation undertaken by the state in relation to UN membership.[114] The high standard of officer training within the defence forces, the internal security role performed in aid to the civil power, and the 'can do' professional working ethos of all personnel, render the defence forces especially suitable for all UN operations. This, however, is something that should not be taken for granted. Despite all the reports or recent years, defence policy still lacks a coherent strategy. The defence forces must be given the resources to maintain the capacity to respond to requests to contribute to peace support operations, when appropriate. There is a very real danger that this could be undermined by 'reforms', combined with government lack of vision. The size of the defence forces is inadequate for the tasks it is intended to fulfil. This situation is all the more critical when it is taken into account that for every battalion or unit on UN or similar service, there should be another in preparatory training, and another standing down. It will not be possible to meet the commitment to the UN Stand By Force Arrangement, and the European Rapid Reaction Force, at the same time.[115] Nor is it clear that the defence forces will be prepared for the security implications of a breakdown or serious para-military threat to the Northern Ireland peace process. Despite protestations to the contrary by the Minister for Defence and the Minister for Foreign Affairs, the numbers just do not add up.[116]

Successive governments have been neither honest nor realistic in their designation of the role of the defence forces, and what is being signalled now is a clear move away from traditional UN operations in favour of the post Cold War model of 'tendered out' or delegated peace support operations. This may well be the way of the future, but what is missing is an honest and clear policy from the government on where Ireland stands on this and related issues.[117] As one recent author put it, 'as the Mother Teresa of the international community',[118] we are uncomfortable with the truth and the dilemmas of the post Cold War era. For many years the real mission of the defence forces was to defend the state from a perceived internal threat, while external security was guaranteed by slipping under the NATO umbrella.[119] When this was combined with an underlying distrust of the military by the political establishment, the consequences for the defence forces were those of a policy of deliberate neglect.

The controversial decision to join the NATO sponsored Partnership for Peace programme, and the commitments under the European Common Foreign and Security Policy have important implications for Ireland.[120] To a large extent the debate over membership of the Partnership for Peace programme took place among political elites and certain interest groups. However, the development of co-operative military relations and operational compatibility with NATO, albeit for peacekeeping/humanitarian purposes, raises important issues for Ireland. The defence forces could benefit from, and contribute to, the stated objectives of the Partnership for Peace.[121]   The Partnership's focus is declared to be on co-operation, training and joint exercises, and its framework document entails participation on a voluntary basis only.[122]   It includes most of the other 'neutral' European states, and former Warsaw Pact members. However, because of its association with NATO, membership of the Partnership for Peace may dilute Ireland's independent middle power identity even more than has already occurred, and it may make forging and maintaining other global links more difficult.

The issues are complex, and the dilemmas confronting Ireland were evident in the debate about participation in the multinational force in the former Yugoslavia.[123]   Military neutrality, however, did not preclude Irish participation in this force, when it was deemed appropriate to do so. In reality, both SFOR and KFOR are NATO forces, albeit operating with the authority of a UN Chapter VII resolution and with non-NATO member contributors. In military terms, Ireland does not possess the capacity to make any significant contribution to such large-scale operations. Irish involvement in these forces sets the scene for a longer-term re-orientation of Irish international peacekeeping. If Ireland is to retain its skills and reputation in the field of peacekeeping, it is necessary to adapt and to participate in the organisations where best contemporary practice is developed. But in doing so, is Ireland contributing to the demise of the UN at the behest of the United States and other permanent members of the Security Council? At the same time, there are some issues that Ireland should not remain neutral in respect of – the genocide, ethnic cleansing, mass rapes, and other crimes against humanity perpetrated in the former Yugoslavia are but one example. The reality is that it has taken a NATO-led force to impose some measure of peace, and prevent the seemingly endless slaughter of so many innocent civilians in the former Yugoslavia. But why have the same NATO powers left the UN strapped for cash and unable to act?   The unilateral NATO response to the Kosovo crisis may provide a more accurate insight into the true nature and purpose of these forces.[124]

The neutral states' tradition of involvement in international peace support operations is confirmed once again by the agreement of European neutrals to send soldiers to serve with the UN-mandated but NATO-commanded KFOR. This participation raises the issue of the compatibility of a policy of political and/or military neutrality with such operations.[125] Ireland is almost unique among the European neutrals in that the Defence (Amendment) Act, 1993, permits the participation of defence forces personnel in any kind of UN military operation.[126] It may be that other states will follow this example, but the experience of Switzerland indicates that nothing should be taken for granted. The situation with regard to Switzerland highlights the difficulties that can arise for genuinely neutral countries. Although not a member of the UN, Switzerland has participated in a number of UN operations.[127] In order to formalise and expedite the process of participation, the Swiss Federal Council enacted a statute in 1993 establishing a standby military force. Like Ireland, peacekeeping is deemed to be an important aspect of Swiss foreign policy. However, the statute was rejected by referendum because the population, among other reasons, considered participation in UN missions a threat to the neutrality of Switzerland.[128] It may be that Irish political leaders had this in mind when they decided not to hold a referendum on Irish membership of Partnership for Peace.[129] The Swiss experience shows that the general public there are wary of the extended parameters of recent UN military operations, and that the threat to neutrality is perceived as very real. The blurring of the distinction between peacekeeping, peace enforcement and enforcement action missions does not help this either.

The risks of involvement for Ireland are not insignificant, as was the case during the Congo crisis nearly forty years ago, but the duty to act as a responsible member of the international community remains and is compelling, in particular, given the shameful record of Ireland and other European countries throughout the Yugoslav conflict. However, NATO makes for an unpredictable bedfellow. Once it gave the UN full co-operation as part of peacekeeping and enforcement missions in Bosnia-Herzegovina. Now it seems to be competing with the UN and to have taken its place in the European area. This may suit the cash-strapped UN in the short term, but what of NATO's plans outside its own area of operations and without UN authorisation? Where do Ireland's interests lie in such a scenario? History should teach us that our interests as a small state lie with the UN, collective security and international law.

Notes

1 Department of Foreign Affairs (1996), *Challenges and Opportunities Abroad, White Paper on Foreign Policy*, Dublin, pp. 149-167, and Department of Defence (2000), *White Paper on Defence*, Dublin, pp. 59-70.

2 *Ibid.*

3 See Department of Defence (1999), *Defence Forces Annual Report*, Dublin, pp. 32-38, and Department of Justice, Equality and Law Reform (1999), *Ireland's Involvement in International Police Missions – A Discussion Paper*, Dublin. For general background see Duggan, J.P. (1991), *A History of the Irish Army*, Dublin: Gill and Macmillan, pp. 249-278, and *An Cosantóir – The Defence Forces Magazine* (October 1995), UN Anniversary Edition.

4 See for example the statement to this effect by the Tánaiste (Deputy Prime Minister) and Minister for Foreign Affairs, Dick Spring, in *The Irish Times*, 6 May 1997; Skelly, J.M. (1997), *Irish Diplomacy at the United Nations, 1945-65*, Dublin: Irish Academic Press.

5 Skelly, *op. cit.* and Kennedy, M. J. (1996), *Ireland and the League of Nations*, Dublin: Irish Academic Press. See also McQueen, N. J. D. (1981), 'Irish Neutrality: the United Nations and the Peacekeeping Experience 1945-1969', DPhil thesis, New University of Ulster, esp. the Introduction, pp. 1-13. Heathcote, N. (1971), 'Ireland and the United Nations Operation in the Congo', *International Relations*, Vol. 111, p. 880. Keatinge, P. (1973), *The Formulation of Irish Foreign Policy*. Dublin, Institute of Public Administration, pp. 7 and 83-86; and (1978), *A Place Among the Nations*. Dublin, Institute of Public Administration, pp. 158-161.

6 *Ibid.*

7 The Defence (Amendment) Act, 1993, amended and extended the Defence (Amendment)(No. 2) Act, 1960, in significant respects. The principle amendment is contained in Section 1, which by defining an 'International United Nations Force' as an international force or body established by the Security Council or General Assembly, goes beyond the previous definition which limited participation to peacekeeping or police type forces. See Murphy, R. (1994), 'Ireland: Legal issues arising from participation in United Nations operations', 1 *International Peacekeeping*, Vol. 1, No. 2, pp. 61-64.

8 *Supra*, note 1.

9 See *White Paper on Defence*, op. cit., p. 12.

10 See criticisms by Murray, T., a former government consultant who reviewed the Defence Forces, *The Irish Times*, 4 March 2000, p. 10. He was especially critical of the treatment of the Naval Service and Air Corps. For the view of the Minister for Defence see *The Irish Times*, 26 April 2000, p. 16.

11 See for example, Cusack, J., *The Irish Times*, 9 February, 2000, p. 3, where a former Chief of Staff asked the Taoiseach to intervene in the dispute.

12 See for example the debate on participation in KFOR, *Dáil Debates*, 507 (852-869), 1 July 1999.

13 *White Paper on Foreign Policy*, op. cit., pp. 191-205.

14 *White Paper on Defence, op. cit.*, pp. 15-18, *The Irish Times*, 31 October and 1 November 2000, pp. 16, 17. At the Helsinki EU Summit of December 1999, it was agreed that by 2003 the EU would be in a position to deploy a 60,000 military force, see *Presidency Conclusions Helsinki European Council Annex IV*, (1999), Brussels, European Council 1999, and Gillespie, P., *The Irish Times*, 20 May 2000.

[15]   See the comments by Kenny, P. and others on 'Kenny Live', 25 April 1998. The two hour RTE television show was exclusively devoted to the defence forces and UN peacekeeping.

[16]   Department of Foreign Affairs (1999), *Ireland and the Partnership for Peace*, an explanatory guide, Dublin, p. 9.

[17]   See, for example, comments by William Norton, leader of the minority Labour party at the time, *Dáil Debate*, 102 (1343), 24 July 1946.

[18]   *Dáil Debates*, 97 (2779-2881), 19 July 1945.

[19]   *Dáil Debates*, 102 (1315-1325), 24 July 1946.

[20]   *Ibid.* According to de Valera, 'the balance of argument would be in favour of getting rid of the veto and of trying to get larger states to accept the rule of law'.

[21]   See the contributions from John A. Costello, a leading member of the main opposition party and future Taoiseach, and others, in *Dáil Debates*, 102 (354-1355 and 1374), 24 July 1946.

[22]   *Ibid.* Dáil Debates, 102 (1403-1408), 24 July 1946. See generally O'Halpin, E. (1999), *Defending Ireland*, Oxford: Oxford University Press, pp. 270-271.

[23]   *Dáil Debates*, 102 (1460), 25 July 1946.

[24]   *Dáil Debates*, 102(1336), 24 July 1946.

[25]   'We in the Government have balanced the pros and cons [of membership]. In our circumstances, although it is impossible to be enthusiastic, I think we have a duty as a member of the world community to do our share in trying to bring about general conditions which will make for the maintenance of peace', *Dáil Debates*, 102 (1325), 24 July 1946.

[26]   Personal interview, senior Department of Foreign Affairs official, Department of Foreign Affairs, Dublin, May 1997; and personal interview, senior serving defence forces officer, Department of Defence, Dublin, May 1997. See Lt. Gen. G. McMahon, (1998), retired Chief of Staff, article, *The Irish Times*, 8 October, p.16 and the statements by MacKernan, P. (1998), General Secretary of the Department of Foreign Affairs, *The Irish Times*, 29 October, p.9.

[27]   Ireland's willingness to participate in SFOR, despite reservations, was also based upon pragmatic considerations and a desire to play as full a role as possible in world affairs for a country of its size and resources, see *Dáil Debates* 479 (514-539), 14 May 1997.

[28]   Keatinge, *op. cit.* and McQueen, N. J. 'Ireland's entry into the United Nations, 1946-1956', in Gallagher T. and O'Connell, J. (eds) (1983), *Contemporary Irish Studies*, Manchester: Manchester University Press, pp. 65-77.

[29]   Fontaine, A. (1970), *History of the Cold War*, New York: Vintage Books, p. 84.

[30]   McQueen, *op. cit.*, p. 69.

[31]   *The Irish Times*, 9-16 December 1955.

[32]   The definition of peacekeeping or preventive diplomacy is taken from Fabian, L. (1971), *Soldiers Without Enemies*, Washington DC: The Brookings Institute, p. 16.

[33]   *Dáil Debates*, 153 (160-1608), 15 December 1955.

[34]   *Dáil Debates*, 159 (139), 3 July 1956.

[35]   These principles were as follows: support for the principles and obligations of the UN Charter; to try to maintain a position of independence; and 'to do

whatever we can as a member of the UN to preserve the Christian civilisation of which we are a part, and with that end in view to support wherever possible those powers principally responsible for the defence of the free world in their resistance to the spread of communist power and influence ... we belong to the great community of states, made up of the United States of America, Canada and Western Europe'. *Ibid.* (127-146).

36   *Ibid.* (137). At the time, neither de Valera nor Aiken of the main opposition party, Fiannna Fáil, raised any opposition to the relegation of this issue in Ireland's foreign policy. This was important because the 'national question' had tended to dominate foreign policy discussions to the detriment of the consideration of more internationally significant issues

37   O'Brien, C. (1969), 'Ireland in International Affairs', Dudley-Edwards, *Conor Cruise O'Brien Introduces Ireland,* London: Deutsch, pp.104-134, esp. pp. 129-132.

38   McQueen, in Gallagher and O' Connell (eds), *op. cit.,* n. 22.

39   Frederick H. Boland, Secretary of the then Department of External Affairs in 1955, was designated as Ireland's first permanent representative at the UN. While Cosgrave's tenure was of short duration, Boland remained as Ireland's permanent representative for five years. He and his successor, C.C. Cremin, were known to approve and support the 'three principles' expounded by Cosgrove. A recent study, however, has challenged the view that the three principles were so influential, Skelly, *op. cit.* n. 4.

40   Aiken was Minister for External Affairs on two separate occasions, for three years from 1951 to 1954, and for twelve years from 1957 to 1969. See Keatinge, *The Formulation of Irish Foreign Policy, op. cit.,* pp. 84-89 and 32-34.

41   *Dáil Debates,* 159 (148), 3 July 1956.

42   Despite strong opposition from the US and the Catholic church, Aiken supported and Ireland voted in favour of the discussion of the representation of the People's Republic of China at the UN. Aiken also put forward plans for military disengagement in Central Europe and general disarmament, which were opposed by the US. These were part of general efforts by him to reduce tensions between the Soviet Union and the West during the Cold War. In addition, Aiken supported some of the small non-aligned new members of the UN, and adopted an independent policy during the Algerian crises. See generally Skelly, *op. cit.,* n. 4.

43   For some interesting background to the pressure put upon the Irish government and the Irish delegation at the UN by the Catholic Church and the United States, see O'Brien, C. C. (1962), *To Katanga and Back – a UN Case History.* New York, Grosset and Dunlap, pp. 21-25.

44   O'Brien, *op. cit.,* n. 37 at p.130.

45   Fabian has examined the semantic confusion surrounding its usage and he drew the following conclusion: 'the term middle power acquired in the United Nations context a variety of connotations. At first it was used in an objective sense to identify those member states with comparatively medium level resources, measured in terms of geography, wealth or military capabilities. It later took on a second meaning according to which middle power endowments were seen as circumstantial and perhaps temporary ... this description was given to countries occupying a political middle on given issues .... A member state could be classified as a middle power for some purposes but not for others ... Middle power membership has thus not taken identical forms in peacekeeping, in debates on colonial or racial rights questions, in disarmament negotiations, or in economic matters – although a Canada, a Sweden, an Austria, or an Ireland has

repeatedly acted out the middle power role on a range of problems'. Fabian, *op.cit.,* p. 88.

[46]   McQueen, DPhil thesis, *op. cit.*, Ch. 6, esp. pp.199-200. The study indicates that Irish voting behaviour in relation to other states compared showed a gradual move towards greater co-operation with Western countries. However, the evidence indicated that this process did not begin in 1961, the date usually assigned to the modification of Ireland's 'independent' stance at the UN. The study found that the process appeared to begin around 1959 at the Fourteenth Session of the General Assembly and to reach an extreme in the 1961 at the Sixteenth Session. After that, co-operation with the US in plenary votes remained more or less steady throughout the 1960s.

[47]   *Ibid.* This close affinity was detectable throughout the period under examination and it appears to be little affected by the supposed right shift in Irish policy after 1961. In fact, the conclusion drawn was that voting behaviour, in terms of co-operation with block leaders, does not offer convincing support for the comment that UN policy underwent a process of deradicalisation after 1961

[48]   Driscoll, D. (1980), 'Is Ireland really "Neutral"?', *Irish Studies in International Affairs*, Vol. 1, No. 3.

[49]   Singer, M. R. (1972), *Weak States in a World of Powers: The Dynamics of International Relations*, New York: The Free Press, pp. 327-328. The Singer and Sensinig study of voting on Cold War issues in the General Assembly from 1955 to 1959 shows that Ireland was a consistent supporter of the United States on such issues. The same was not the case in respect of the states considered truly non-aligned in the international system

[50]   See Bowett, D. W. (1964), *United Nations Forces*, London: Stevens, esp. pp. 99-103; White, N. (1997), *Keeping the Peace, 2nd. Ed.*, Manchester: Manchester University Press, p. 253, and James, A. (1990), *Peacekeeping in International Politics*. London: Macmillan, pp. 210-223.

[51]   Skelly, *op. cit.*, pp. 268-269.

[52]   Full details are contained in Department of Defence (2000), *Defence Forces Annual Report 1999*, Dublin, pp. 32-38. See also Department of Defence (1997), *Department of Defence and Defence Forces Strategy Statements 1997-1999*, Dublin, p. 8. When the term defence forces is used, it refers to the Permanent Defence Forces established under Section 18(a) of the Defence Act, 1954, and includes army, navy and air corps.

[53]   *Ibid.*

[54]   As far back as 1986, the then Chief of Staff commented publicly that much of the equipment was either obsolete or obsolescent, see interview, Lt. Gen. T. O'Neill (1986), *The Irish Press*, 1 April. For a more current analysis, see Cusack, J. (1999), *The Irish Times*, 9 October, p. 11.

[55]   The Chief of Staff, Lt. Gen. C. Mangan (2000) recently described the forces as 'moving from a garrison-based organisation, dominated by ATCP (aid to the civil power) and security duties, to having a significant part of the defence forces prepared to deploy with a rapid reaction force for European operations', reported in *The Irish Times*, 15 November, p. 9.

[56]   This description would not be accepted by many serving defence forces personnel, personal interview, *op. cit.*, n. 26.

[57]   *The Irish Times*, 18 July 1960 and Duggan, op. cit., p. 250.

[58] In all 6,197 Irish personnel served with the peacekeeping force in the Congo and twenty-six of these lost their lives

[59] There was a substantial military commitment to ONUC; Ireland was a permanent member of the Congo Advisory Committee; an Irishman, Frederick Boland, became President of the General Assembly; another, Lt. Gen. Sean McKeown, became Force Commander for a time, and Conor Cruise O'Brien became the Secretary-General's special representative in the Congo. See Skelly, *op. cit.*, pp. 266-283.

[60] Between April 1964 and October 1973 over 9,000 Irish personnel served with this force. At one stage there were over 1,000 troops in Cyprus while the strength of the army was less than 8,000 personnel.

[61] Security Council Resolution 340, 25 October 1973.

[62] *Dáil Debates*, 268 (797-830), 30 October 1973. The group was later augmented by another infantry company (130 men approx.) and it crossed the Suez canal on 9 November 1973. It was replaced by the 26 Infantry Group on 26 April 1974.

[63] See statement by Minister for Foreign Affairs, Garret Fitzgerald, *Dáil Debates*, 273 (692-693), 6 June 1974, see also the statement by the Minister for Defence, *Dáil Debates*, 273 (1715-1716), 27 June 1974.

[64] When the motion to approve the despatch of the contingent to UNEF II was being debated in the Dáil, the Minster for Defence and others had emphasised the need to recruit more volunteers for the army, due to the security situation in the country. Dr Fitzgerald said at the time that 'it was not without careful thought' that the government agreed, see *Dáil Debates*, 268, (797-830), 30 October 1973.

[65] Personal interview, UN Department of Peacekeeping Operations official, Pisa, Italy, June 1997.

[66] *Dáil Debates*, 306 (595-613), 9 May 1978. In July 1977, the UN requested that Ireland contribute a full contingent once again to UNFICYP in Cyprus. However, owing to a later decision to reduce the overall size of the force, the request was not maintained. There have been forty-five Irish casualties with this peacekeeping force; this figure includes Private Kevin Joyce who was taken captive on 27 April 1981. He is still categorised as missing in action.

[67] See *Dáil Debates*, 361(1088-1091), 5 November 1985 and 357 (428-434); and The Irish Times, 11 June 1985. However, in October 1985, the then Taoiseach, Garret Fitzgerald, warned that the participation of Irish troops in UNIFIL could be put in jeopardy if Israeli forces continued to prevent them fulfilling their mandate, *The Irish Times*, 21 October 1985, p.1 and *The Sunday Tribune*, 20 October 1985, p.1.

[68] See, for example, reports by Fagan, K. (1998), *The Irish Times*, 21 September 1998, p.10; Cusack, J. (1994), 16 July and 24 October 1995; Myers, K. (1995), 25 November in the same paper, and Marcus, J. (1984),'Irish Defence Policy: Debate on Neutrality', *Janes Defence Weekly*, 4 August 1984, pp.152-154.

[69] O'Halpin, *op. cit.*, p. 272.

[70] Figures supplied by Military Archives, Dept. of Defence, Dublin, August 1997.

[71] This is not to deny that the ONUC operation in the Congo did involve a number of mandate changes and enforcement operations on the ground. See Higgins, R. (1980), *The United Nations Operation in the Congo (ONUC) 1960-1964*, London: Royal Institute of International Affairs; Lefever, E. W. (1965), *Crisis in the*

Congo, Washington: The Brookings Institute, and James, A. (1994), 'The Congo Controversies', *International Peacekeeping (Kluwer)*, Vol. 1, No. 1, pp. 44-58.

72   See generally Murphy, R. (1999), 'Legal Framework of UN Forces and Issues of Command and Control of Canadian and Irish Forces', 4 Journal of Armed Conflict Law, pp. 41-73; and Murphy, R. (1994), 'Ireland: Legal issues arising from participation in United Nations operations', *International Peacekeeping (Kluwer)*, Vol. 1, No.2, pp.61-64.

73   *Ibid.*

74   *The Irish Times*, 10 August 1994 and the *Irish Independent*, 6 August 1994. In 1984, the defence forces were described by one commentator as 'a small but highly professional Defence Force', and he went on to say that Ireland 'faces the essential dilemma of all small nations seeking to provide their own security with limited resources', while at the same time 'Irish troops have served with distinction in the Congo, Cyprus and the Middle East in UN sponsored peacekeeping activities', Marcus, J., 'Irish Defence Policy: Debate on Neutrality', *Janes Defence Weekly*, 4 August 1984, pp. 152-154.

75   Department of Defence (1996), *Defence Forces Review Implementation Plan*, Dublin, February.

76   Personal interviews, defence forces personnel during 1996 and 1997. In addition, the *Report of the Commission on Remuneration and Conditions of Service in the Defence Forces (1990)*, Government Publications/Stationary Office, Dublin, was a damning indictment of not just pay and conditions, but bureaucratic and ineffective structures, and a remarkably militarily ineffective organisation.

77   Defence Forces Review Implementation Plan, *op cit.*, pp. 105-106.

78   *Ibid.*, Executive Summary, pp. i and ii. The reorganisation of the defence forces was to be based on a three brigade structure, with a manpower level of 11,500. See also Department of Defence (1996), *Department of Defence and Defence Forces Strategy Statements 1997-1999*, Dublin, pp. 37-41.

79   Personal interview, *op. cit.*, n. 26, see also *Department of Defence and Defence Forces Strategy Statements 1997-1999*, op. cit., pp. 5-9.

80   Defence Strategy Statements, *op. cit.*, p. 13.

81   See *Dishonoured Legacy, Report of the Commission of Enquiry into the Deployment of Canadian Forces to Somalia (1997)*, Ottawa: Canadian Government Publishing, also available at <http://www.dnd.ca.somaliae.htm> (English version).

82   Janowitz, M. (1960), *The Professional Soldier.* New York: Free Press. The term 'constabulary' was probably an unfortunate choice of word as it conjures up an image of the unarmed British 'bobby' keeping the peace along his beat.

83   *Ibid.* See also Dandeker C. and Gow J., 'Military Culture and Strategic Planning', in Schmidl E. (2000), *Peace Operations Between War and Peace*, London: Frank Cass, 58-79.

84   Segal, D.R. and Wechsler Segal, M. (1993), *Peacekeepers and their Wives.* London, Greenwood Press, p. 9. This view of the defence forces is from sixteen years service therein, and extensive interviews and conversations with Irish military personnel. Furthermore, the participation in UN missions in the cause of peace has been part of the stated mission of the Defence Forces since the 1960s.

85   Jackson, J. A. (1968),'The Irish Army and the Development of the Constabulary Concept' in Van Doorn, J. (ed.), *Armed Forces and Society*, The Hague: Sociological Essays.

[86]   Plans are now in place to change this, and it is planned to send smaller composite units to more missions, similar to that of UNAMET in East Timor, interview, senior officer, November, 2000.

[87]   Although from time to time the defence forces have encountered difficulty filling places in the UNIFIL battalion, personal interview, *op. cit.*, n. 26. At present, around thirty technical staff have been detailed for service with UNIFIL owing to the need to complete work arising from the redeployment following the Israeli withdrawal. In October 1984, an army medical doctor instituted proceedings in the High Court to restrain the Minister for Defence from sending him to Lebanon as part of the Irish contingent with UNIFIL. He claimed his health would be damaged by such service. His action was unsuccessful. *The Irish Times*, 26 October 1984. However, this was an exceptional case.

[88]   This fact was acknowledged to some extent by the Minister for Defence, Paddy Donegan, in 1974 when announcing the withdrawal of Irish troops from UNEF II. He said he wanted 'our troops to know it was only a temporary measure', because he knew the opportunity to serve abroad is a considerable incentive for young people to join the army. See *Dáil Debates*, 273 (1715-1716), 27 June 1974.

[89]   *The Irish Times*, 29 July 1963

[90]   Given the relatively small size of the defence forces, a large number of officers have also served in senior command and staff appointments with UN missions. See the article by Lt. Col. M. Shannon (1989), 'Thirty Years of Peacekeeping, A Perspective on Staff Appointments', *An Cosantóir*, April 1989.

[91]   Defence Forces Review Implementation Plan, *op. cit.*, pp. 105-106.

[92]   See Lt. Col. O. McDonald (1997), 'Peacekeeping Lessons Learned: An Irish Perspective', *International Peacekeeping (Kluwer)*, Vol. 4, pp. 94-103. The school provides general and mission specific national and international courses and training for peacekeeping duties. It is also responsible for keeping abreast of developments in the field and the development of a peacekeeping doctrine.

[93]   Personal interview, Col. R. Bunworth (1985), Dublin. Col. Bunworth was the Officer Commanding Southern Command and also Assistant Chief of Staff of the defence forces prior to his retirement. He had extensive experience with the UN in the Middle East and he was chairman of the Israeli Syrian Mixed Armistice Committee in 1967, and Chief of Staff of UNTSO during 1973 and 1974.

[94]   At a late stage the Irish battalions with ONUC were supplied with helicopters, and armoured cars were dispatched from Ireland.

[95]   That is not to say that certain incidents, especially in the Congo, did not amount to prolonged fire-fights to seize or defend strategic locations. These incidents, such as the 'siege of Jadoville' and 'the tunnel', or the battle for At-Tiri in Lebanon had all the ingredients of a full-scale military operation. However, they were nonetheless exceptions to the general rule that confrontations were usually of short duration and in most cases the UN troops managed to contain them by means of restraint and forbearance in spite of what often amounted to extreme provocation.

[96]   In February 1986, the defence portfolio was relegated even further when the Minister, Paddy O'Toole, was given responsibility for the Department of An Gaeltacht in addition. The present Minister for Defence is also responsible for the Department of the Marine.

[97]   In 1949, the Minister for External Affairs, Sean McBride, when answering a question in the Dáil regarding NATO membership stated: 'As long as partition

lasts, any military alliance or commitment involving joint military action with the state responsible for partition must be quite out of the question', *Dáil Debates*, 114 (323-326), 23 February 1949. See also Dudley Edwards (ed.), *op. cit.*, pp. 118-127, Keatinge, *A Place Among the Nations, op.cit.,* pp. 93-99.

98 O'Halpin, *op. cit.,* p. 261.

99 The situation the army found itself in during this period has been succinctly stated by one commentator as follows: 'Much (of the army's) equipment became increasingly outdated, and although some items, such as small arms and uniforms were renewed, this was done without any clear idea of the army's mission. More seriously, opportunities for training were limited and career prospects were restricted. Only in the early nineteen sixties did large scale participation in UN peacekeeping operations lift professional morale out of the routine rut of state ceremonials, guard duty, civilian emergencies and horse shows', Keatinge, *A Place Among the Nations, op.cit.,* p. 93.

100 For certain disadvantages associated with participation, see Murphy, R. (1998),'Ireland and Future Participation in Peacekeeping Operations', *International Peacekeeping* (F. Cass), Vol. 5, No. 1, pp. 22-45 at 37.

101 The factors that will inform consideration of such requests will include: an assessment of whether a peacekeeping operation is the most appropriate response to the situation; consideration of how the mission relates to the priorities of Irish foreign policy; the degree of risk involved; the extent to which the particular skills or characteristics required relate to Irish capabilities; the existence of realistic objectives and a clear mandate which has the potential to contribute to a political solution; whether the operation is adequately resourced; and the level of existing commitment to peacekeeping operations and security requirements at home; see *White Paper on Defence, op. cit.,* p. 63 and *White Paper on Foreign Policy, op. cit,* pp.194-195. The White Paper on Defence outlined additional factors for consideration, including ongoing developments in UN peace support operations, the evolution of European security structures, and the resource implications for the defence budget.

102 Comdt. B. O Keeffe (1998), spokesperson for the commissioned officers (RACO), RTE 9 O Clock News, 11 May.

103 See *The Irish Times*, 11 May 1998.

104 *White Paper on Defence, op. cit.,* p. 61. See articles by Cowan, B., Minister for Foreign Affairs, *The Irish Times*, 18 November 2000, p. 9, and *The Examiner,* 14 July 2000, p. 15.

105 See the *Nice Treaty White Paper*, Dublin: Government Publications, March 2001, and *The Irish Times*, 29 March 2001, 8. See also Maguire J. (1999), *Defending Peace – For an Alternative to NATO/PfP and a Militarised Europe,* Afri, Dublin, (1999); and Afri Position Paper No. 2 (1999), *Towards Real Security – A Contribution to the Debate on Irish Defence and Security Planning,* Dublin (1999), and Comhlamh, Focus, Issue 62, Dublin (Aug/Sep 2000), 16-24.

106 The criteria are as follows: that the operation derives its legitimacy from decisions of the Security Council; that the objectives are clear and unambiguous and of sufficiency and urgency and importance to justify the use of force; that all other reasonable means of achieving the objectives have been tried and failed; that the duration of the operation be the minimum necessary to achieve the stated objectives; that diplomatic efforts to resolve the underlying disputes should be resumed at the earliest possible moment; that the command and control arrangements for the operation are in conformity with the relevant decisions of

the Security Council and that the Security Council is kept fully informed of the implementation of its decision. *White Paper on Foreign Policy, op. cit.,* pp. 199-200.

[107] Lt. Col. E. Reumiller (1997), 'Canadian Perspectives and Experiences with Peacekeeping', paper delivered to seminar on Conflict Resolution and Peacemaking/Peacekeeping: the Irish and Canadian Experiences, Dublin, Association of Canadian Studies in Ireland.

[108] See reported warning by Defence Forces Chief of Staff that Irish peacekeepers are facing competition, The Irish Times, 5 October 1995; and the Defence Strategy Statements, *op. cit.,* p.15.

[109] The Irish Defence forces established a UN Training School in 1993, and agreed to participate in UN Stand-By forces in 1996. See also 'Improving the UN's Rapid Deployment Capability: A Canadian Study', February 1995; 'A UN Rapid Deployment Brigade: the Netherlands Paper', January 1995; and 'A Multifunctional UN Stand By Forces High Readiness Brigade: Chief of Defence, Denmark', 25 January 1995.

[110] Personal interview, Department of Foreign Affairs official, op. cit., n. 26. See also *Dáil Debates,* 472 (701-725), 4 December 1996 and *The Irish Times,* 22 and 28 November 1996.

[111] *Dáil Debates,* 479 (514-539), 14 May 1997 and *The Irish Times,* 23 January, 28 April and 8 May 1997.

[112] Personal Interviews, *op. cit,* n. 26. See also Department of Foreign Affairs (1999), *Ireland and the Partnership for Peace,* an explanatory guide, Dublin. It had been hoped to send a company strength contingent to SFOR, but some fifty personnel in a military police capacity was ultimately agreed.

[113] *Dáil Debates,* 507 (852-86), 1 July 1999. See also *The Irish Times,* 31 August 1999 and 1and 2 July 1999.

[114] The Defence (Amendment) Act, 1993, see Murphy, R. (1999), 'A Comparative Analysis of the Municipal Legal Basis for Canadian and Irish Participation in United Nations Forces', 38 *Revue de Droit Militaire et de Droit de la Guerre/The Military Law and the Law of War Review,* pp. 163-208.

[115] See reports by Cusack, J., *The Irish Times,* 5 February 2000, p. 3, and Murray, N., *The Examiner,* 14 July 2000, p. 1, and Lt. Gen. G. McMahon (2000), former Chief of Staff, article in *The Irish Times,* 26 July, p. 16. For an alternative view, see Jack McConnell, Press Officer, Department of Defence, letter, *The Irish Times,* 1 August 2000, p. 13.

[116] See speech by Cowan, B. (2000), Minister for Foreign Affairs, to the UN General Assembly, Department of Foreign Affairs, Dublin, September 2000, and de Breadún, D., *The Irish Times,* 16 September 2000, p. 13, and the denial of the reduction in UN role by the Minister for Defence reported in Roche, B., *The Irish Times,* 2 August 2000, p. 4.

[117] See generally Maguire, J. (1999), *op. cit.;* Afri Position Paper No. 2, *op. cit.,* and Comhlamh (2000), Focus, Issue 62, Dublin, pp. 16-24.

[118] O'Halpin, *op cit.,* p. 353.

[119] See English, A. J. (1987), 'The Irish Republic – Odd Man Out of European Defence', *Jane's Military Review,* London: Jane's Publishing, p. 31 and Mac Sweeney, B. (1998), 'Irish Defence in the Context of Irish Foreign Policy', *Irish Studies,* Spring, p. 51.

[120] Ireland formally joined the Partnership for Peace programme in December 1999, see *The Irish Times,* 2 December 1999, p.3. See also Doherty, R. (2000),

'Partnership for Peace: the sine qua non for Irish Participation in Regional Peacekeeping', *International Peacekeeping* (F. Cass), Vol. 7, No. 2, pp. 63-82; and *Challenges and Opportunities Abroad, op. cit.,* pp.128-140, Defence Strategy Statements, op. cit., pp.7-9, and Afri, *Towards Real Security, op. cit.,* pp. 2-7 and Gillespie, P., *The Irish Times*, 30 September 2000, p. 13.

121 It is difficult to take issue with the first three stated objectives of the Partnership for Peace, namely, transparency in defence planning, ensuring democratic control of defence forces, maintenance of capability and readiness to contribute to UN and the Organisation for Security and Co-operation in Europe (OSCE) operations.

122 *Challenges and Opportunities Abroad, op. cit.,* pp. 129-131.

123 For an examination of the security issues, see Keatinge, P. (1996), *European Security – Ireland's Choices*, Dublin: Institute of European Affairs.

124 See Murphy, R. (2000), 'Kosovo: Reflections on the legal aspects of the conflict and its outcome', *Irish Studies in International Affairs*, Vol. 11, pp. 7-30; and Maguire, J. *op. cit.,* at pp. 60-64.

125 See Dragon, S. (1999), 'Permanent Neutrality and Peacekeeping', *International Peacekeeping (Kluwer)*, Vol. 5, Nos. 1-2, pp. 37-40.

126 See Murphy, R. (1999), 'A Comparative Analysis of the Municipal Legal Basis for Canadian and Irish Participation in United Nations Forces', *op. cit.,* pp. 163-208.

127 Switzerland participated in many operations, for example, UNEF, ONUC and UNFICYP. A Swiss military medical unit was first sent to Namibia in 1988. Since then Switzerland has regularly contributed to peacekeeping operations through such units.

128 Dragon, *op. cit.,* p. 38.

129 See *The Irish Times*, 2 December 1999, p. 3. A major source of controversy arose from the fact that one of the government parties, Fianna Fáil, had promised before gaining power that it would hold a referendum on the issue. It changed its mind in government. For the terms of Irish membership, see *The Irish Times*, 6 October 1999, p. 6 and 2 December 1999, p. 3.

Chapter 2

These Islands and the European Dimension[*]

Brigid Laffan

Patrick Keatinge's seminal work on Irish foreign policy – *A Place Among the Nations: Issues of Irish Foreign Policy* – published in 1978 captures the complexity of relations between Great Britain and Ireland and the dominance of Anglo-Irish relations in Irish foreign policy. Long before the establishment of the Irish state, Britain's Ireland was a presence in the international system and the Irish engagement with the world outside involved a search for a non-imperial external environment. Ireland's search for independence, identity, security, unity and prosperity, the key issues identified by Keatinge in the 1978 volume, were for long mediated by what he calls the 'British Isles sub-system' (Keatinge, 1978, p. 228). That sub-system was characterised by dominance, dependence and 'unequal sovereigns' (Keatinge, 1986). In the final chapter of the 1978 volume, the author provided an overview of the three levels of international activity that were likely to impinge on Irish foreign policy after 1978 – the global, the regional (EU) and the level of the 'British Isles sub-system' (Keatinge, 1978, p. 225).

It would have been impossible to predict the profound changes that have characterised all three levels in the period since that volume was completed in the 1970s. We have witnessed the end of the Cold War, the reunification of Germany, the collapse of the Soviet Union and the arrival on the international scene of some twenty new states. The changes in the dynamic of European integration have been no less profound. Few would

[*] An earlier version of this paper was presented to a round-table meeting entitled 'Redefining Relationships: North-South and East-West Links in Ireland and Britain in the New Millennium', University College Dublin, 8 January 1998.

have predicted in 1978 the completion of the internal market, the euro, the European Security and Defence Policy (ESDP), additional European treaties and a Union that was embarking on continent-wide enlargement. The objective of this chapter is to analyse the changes within the 'British Isles sub-system' in the context of the regional or EU level of activity. The key claim of this chapter is that joint membership of the European Union transformed relations between the two states and assisted them in their continuing search for ways of managing and perhaps resolving the communal conflict in Northern Ireland. Although American diplomacy was central to the Good Friday Agreement, the agreement itself owes much to the changing context of statehood in Europe.

British and Irish membership of the European Union (EU) since 1973 has had profound effects on the economies and polities of both states. The decision to join the Union represented the most significant foreign policy decision taken by either state in the post-war period. EU membership involved participation in an additional arena of public policy making, acceptance of an extra-national constitutional and legal system, and a commitment to an evolving set of political structures at EU level. It had important effects on legal and political sovereignty by embedding both states in a federal legal order and in a system of pooled or shared sovereignty. By sheer coincidence, the outbreak of communal conflict in Northern Ireland coincided with the decision by the EU to open accession negotiations with Britain, Ireland, Norway and Denmark in 1968-69. Neither Britain nor the Republic of Ireland was principally concerned with the potential impact of EU membership on the conflict in Northern Ireland when they sought and secured EU membership. However, EU membership altered the context of relations between successive British and Irish governments, impinged on relations between the two communities in Northern Ireland and had an impact on strategies for conflict resolution. This chapter addresses the 'European' dimension of relations between the United Kingdom and Ireland in the first section, and then proceeds to analyse the 'European' dimension of conflict resolution/ management in Northern Ireland.

British-Irish relations in the EU

Joint membership of the EU altered the context of British/Irish relations in a radical manner by providing the Irish economy, polity and society with a highly institutionalised and rule-bound context within which it could adapt to economic and political internationalisation. The EU system offered a far more benign external environment for small states than balance of power systems or empire. EU membership enhanced the presence of the Irish state in the European and global arenas and the European market gave the Irish economy the opportunity to diversify and expand. It provided a continental home for the Irish economy and polity that enabled Ireland to move from dependence to interdependence. The formal equality of the British and Irish states in the EU moderated and tamed the asymmetrical relationship between the two countries and embedded their relationship in a wider multilateral framework. Both states became part of an evolving continental polity.

In the Union, 'the patron-client pattern was dissolved; in the new circumstance British ministers and diplomats could see their Irish counterparts as clever partners in Europe. Without this transformation it is almost impossible to see how Dublin-London relations could have been transformed as they were between the mid-seventies and the mid-eighties' (Kennedy, 1994, p.177). The EU offered the Republic an escape from excessive economic dependence on Britain, clearly apparent in the changing geographical pattern of Irish exports. In 1971, the UK market absorbed 61 per cent of Irish exports; the proportion had fallen to 25 per cent by 1998 (McAleese, 1998). Although material considerations played a pivotal role in Ireland's decision to apply for membership, the EU was a powerful symbol of Ireland's place in the European order as an independent small state with a seat at the table. The significance of this was seen as early as 1975 during Ireland's first presidency of the Council of Ministers. The European Union became central to the state's external identity, as highlighted by the 1996 White Paper on Foreign Policy, which concluded that:

> Irish people increasingly see the European Union not simply as an organisation to which Ireland belongs, but as an integral part of our future. We see ourselves increasingly as Europeans (Government of Ireland, 1996, p.59).

Such a statement would be inconceivable in a British, Danish or Swedish White Paper on foreign policy.

EU membership was a project for Ireland's future that also vindicated one of Ireland's strongest traditions, nationalism.

Ireland's engagement with Europe was part of a 'very deep longing for an alliance, a friendship that was non-imperial and psychologically satisfying, combined with a culturally determined wish to be self-sufficient and to be true to no one but one's collective self' (Garvin, 2000, p. 37). Participation in the EU was intimately linked to the national project of economic and social modernisation. Ireland's decision in the late 1950s and early 1960s to switch from protectionism to an outward orientation was a highly conscious and strategic one. It was intended to achieve an exporting economy by re-orienting the indigenous economy and attracting inward investment. In order to do this Ireland had to embrace free trade and multilateralism in the context of the EU. Paradoxically, sharing sovereignty in the EU provided successive Irish governments with a wider range of strategic policy choices than would have been possible if Ireland remained locked into an uneven and dependent relationship with the UK. Within two years of membership, when Britain engaged in a re-negotiation of its terms of membership in 1975, the then Irish government decided that even if the UK withdrew following the 1975 referendum, Ireland would remain in the Union. This was followed by the decision in 1978 to join the EMS without Britain and to join the single currency in the first wave. In both these instances, the Irish government was prepared to adopt an EU policy, which had the potential to drive a wedge between North and South. There has been a relatively easy fit between the dynamic of European integration, EU policy regimes and Irish preferences. This has enabled successive Irish governments to display a *communautaire* approach to the development of the EU in stark contrast to the controversial nature of the EU in domestic UK politics. The UK has never exercised the influence in the EU that its size would warrant although this may be changing under Tony Blair (Gillespie, 2000). Well schooled in the elusive nature of formal sovereignty, Irish politicians and administrators embraced the sharing of sovereignty unlike their UK counterparts for whom sovereignty remained a core political value.

Joint membership of the European Union provided British and Irish ministers and officials with a forum for continuing contact across the range of public policy issues. EU meetings, particularly European Councils, provided British and Irish prime ministers with an informal arena to discuss Northern Ireland at the margins of EU deliberations. Bilaterals became such a common occurrence that officials began to prepare for them as a matter of routine. In addition to the business content of such meetings, they provided an important opportunity for relationship building between the heads of government. Opportunities for informal contact meant that even when Anglo-Irish relations were at a low ebb, there was not a complete breakdown in communications. The Milan European Council in 1985 opened the way not only for the Single European Act but also the Anglo-Irish Agreement (Fitzgerald, 1991, p.551). Both governments sought to keep the question of Northern Ireland separate from their relationship in the Union. The Irish government was never tempted to try to raise the issue in the context of European Political Co-operation (EPC) and devoted far greater diplomatic resources in getting the US actively involved in conflict resolution. That said, the EU was regarded as a means of internationalising the question of Northern Ireland. In addition, given that Northern Ireland was part of the EU as a region of the United Kingdom, European institutions were external parties to the problem and gradually developed and interest in and a policy approach to the problem. EU institutions, notably, the Commission became very interested in Northern Ireland.

The development of an EU involvement

During the referendum on EU membership in 1972, there was a naive belief in the Republic that joint membership of the Union would spirit the border away and that European integration would foster Irish unity almost by stealth. In an integrating Europe, the border would gradually decline in economic and political salience. A 'borderless Europe' implied a 'borderless' Ireland. Such expectations, although understandable, were based on the assumption that the EU was considerably more integrated than in fact it was, and that its development was leading to traditional statehood. It ignored the imbalance in the Union between its impressive economic power and much weaker degree of political integration. The disintegration of Europe's traditional nation states is a continuing theme in discussions of European regionalism. Proponents of a 'Europe of the Regions' saw such a project as offering the prospect of transcending the British and Irish states and thereby providing a lasting solution to the Northern Ireland conflict in a frontier-free Europe (Kearney, 1988). Although regionalism is a growing phenomenon in Europe over the last twenty years, it is unlikely to transcend the traditional nation states, as each regionalism is highly contingent on the constitutional and political environment within which it evolves (Laffan, O'Donnell and Smith, 1999, p. 21). Post-Agreement Northern Ireland finds itself in a Europe of growing regional activism and multi-levelled governance.

Scholarly assessments of the EU role in Northern Ireland have tended to downplay the Union's role and to conclude that the EU was essentially a 'by-stander' that had not weakened the conditions of communal conflict (Rouane and Todd, 1996: Teague, 1996). It had altered relations between the two states and the two communities involved in the conflict (Bew and Meehan, 1994: Hainsworth, 1981: O'Cleireacáin 1983). The development of an EU dimension can be analysed under four main headings; the EU as a political arena, EU policies and reports on Northern Ireland, the EU as a model of negotiated governance and the EU in Northern Ireland.

The EU as a political arena

The EU was not just an external party to Northern Ireland but an additional arena of politics above the UK and Irish states. Northern Ireland was part of this evolving and increasingly complex layer of politics and economics. Like all of Europe's regions and states, Northern Ireland had interests to represent and public goods to secure in the EU. As in all political systems voice and representation mattered. Formally, Northern Ireland was represented in the Union's policy process by London-based ministers and civil servants. The UK system for managing EU business was based on the dominance of the 'lead ministry' with highly centralised mechanisms of co-ordination emanating from the Cabinet Office. This system favoured sectoral ministries rather than the three territorial ones because they did not have the status as lead ministries in any field. The representation of Northern Irish, Scottish or Welsh interests in the EU Council of Ministers had to pass through the processes of UK preference formation before they reached the table in Brussels. It has been argued that the UK system did not adequately represent the specific regional interests of the component parts of the UK. Specifically in relation to Northern Ireland, farming and community interests have felt poorly represented by the UK. Northern Ireland faces the additional problem of not having ministers in the British

Cabinet who could argue for its interests in cabinet debates (Bew and Meehan, 1994).

Concern with the under-representation of Northern Ireland in Brussels led to the opening of the Northern Ireland Centre in Europe in 1991. The Centre resembled the growing number of regional offices found in Brussels. It is a public/private partnership involving the Chamber of Commerce, local authorities, employers, trade unions and voluntary groups. Crucially, it received cross-party support. Both by its activities in Brussels and in Northern Ireland, the Centre provides an example of the way in which the EU experience had led to the establishment of common ground where the various parties and sectors in society work together to define and pursue a common agenda for Northern Ireland in relation to EU policies. The Centre established a working group involving the key chief executives of the Councils and Northern Ireland's members of the Committee of the Regions. Its Concordia project was designed to develop an active social partnership. In November 1998, it organised a four-day working visit for members of the Assembly to Brussels. Such developments would be regarded as routine and mundane in most political systems, but were difficult to develop in Northern Ireland. The participants regarded the fact that the visit took place as the beginning of normal politics. The EU agenda and the need to respond to the development of EU policies provided political space and political opportunities for co-operative and collaborative work. The question of representation in Brussels was re-opened in the context of the evolving constitutional changes in the United Kingdom and must also be addressed in relation to the implementation of the Good Friday Agreement.

The absence of direct ministerial representation in Brussels meant that Northern Ireland's three MEPs play a pivotal political role in links to the Brussels arena. European Parliament (EP) elections provided an electoral contest every five years and an arena within which to conduct party politics. Since the first direct elections in 1979, John Hume of the SDLP and Ian Paisley of the DUP have represented Northern Ireland. The UUP was represented by John Taylor and is now represented by Jim Nicholson. The three MEPs collaborate in the EP on policy issues while at the same time differing in their attitudes towards the EU and the role of the EU in Northern Ireland (Bew and Meehan, 1994). During the negotiations on the Community

Initiatives for 1994-99, considerable work was undertaken in relation to the eligibility of Belfast and Derry for this programme. The creation of the Peace and Reconciliation fund emerged from a Task Force established by Jacques Delors on the prompting of the three MEPs. Their three assistants in the EP worked closely with the Commission in the design of the programme. Given the importance of the agricultural agenda to Northern Ireland, each of the three main parties – UUP, SDLP and DUP – pay particular attention to this policy area and in the period before the establishment of the Executive, gave responsibility for it to Jim Nicholson, Denis Haughey and Nigel Dodds. They formed a close working relationship that has been a valuable means of establishing a network of communication, which can then be utilised on other issues. Co-operation on policy issues cannot, however, disguise divergence on the EU and its role in Northern Ireland.

Party attitudes towards Europe and an EU role in conflict resolution divide along communal lines. Nationalist opinion is generally supportive of European integration, whereas unionist opinion is far more sceptical. Unionist opinion is in line with British attitudes, whereas nationalist opinion is in line with opinion in the Republic of Ireland, albeit at a somewhat lower level of support (Reinhardt, 1996, p.10). Among the political parties, the SDLP and the Alliance Party are the most pro-European. John Hume has moulded the pro-European stance of the SDLP. Hume, in particular, played the European card with skill and used his position in the EP's socialist grouping to garner support for his analysis of the conflict and its resolution. In the EP, Hume successfully appropriated the European agenda and put it to use to promote his analysis of Northern Ireland. The SDLP went furthest in its support for an active EU role in the governance of Northern Ireland. In 1992, the SDLP proposed that the EU Commission should nominate one member of a six member Commission that would govern Northern Ireland. The proposal found little support from other political parties, the British government and the Commission itself (Bew and Meehan, 1994). Partly because of the Hume approach and his success, the unionist parties were defensive about an EU dimension and intergovernmental in their approach to European integration. The UUP favours intergovernmental co-operation among Europe's nation states but would not support radical federalisation, which might undermine the United Kingdom and its position in it. The UUP may have developed a more nuanced and less oppositional approach to the EU had it not been for the strident anti-European analysis introduced to the party by Enoch Powell. Their large farming supports benefit from the common agricultural policy. The DUP is fundamentally opposed to the EU, seeing Brussels as part of a wider Roman Catholic plot to control the continent. Both unionist parties have opposed the political involvement of the EU in Northern Ireland while accepting functional co-operation, if it can be ring-fenced.

EU policies – an assessment

The EU's role in Northern Ireland has evolved on the basis of its policy regimes and functional competence in agriculture, market integration and regional policy. The latter is one of the most visible of the EU's policy regimes in Northern Ireland. The establishment of the European Regional Development Fund (ERDF) in 1975 strengthened the development of a European regional policy. The Commission from the outset favoured a role for EU regional policy in alleviating obstacles to the economic development of border areas. The Commission wanted to transform Europe's borders from barriers into bridges. Cross-border co-operation formed a central part of the policy in this domain. The Irish government supported Commission preferences and argued that the non-quota section of the European Regional Development Fund (ERDF) should be used to finance cross-border projects. Once the possibility of cross-border projects was included in the regulations, the EU had a policy instrument to promote such projects in the context of the Irish border. Their development was slow, tortuous and contested. They began with a series of low-key reports outlining the economic problems of the border region and strategies for development. In the late 1970s, the Londonderry/Donegal Communications Study and the Erne Catchment Area Study were co-financed by the Commission, in addition to a number of programmes for tourism, small business and handicrafts. This was followed by a report on *Irish Border Areas* by the Economic and Social Committee in 1983, which recommended a strengthening of cross-border initiatives and the use of EU budgetary mechanisms to finance such initiatives. In addition to cross-border projects, the Commission recognised Northern Ireland as a region deserving of special treatment (objective one status) in the context of its regional policy. It ranked, together with the Republic, as a priority area for structural fund monies.

In the late 1970s and early 1980s, financial transfers became a key and enduring feature of the Union's policy towards Northern Ireland. The significance of budgetary instruments owed much to the fact that the Union had a sound treaty basis for involvement in the economic domain.

The visibility and salience of EU policies was enhanced by the reform of the structural funds and their increased financial resources after 1988. The new regulations required the development of an integrated plan covering all sectors which was then submitted to the Commission, which in turn agreed a Community Support Framework (CSF), a package of financial aid over a number of years. The Commission favoured what it called a partnership model for the development of such plans. This implied that there was extensive consultation by government of political parties and societal groups in the establishment of priorities and programmes. Because of the increase in financial resources and the manner of their delivery, the distribution of the funds became politicised with more and more groups seeking involvement in the programming process. Because of the weakness of the political process in Northern Ireland, the civil service and particularly the Department of Finance and Personnel (DFP) dominated the process at the outset. The department came under pressure from the political parties and the Commission to strengthen the consultative process. A key feature of the reformed fund was a Community initiative entitled Interreg that was specifically designed to promote cross-border co-operation and integration. This provided an opportunity to up-grade the relatively low-key co-operation, which had been built up during the 1980s. In practice, funding from Interreg 1 went to separate projects on either side of the border. The next programming period, 1993-99, required a review of the mechanism for cross-border co-operation. Both the National Plan submitted by the Republic to Brussels and the Single Programming Document submitted by the authorities in Northern Ireland contained a chapter on cross-border co-operation, which identified five priority areas. What is known as the common chapter contained no new initiatives nor were there proposals for enhanced co-operation between the two adminis-trations (Kennedy, 1994, p. 61.) The experience of implementing the Interreg programme did, however, lead to cross-border mobilisation in the border region as local politicians and voluntary groups sought to improve co-operation. Three cross-border networks – the North West Cross Border Group, the East Border Committee and the Irish Central Border Area Network – evolved from the 'bottom-up' with a new approach to cross-border co-operation. The networks were determined to develop cross-border co-operation that went beyond the formal networks establishment by civil servants.

Once EU policies began to impinge on Northern Ireland as a region, it was inevitable that attention would be drawn to the conflict itself. Whereas the Commission and the Council of Ministers restricted their involvement to functional co-operation within the ambit of EU policy regimes, the European Parliament became increasingly involved in debating the political dimensions of the conflict. Between 1981 and 1984, the European Parliament paid growing attention to political conditions within Northern Ireland. The Maze hunger strike was debated in 1981 and the use of plastic bullets condemned in 1982. This was followed by a major report issued in March 1984, known as the Haagerup Report after the Danish MEP who was the main rapporteur, on the situation in Northern Ireland. The commissioning of a report on Northern Ireland by the Political Affairs Committee of the Parliament was extremely controversial because it raised questions about the blurring of the boundary between what could be considered as the internal affairs of a member state and the competence of the Union. The British government was extremely unhappy about the report and the prime minister instructed the Conservative MEP's to try to block the commissioning of the report. Unionist politicians were also implacably opposed to the intervention of the EP in the political and constitutional affairs of Northern Ireland.

The resolution which accompanied the report, set out the role that the EU should play in relation to Northern Ireland, in addition to views about the perceived role of other actors. The report strongly endorsed an Anglo-Irish framework for the resolution of the conflict because it was replete with references to the need for 'the closest possible co-operation between the United Kingdom and Irish Governments' and 'for expanding and enlarging their mutual co-operation' (EP, 1984, p. 9). Concerning the EU itself, the report highlighted the role of EU expenditure and called on the Commission and the Council of Ministers to develop an integrated plan for the development of Northern Ireland. This was very much in line with what the EU was already doing, notably with respect to the Integrated

Programme for Belfast. The political importance of the report should not be underestimated in that it emphasised the importance of Anglo-Irish relations and recognised the interest of the Republic in Northern Ireland. It has been argued that 'the real significance of Haagerup was that it showed the extent to which an essentially nationalist analysis of the problem was being accepted by external neutrals, as was the idea that progress towards a solution lay in the broader Anglo-Irish context' (Kennedy 1994, p.179). Since Haagerup, the EU has supported and endorsed all political agreements between Britain and Ireland. The Commission responded to the Anglo-Irish Agreement by creating a Northern Ireland committee in its services which was followed by an EU donation to the Ireland Fund in 1989. Following the cease-fires in 1994, the Commission established a Commission Task Force which designed the Peace and Reconciliation Fund (1995-99), approved by the Essen European Council at the end of 1994. The Berlin European Council in March 1999 agreed to the continuation of the Peace Fund into the next financing period (2000-2006).

The EU as a model

The European Union, established as a peace project in the context of Cold War Europe, offered a model of inter-state relations that rested on co-operation, interdependence, mutual understanding and civic statehood. Its founding ideology was based on reconciliation and the transformation of neighbours into partners in a collective project. John Hume appropriated the rhetoric of European integration, arguing constantly that if conflict on the scale of two world wars could be resolved through dialogue, then so could the conflict in Northern Ireland. In addition to the rhetoric of integration, participation in the EU offered alternative models of politics and political order.

First, the iterative and intensive EU Treaty negotiations, with no final settlement in prospect, underlined the adequacy of partial agreement. Second, the investment in the EU in building institutions drew attention to the importance of institutional innovation in promoting collective action and in socialising political actors into new procedures and norms of policy making. Third, the emphasis in the Union on problem-solving pragmatic politics was a useful antidote to the zero-sum bargaining of politics in Northern Ireland. Fourth, the sharing of sovereignty in the EU highlighted the divisibility of sovereignty in contemporary Europe. The language and style of politics in the EU – partnership, problem solving, experimentation, innovation, unending negotiations – offered a way of doing things which must characterise the implementation and operation of the Agreement if it is to become a living settlement. The institutions of the Good Friday Agreement outlined below echo a number of the institutional and procedural features of the EU. The d'Hondt system used for the allocation of political offices according to the share of seats in the European Parliament is used for the allocation of ministerial office to the parties in the Northern Ireland Assembly. The North-South Ministerial Council which meets in plenary and in different sectoral formations is not unlike the Council of Ministers, and meetings of the British and Irish heads of government resemble the European Council.

The EU in Northern Ireland

Membership of the European Union brought Commissioners, their officials and EP groups to Northern Ireland. A number of high-ranking Commission officials, notably Carlo Trojan, former Secretary General of the Commission was personally very committed to Northern Ireland. The Commission officials who sat on programme monitoring committees brought with them their experience of different administrative and political systems and could be regarded as neutral in terms of the division between the communities. With the growing salience of the EU, more and more groups within Northern Ireland became active in transnational projects and in Brussels based lobbying groups.

Knowledge and interest in the EU is expanding beyond the narrow confines of the mandarins in the civil service. The preparation of the Single Programming Document for structural fund finance provided opportunities for the identification of areas of common interest. The Peace and Reconciliation Fund (PRF) led to the establishment of new mechanisms of co-operation which enabled people to see the potential for co-operation when the dynamic was changed. It was an important validation and endorsement of the cease-fires and created political space for new developments. It forced politicians and wider civil society groups to take on the responsibility for resource allocation.

The Fund was administered by the NI Partnership Board that consists of the political parties, the voluntary and community sector, and the social partners. The Board managed the programme that was largely administered by twenty-six District Partnerships. At local level, there were funding mechanisms, which push the political parties towards agreement on resource allocation which, in turn, promote effective working mechanisms. Clearly, the performance of the partnerships was patchy and there continues to be tension between the politicians and wider civil society groups. The Commission regarded the delivery mechanisms and the inclusive nature of the process as a model for mainstream EU funding (Wolf-Mathies, 1998). The Peace and Reconciliation Fund (PRF) will continue in the next funding period with minor changes in the mode of delivery.

The Good Friday Agreement

The constitutional settlement embodied in the Good Friday Agreement represented a complex set of institutional and political arrangements within Northern Ireland, between North and South and between Britain and Ireland. Important landmarks in the lead-up to the Agreement were the Anglo-Irish Agreement (1985), the Downing Street Declaration (1993) and the Framework Document (1995). The Anglo-Irish Agreement had little EU content other than a reference to the determination of both governments to develop close co-operation as partners in the EU. The 1995 Framework Document contained a much stronger reference to the EU. It referred to 'an agreed approach for the whole island in respect of the challenges and opportunities of the European Union', to the implementation of EU programmes 'on a cross-border or island wide basis' and to 'joint submissions' to the EU (Framework Document, 1995 paragraph 26).

The Good Friday Agreement itself is replete with references to European issues.

Strand One: This strand consists of an elected Assembly and an Executive Authority headed by a First Minister and Deputy Minister. The duties of the latter consist in part of co-ordinating the work of the Executive and managing the external relationships of the administration. The December 1998 agreement on the Executive established eleven departments, all of which have a European dimension. Many of them, notably Regional Development, Social Development and Enterprise, Trade and Investment have overlapping responsibilities in an EU context. Given the distribution of portfolios across the political parties, there are likely to be considerable turf battles about departmental responsibilities at the outset. Control of economic policy is a looming battle because there is an Economic Policy Unit and a Policy Innovation Unit in the Office of the First Minister and Deputy Minister, the Department of Enterprise, Trade and Investment has responsibility for Economic Development Policy and the Department of Finance and Personnel is likely to want to continue to play its traditional Treasury role. Responsibility for European matters was allocated to the Office of the First Minister and Deputy Minister, which co-ordinates the European briefs of the other departments and has developed relations with a range of EU players. The appointment by Seamus Mallon of two former senior Commission officials as advisors suggests that the SDLP intended to have a large input into the development of European policy. The UUP had no corresponding expertise at the outset. Prior to the formation of the Executive, the Department of Finance and Personnel (DFP) had the central co-ordinating role within the Northern Irish administration. It remains the lead player in developing and negotiating the Community Support Framework and Community Initiatives with the Commission. Because of direct rule, civil servants in Northern Ireland have had far less political direction in policy development than is the norm in a democratic system of government. The representation of Northern Ireland's interests in Europe had to be re-negotiated with London. The model followed the mechanisms that were negotiated with Edinburgh and Cardiff. Whitehall was determined to maintain overall control of the UK's European policy but had to agree standard operating procedures with the devolved administrations. Depending on the political complexion of these administrations, the relationship on EU affairs may be co-operative or conflictual (Robbins, 1998). The experience in other countries, notably Germany, Belgium and Spain, suggests that there will be tensions about EU business.

Strand Two: There were a number of references to EU matters in Strand Two. First, the North-South Ministerial Council has a remit to consider the European Union dimension of relevant matters, including the implementation of EU policies and programmes under consideration in the EU. Arrangements must be put in place to ensure that the views of the Council are taken into account and represented appropriately at relevant EU meetings (Good Friday Agreement, Strand 2, Paragraph 17) This was deliberately ambiguous and offered the prospect that the views of the Council on EU matters may simply be noted by the relevant channels, or it could mean that members of the Council participate in Irish delegations to the Council and its working parties. This clause may have significant consequences for Ireland's management of EU policy in the long term. To date, EU business has not impinged all that much on the work of the North South Ministerial Council.

The second EU dimension in Strand Two related to the implementation bodies proposed in the Agreement. In the December 1998 agreement on implementation bodies, it was decided to establish an implementation body for Special EU Programmes. The body was given responsibility for the existing cross-border programmes, the development of the Community initiatives in the next programming period and their implementation. An implementation body on EU programmes was high on the SDLP's shopping list and was agreed by the UUP, albeit with reservations.

Cross-border co-operation to date has had a modest impact on co-operation and integration in border regions. There are three models for the development of cross-border initiatives based on:

- parallel or back to back implementation
- joint planning but separate implementation
- joint planning and implementation.

To date the implementation of cross-border initiatives on the Irish border has been largely characterised by the first model with an attempt to move to model two in the 1994-99 programming period. The implementation of the Special EU Programme Body (SEUPB) was clearly designed to move the process to the third model with joint planning and implementation. This implied institution building and the allocation of sufficient administrative staff to the implementation body. There are formidable barriers to this. The unionists remain sceptical about cross-border co-operation and will try to limit it to clearly defined and targeted projects. They are suspicious of rolling unity and the potential spill-over from the economic to the political. The administrative barriers are also formidable in that both civil services have a long tradition of working within their distinctive administrative cultures and jurisdictions. It is unclear just how much political and administrative capacity will be invested in the management of change and in creating the capacity for innovation and experimentation. If the implementation bodies are to promote cross-border co-operation, they will have to have sufficient capacity and policy space to generate new ideas and new processes of politics.

The SEUPB was established under an Agreement between the government of Ireland and the government of Great Britain and Northern Ireland in March 1999 and came into effect on 2 December 1999. It is directly accountable to the North/South Ministerial Council which in turn is accountable to the Oireachtas and the Northern Ireland Assembly. Its work was hampered in the early period by the suspension of the Executive but in the latter half of the year 2000 it began the slow process of establishing itself in the institutional landscape of Northern Ireland and the Republic. The SEUPB finds itself at the confluence of a number of different changes – regionalisation in the Republic, changes in the EU guidelines on cross-border co-operation, the evolution of the new institutions and 'bottom-up' mobilisation in the border region. It must establish itself as a new organisation in the context of a fluid and dynamic external environment.

Strand Three: The EU dimension to Strand Three manifested itself in the suggestion that EU matters were suitable for discussion by the British-Irish Council. Moreover, the stipulation that two or more members were free to develop bilateral or multilateral arrangements has encouraged the development of political and policy links between Dublin, Cardiff and Edinburgh. It will act as an additional spur to the Ireland-Wales Interreg programme. The development of multiple relations between the component parts of the two islands, will over time lead to 'these islands' emerging as a sub-system in the EU, not unlike the Benelux, Franco-German relations and Nordic Co-operation. Enlargement to the East and the addition of many more states will in any case promote the growth of more sub-system groupings in the EU.

Conclusions

This chapter analysed the dynamic role that joint membership of the European Union has played in the changing relations between Britain and Ireland and North and South. It demonstrated just how much has changed since Patrick Keatinge confronted the problem of the future in the final chapter of the volume, *Issues in Irish Foreign Policy*, in 1978. In the period since then, the Irish State and its political élite have continued to grapple with the dilemmas of British-Irish relations and the continuing conflict in Northern Ireland. The Good Friday Agreement concluded in April 1998 and subsequent legalisation went a long way towards providing a constitutional settlement for conflict management if not conflict resolution in Northern Ireland. Its achievement showed just how far British-Irish relations had evolved and developed since the trauma of 1968-69. Tony Blair's address to the Oireachtas in November 1998 provided a symbolic marker of the change.

The outbreak of communal conflict in Northern Ireland coincided with accession negotiations to the EU and subsequent membership. Without the embedding of both states in the wider system of European integration and without the model of politics offered by the EU, it is unlikely that both states and other political actors could have found the political capacity and the institutional models to craft the Good Friday Agreement. The EU made an essential contribution to the changing relations between Britain and Ireland and to conflict management *in* Northern Ireland. The Good Friday Agreement is being implemented in the context of an unsettled UK, which together with the Republic is embedded in an unsettled and enlarging Europe. Moreover, it is being implemented in a very unstable political and institutional environment in Northern Ireland with continuing crises about the future of policing and decommissioning. It is impossible to predict if the Agreement can withstand repeated crises or if its institutions can become embedded in the institutional landscape of these islands. The 'problem of the future' remains. Patrick Keatinge uses a quote from Hedley Bull to introduce his final chapter on 'The Problem of the Future' which ends as follows: '(I)t is better to recognise that we are in darkness than to pretend that we can see light' (Keatinge, 1978, p.223). The Good Friday Agreement undoubtedly represented light in the context of the dark days of conflict in Northern Ireland and Patrick Keatinge's work on Irish foreign policy was the first serious attempt by an international relations scholar to shed light on Ireland's role in the world. We are indebted to him for his path-breaking scholarship and his pedagogic contribution.

References

Bew, P. and Meehan, E. (1994), 'Regions and borders: controversies in Northern Ireland about the European Union', *European Journal of Public Policy*, 1:1, pp. 95-113.

European Commission (1998), *Peace and Reconciliation Fund*, Docs. EC 98/63.

European Parliament (1984), *The Haagerup Report on the Situation in Northern Ireland*, Doc. 1-1526/83.

Framework Document (1995), in Cox, M., Guelke, A. and Stephen, F. (eds.) (2000), *A Farewell to Arms?* Manchester: Manchester University Press, pp. 338-41.

Fitzgerald, G. (1992), *All in a Life*, Dublin: Gill and Macmillan.

Good Friday Agreement (1998), Agreement Reached in the Multi-Party Negotiations.

Government of Ireland (1996), *Challenges and Opportunities Abroad: White Paper on Foreign Policy*, Dublin: Government Publications.

Gallagher, E. (1984), 'Anglo-Irish Relations in the European Community', Address to a conference of the Royal Irish Academy on 23 November 1984.

Garvin, T. (2000), 'The French are on the Sea', in O'Donnell, R. (ed.), *Europe: The Irish Experience*, Dublin: IEA, pp. 35-43.

Gillespie, P. (ed.) (2000), *Blair's Britain, England's Europe: A View from Ireland*, Dublin: IEA.

Hainsworth, P. (1981), 'Northern Ireland: A European Role?, *Journal of Common Market Studies*, 20:1, pp. 1-15.

Hainsworth, P. (1996), 'Northern Ireland and the European Union', in Aughey, A. and Morrow, D. (eds.), *Northern Ireland Politics*, London: Longman, pp. 129-138.

Kearney, R. (1998), *Across the Frontiers: Ireland in the 1990s*, Dublin: Wolfhound.

Keatinge, P. (1978), *A Place Among the Nations: Issues of Irish Foreign Policy*, Dublin: IPA.

Keatinge, P. (1986), 'Unequal Sovereigns: the Diplomatic Dimension of Anglo-Irish Relations', in Drudy, P.J. (ed.), *Ireland and Britain since 1922,* Cambridge: Cambridge University Press.

Kennedy, D. (1994), 'The European Union and the Northern Ireland question', in Barton, B. and Roche, P. J. (eds.), *The Northern Ireland Question: Perspectives and Policies*, Aldershot: Avebury, pp. 166 88.

Laffan, B., O'Donnell, R. and Smith, M. (1999), *Europe's Experimental Union: Rethinking Integration*, London: Routledge.

McAleese, D. (2000), 'Twenty-five Years "A Growing"', in O'Donnell, R. (ed.) *Europe: The Irish Experience*, Dublin: IEA, pp. 79-110.

O' Cleireacain, S. (1983), 'Northern Ireland and Irish Integration: The Role of the European Communities', *Journal of Common Market Studies*, 22: 2, pp. 107-24.

Reinhardt, N. (1996), 'Public Attitudes towards the European Union', in Browne, M. and Kennedy, D. (eds.) *The Dynamics of Conflict in Northern Ireland*, Cambridge: Cambridge University Press.

Robbins, K. (1998), 'Britain and Europe: devolution and foreign policy', *International Affairs,* 74:1, pp. 105-118.

Rouane, J. and Todd, J. (1996), *The Dynamics of Conflict in Northern Ireland*, Cambridge: Cambridge University Press.

Teague, P. (1996), 'The European Union and the Irish Peace Process', *Journal of Common Market Studies*.

Wulf-Mathies, M. (1998), 'Visit of the Northern Ireland Assembly', address 4, November 1998.

Chapter 3

Ireland's Official Aid Programme[*]

Helen O'Neill

Introduction

In 1974, a year after joining the European Economic Community (EEC now EU), Ireland established its bilateral aid programme. Total expenditure on official development assistance (ODA), both bilateral and multilateral, was IR£1.5 million. In 1999 – when Ireland celebrated twenty-five years of its aid programme and it got a new logo and a new name (Ireland Aid) – ODA exceeded IR£181 million which was well over one hundred times that original amount. Related to GNP, the 1974 aid figure represented 0.05%. In 1999 – if the estimate for GNP of IR£51 billion turns out to be correct – it was 0.31%. Admittedly, this falls far short of the UN aid target 0.7% and is still below the 0.4% 'average country effort' for EU member states today. Nevertheless, on this measure, Ireland had already climbed into the upper half of the 'donor league table' in 1997 and remained there in 1998 having already overtaken the DAC average three years earlier. In the intervening years, the world economy and polity has changed dramatically and the global context within which aid programmes operate today is very different from what it was when the Irish aid programme was launched in 1974.

Before comparing these two periods, however, it is appropriate to define what is meant by foreign aid. It is also appropriate to examine the main reasons why donor countries

[*]   I would like to thank officials in the Department of Foreign Affairs (Ireland Aid), the Department of Finance and the Department of Enterprise, Trade and Employment for very useful discussions and for supply of unpublished data. This chapter was completed for publication prior to the Spring 2002 publication of the Report of the Ireland Aid Review Committee (http://www.gov.ie/iveagh).

are motivated to give foreign aid and why their developing country partners tend to welcome it.

What is foreign aid?

While donors might like to count all their financial transfers to developing countries as part of their foreign aid budgets, the members of the DAC have agreed strict rules regarding what is, and what is not, to be defined as what it calls 'official development assistance' or ODA. This term excludes military equipment and export credits extended to developing countries at market rates of interest. The term includes transfers to developing countries and to multilateral institutions – such as the World Bank and the United Nations Development Programme – which are provided by official agencies, including state and local governments which are concessional in character and contain a grant element of at least 25%. The transfers may be in cash, or kind or expertise but their main objective must be 'the promotion of economic development and welfare of developing countries' (OECD/DAC, 1972, p. 171).

Motivations for giving and receiving foreign aid

The three main reasons why donors give aid are cited as: humanitarian (because of a moral obligation to help poor people); political (globally, to promote world peace and global development; domestically to provide aid to 'friendly' countries in order to defend national interests or security); and economic (externally, by promoting economic benefits for developing countries through transfers to them of scarce foreign exchange or technical assistance; domestically, by promoting economic benefits for the donor country through expansion of investment opportunities, export markets, and ensuring secure sources of raw materials and energy). Developing countries can also have a mixture of motivations for welcoming aid inflows. Aid can be a means of strengthening the political position of developing country governments. It can also be perceived as essential to the process of economic and social development by supplementing scarce domestic resources including foreign exchange and skills.

The global environment for aid in 1974

The 1960s had been a period of unprecedented growth and strong commodity prices in the world economy. It was also the decade when most of today's developing countries, including most of those in sub-Saharan Africa, had achieved their political independence. As a result, the 1970s began with great hopes on both economic and political fronts. It was designated the 'development decade' by the United Nations and most industrialised countries accepted an aid target for donors of 0.7% of their GNP although most of them did not commit themselves to a time frame for reaching it. In 1974, at a Special Session of the UN General Assembly, developing countries as a group called for restructuring of international economic institutions and a new international economic order (NIEO). Ireland, working with other 'like-minded' countries such as Canada and the Scandinavians, supported the developing countries in their call for the NIEO. In 1975, the first Lomé Convention was signed between the EEC and independent African, Caribbean and Pacific (ACP) countries.

The 'trickle-down' theory, which claims that all boats are lifted by the rising tide ('as the rich get richer, the poor also get richer') was widely accepted by policy makers during those years of strong economic growth. Although this theory was questioned by development economists, its inverse ('when the rich get poorer, the poor get poorer still') certainly seemed to operate in times of slow or declining economic activity. When the world economy went into recession following OPEC's oil price increases of 1973 and 1979, global growth declined but it shrank most dramatically in oil-importing developing countries as demand for their raw material exports fell and commodity prices collapsed. Indeed, the seeds of the third-world debt problem were sown during that period as developing countries borrowed heavily in an effort to maintain their development programmes. Interestingly, despite the world recession, aid flows from the large donors remained high throughout the 1970s (and the 1980s), motivated as they were by the strategic interests of the Cold War period.

The global environment for aid at the beginning of the twenty-first century

Once the Cold War was over in the early 1990s, the end of the arms race between the US and former Soviet Union (FSU) was expected to produce a 'peace dividend' and a substantial increase in funds available for development purposes. The opposite occurred. Now that the so-called Third World was no longer needed as the theatre in which superpower rivalries were played out, the global environment for aid became less positive than it had been in the 1970s and 1980s. Within two years of the break-up of the Soviet Union, global aid flows began to fall –

reflecting the fundamental shifts that quickly occurred in the strategic and political interests of the Cold War era's two superpowers. Between 1992 and 1997, total aid from DAC member states fell from US$60.8 billion to US$47.6 billion or from 0.33% to 0.22% of their combined GNPs (OECD/DAC, 1999). Aid from the FSU dried up completely. For many of the heavily indebted developing countries, this outcome has been particularly ironic. Having come through the 'lost development decade' of the 1980s, during which many of them experienced negative growth rates, but having finally begun to experience some of the benefits of the economic and political reforms they launched under structural adjustment programmes, they perceive themselves to be penalised rather than rewarded for their efforts. They argue that what they need is more, not less, aid.

To be sure, some positive signs are emerging. Aid flows from DAC member states rose to US$51.5 billion in 1998 – finally reversing a five-year period of decline. They rose again (to US$56 billion) in 1999, a welcome consolidation of, it was hoped, a sustainable recovery. More intensive efforts are being undertaken to tackle the debt problems of the poorest countries including the Jubilee 2000 initiative and improvements in the world Bank/IMF debt reduction initiative for highly indebted poor countries (HIPC). Donor and host governments are forging more equal partnerships within their aid relationships. Developing country governments are making greater efforts to promote more participatory development strategies designed to eliminate absolute poverty inside their countries. There is an increasing focus on promotion of human rights, democracy, good governance, gender equality, and environmental and socio-economic sustainability. The overall objective of both development strategies and aid strategies is stated in terms of the promotion of a more holistic 'human development'. Nevertheless, a recent World Bank report admitted that progress toward meeting international targets for human development is in danger of stalling after a generation of improvement as the spread of HIV/AIDS in sub-Saharan Africa wipes out hard-won improvements in life expectancy and as the costs of servicing debts and coping with political conflicts and other man-made disasters lead to cuts in education and health budgets. In 2000, DAC aid flows fell back again (to US$53 billion)

Motivations and objectives of Ireland's aid programme in the 1970s

From its beginnings in the 1970s – and not surprisingly, given that missionaries had pioneered Ireland's involvement in developing countries – the Irish aid programme was imbued with a strong humanitarian motivation. Early ministerial speeches and departmental documents stressed a 'moral obligation' to help 'poor countries and poor people' and to 'promote the development of developing countries' (Fitzgerald, 1973). The production of direct economic benefits was not to be pursued. Any 'commercial advantages and opportunities that presented themselves' could be availed of but they were to be expected from participation of Irish companies in multilateral aid programmes and in the implementation of indigenously funded projects in resource-rich developing countries rather than from the bilateral aid programme (O'Kennedy, 1979, p. 2). Interestingly, promotion of human rights – a huge issue at the global level today – was also included in the aims of the Irish aid programme as early as 1979. A realisation of the existence of a 'mutuality of interests' which 'inextricably bound' Ireland's future and that of developing countries was spelled out early on (O'Keefe, 1981, p.8). Poverty reduction, satisfaction of basic needs, an equitable internal distribution of the benefits of economic development, and promotion of self-reliance were repeatedly cited as the main aims of the programme from its earliest days. The geographic focus was on a small number of low-income 'priority countries' in sub-Saharan Africa and the sectoral focus was on agricultural and rural development, health, and education. All aid was in grant form and remains so today. As a result, the Irish aid programme creates no debt – although it is now getting involved in debt relief programmes, not only with its priority country partners, but also multilaterally through World Bank and IMF initiatives. Finally, it is appropriate to note that, as early as 1973, the then Minister for Foreign Affairs was describing development co-operation as one of the 'basic objectives of Irish foreign policy' (Fitzgerald, 1973).

Aims and principles of Ireland's aid programme today

At the beginning of the new century, while the overall objectives established over twenty-five years ago remain at the centre of Ireland's aid programme, the range of activities, matched by new expenditure headings, designed to achieve these aims, has become wider and more complex in line with international developments and the new global context for aid. The 1997 strategy statement of the Department of Foreign Affairs, *Pursuing Ireland's External Interests* (DFA 1997), spelled out the aims of Ireland's development co-operation policy as follows: 'To contribute to the development needs of poor countries in partnership with the governments and people of those countries and in line with their priorities; support a process of self-reliant, sustainable, poverty-reducing and equitable growth and development, in particular in the least-developed countries; advance the concept of sustainable development in all its aspects including material well-being, human rights, fundamental freedoms, gender equality, protection of the environment, support for civil society and processes, as well as mechanisms to prevent, resolve and recover from conflict; ensure rapid and effective response to humanitarian emergencies; maintain coherence in all aspects of Ireland's relations with developing countries; and promote active participation by Ireland in multilateral institutions concerned with development'. The document also stresses that development co-operation policy is 'an integral part of Irish foreign policy' which works toward the overall goals of 'international peace, security, and a just and stable global economic system'.

Thus, the 'guiding principles' that inform Ireland Aid's bilateral aid programme today can be summed up as: participation and local ownership; a focus on poverty reduction; gender sensitivity; and sustainability. The restating of the guiding principles has been accompanied over the years by some reinterpretation of associated concepts, the most important of which I call the three Ps (O'Neill, 1999, p. 300).

The first is *poverty* reduction. Back in the 1970s, poverty was identified with low incomes. But when I asked members of a local development committee in Ethiopia last year to define poverty, their response that it is 'powerlessness and vulnerability, lack of information, and lack of basic material needs' reflects the newer interpretation of the concept – and one that informs Ireland Aid's development aid strategy throughout sub-Saharan Africa.

The second P is *participation* and its associated concept of local ownership. Together, these ensure that the people to whom development programmes and projects are supposed to deliver benefits are fully involved in the process from the stage of problem analysis though project design, implementation, monitoring, and evaluation.

The third P is *partnership*. In the 1970s, this concept was preached by donors but practised only to a very limited extent: they kept a tight grip on the purse strings and used only expatriate technical experts to plan and manage projects. Today, Ireland's aid programme, in common with those of many other donors, is trying to ensure that the partnership principle works at two mutually-reinforcing levels: internationally, by giving more 'ownership' of aid programmes to developing country governments (for example, though budgetary support for sector-wide programmes); and nationally, by working within local structures and using local experts, while encouraging more democratic political processes that bring poor people more effectively into the development process. A senior official in the Ethiopian administration told me during my visit that he was very positive about Ireland Aid 'because it works within Ethiopian structures and uses 90% Ethiopian staff'.

Ireland's foreign aid targets

Since the bilateral aid programme was launched in 1974, one of the most debated issues in development fora in Ireland has been the size of the aid budget – and related concerns such as the precise increases that successive governments were committing themselves to, and the progress (or at times retrogression) that was being made in relation to reaching the UN target of 0.7% of GNP. Without rehearsing the often tortuous analyses that have been produced over the years (and especially in the late 1980s when ODA fell sharply in line with overall cuts in public expenditure), it can be stated that no end-of-period target, either in money terms of in percent-of-GNP terms, set by any Irish government, has ever been met.

According to the 1993 *Strategy Plan* for Irish aid (DFA 1993), ODA should have increased by 0.05% of GNP each year from 1993 through 1997 'so as to make steady progress towards achieving' the UN target of 0.7% of GNP and specifically to have reached a medium-term target of 0.4% of GNP by 1997. Targets for nominal flows of ODA were set at around IR£90 million for 1995, IR£110 million for 1996, and IR£135 million for 1997.

As can be seen from Table 1, total expenditure has increased strongly and steadily since 1993. In 1995, expenditure overshot the target by nearly IR£7 million and in 1996 the overshoot was a more modest IR£2 million. However, in 1997 it

Table 1: Ireland's ODA, selected years 1974-2000 (IR£m and %)

	1974	1978	1984	1988	1994	1998	2000[a]
Total ODA (IR£m)	1.50	8.40	33.20	32.40	75.20	139.60	200.90
Bilateral aid[b]	0.20	2.70	13.30	14.30	39.50	86.80	131.50
Multilateral aid	1.30	5.70	19.90	18.10	35.70	52.80	69.40
Bilateral as % ODA	13.00	33.00	40.00	42.00	51.00	60.00[c]	62.10
ODA as % GNP	0.05	0.13	0.22	0.18	0.24	00.30	0.31[e]

a = allocation   b = including administration costs and tax deductability   c = bilateral aid (excluding administration costs and tax deductibility) as a percentage of total ODA   e = estimate

Sources: Department of Foreign Affairs, *Ireland's Official Development Assistance,* various years and data supplied in June 2000

fell short of the target by over IR£10 million or nearly 8% and, as a percentage of GNP, ODA of IR£124.1 million actually fell to 0.27%. Another target announced in the 1993 strategy plan was to achieve a two-to-one ratio of bilateral to multilateral aid. As can be seen from Table 1, that target also remains elusive.

Clearly, the fact that the Irish economy has been growing at remarkable rates since 1994, would have prevented the percentage-of-GNP target from being achieved in recent years unless the allocation in Irish pound terms had been increased significantly compared with the 1993 planned allocations. Indeed, it is worth noting that in none of the years between 1995 and 1997 did the ODA allocation increase by 0.05% of the GNP – whether the calculation is made on the basis of the current year's GNP or that of the previous year. In any case, in the absence of precise information on the rate of growth of GNP for 4-5 year periods ahead, it is not possible to set targets for both the nominal level of ODA and percentage-of-GNP that such levels would represent.

In July 1997, the Minister of State at the Department of Foreign Affairs, Liz O'Donnell, reported that the new government had committed itself to continue the pattern of steady increases in ODA and had set 'an ambitious – but attainable – target of 0.45% of GNP by the year 2002' (Department of Foreign Affairs, 1997). At the United Nations Millennium Summit, held in New York in September 2000, the Taoiseach, Bertie Ahern, described the 0.45% of GNP target as an 'interim target' and pledged that Ireland would reach the UN

0.7% of GNP target by the end of 2007 (Ireland 2000). In nominal terms, these commitments imply expenditures of around IR£365 million by the end of 2002, or a doubling of the 1999 out-turn figure, and a further doubling of the 2002 figure to around IR£800 million by the end of 2007. In October 2000, the Department of Finance agreed that the aid budget would reach 0.35% of GNP by the end of 2001.

Given that only five countries (Norway, Sweden, Denmark, Luxembourg and the Netherlands) currently meet or exceed the UN aid target, the Taoiseach's pledge is enormously significant, both in terms of the signal it sends to all donors and receivers of aid at a time when global aid flows need renewed impetus, as well as in terms of Ireland's aid policy and its place within the nation's overall foreign policy – and indeed domestic economic and social policy. Speaking at a meeting of the Foreign Policy Association in New York on 8 September 2000 on 'Ireland in the Wider World', the Taoiseach re-echoed earlier statements underlining the humanitarian motivation of Ireland's aid programme when he referred to his pledge to reach the UN aid target: 'Our ability to make such a decision crystallises the transformation that has taken place in Irish society and the Irish economy over the last two decades. We have now unprecedented prosperity in Ireland, but we remain a deeply concerned and caring people' (Ireland, 2000).

Irish Aid performance since 1974

Table 1 shows the growth of Irish aid flows between 1974 and 1999 and the allocation for 2000 in terms of both nominal amounts and percent-of-GNP. It also shows the way in which the division of the overall budget between bilateral and multilateral aid has evolved over the years. (It should be noted, in this regard, that the figures for bilateral aid, both in nominal and percentage terms, given in Table 1 are higher than those in Tables 2 and 3 – arising from the inclusion in them of administration costs and tax deductability). A relatively recent and very helpful development has been the confirmation by the Department of Finance that Irish aid will in future receive assurances on a three-year rolling basis regarding annual allocations for the bilateral side of the aid budget. In 1999, the commitments for bilateral aid for 1999, 2000, and 2001 had been set at around IR£104m, IR£136m, and IR£159m respectively while allocations for total ODA for the three years are estimated at IR£171m, IR£184m, and IR£207m. In the latter part of 2000, it was already clear that total ODA expenditure for the year would exceed IR£200 million. Following the pledge to reach the UN target by the end of 2007, the 2001 budget was already being revised upward to over IR£250 million.

Geographic distribution of Irish aid

From its beginnings, Ireland's bilateral aid programme has been focused on a small number of so-called priority countries. Five were selected in 1974: Lesotho, Zambia, Tanzania, Sudan, and India. India was soon dropped for practical reasons – mainly because its size was considered inappropriate for the small Irish programme – and Sudan was dropped in more recent times. In 1994, two new countries, Ethiopia and Uganda were added and in 1996 Mozambique brought the total to six. All are located in sub-Saharan Africa. They are very poor and classified as 'least-developed' by the United Nations and the World Bank. All rank low in terms of human development indicators (including percentage living in absolute poverty; life expectancy; adult literacy; infant mortality; access to safe water, sanitation, and health services). In 1975, 17% of total bilateral aid was spent in the priority countries; in 2000 the figure is estimated at 47 %. Other countries in receipt in assistance in recent years from the bilateral programme include: Albania, Bangladesh, Cambodia, Eritrea, Ghana, Malawi, Namibia, Nigeria, Occupied Territories, South Africa, Sudan, Vietnam, and Zimbabwe.

Sectoral distribution of Irish aid

A cursory examination of expenditure over the years might suggest that there has been little change in the distribution of Irish aid by sector. The 1973 policy statement referred to a programme that would show 'balanced growth in all its sectors' but 'particularly where Ireland has a special interest or competence'. However, because the programme in the 1970s could best be described as a collection of projects, and because most of the aid was delivered through Irish technical assistance, it tended to focus on rural development as well as education and health since these were the sectors within Ireland that could provide technical expertise at that time. Ireland also responded to specific requests from its partner countries. The result was a type of supply and demand balance.

Today, the focus is still on rural development, education, and health. However, it is a very different programme. Both its drivers and its delivery mechanisms are very different from what they were twenty-five years ago. First, there have been very significant shifts *within* the sectors. The amount of aid being provided to hospitals and universities has been severely cut back. Within the health sector, the focus is on primary healthcare; within education, on primary and informal schools, teacher training, and adult literacy. Within rural development, the focus is on food security, rural roads, provision of clean water and sanitary services, and micro-credit (especially for women). Sensitivity to the gender implications of all aspects of the aid programme is very noticeable. Assistance is also provided to promote human rights and democracy. Indeed, in recognition of the importance of politics within the process of development, the rural development programme includes training of local officials and members of local development committees. This training is designed to help them to conceptualise about poverty and development and to be sensitive to the rights of individuals, especially the poorest ones.

Second, the bilateral aid programme is now demand-driven. It responds to stated needs in the partner countries and has to fit in with local structures. The number of Irish technical experts has been reduced significantly (although the need to build up capacities within national administrative structures calls for training in a wide range of skills; this type of expertise is still provided through Ireland Aid, often in Ireland). Third, the Irish bilateral aid programme is no longer a collection of 'project islands'. Most aid to the priority countries is delivered in the form of integrated programmes at sub-national level (area-based programmes) selected in consultation with governments in the priority countries. More recently, Ireland Aid has got involved in what are called sector-wide approaches (SWAps) and programme aid where aid is provided to some priority countries in the form of general budgetary support to sectors such as health and education. Of course, the priority governments would prefer if most aid were provided in the form of programme or sectoral budgetary support. However, until administrative capacities and auditing procedures and co-ordination among donors are much stronger, SWAps and programme aid will remain a relatively small part of the programme.

Table 2: growth of the bilateral aid programme
during the 1990s and allocation 2000 (IR£m)

	1992	1994	1996	1998	1999	2000[a]
Priority countries	6.6	14.9	25.1	42.2	44.1	58.6
Lesotho	2.0	4.0	4.2	4.7	5.2	6.0
Tanzania	2.6	4.1	5.0	10.1	7.7	13.1
Zambia	1.5	3.4	5.5	5.9	5.9	5.9
Sudan	0.5	0.6	-	-	-	-
Uganda	-	1.1	2.2	5.1	7.4	10.0
Ethiopia	-	1.1	7.0	11.3	11.6	16.2
Mozambique	-	0.6	1.2	5.1	6.3	7.4
Other countries	0.5	3.5	5.5	5.2	4.3	6.0
Co-financing with NGOs	1.7	3.2	6.8	6.4	7.1	8.8
Co-financing with multilaterals	0.4	1.5	1.4	2.1	2.7	3.1
Education and training	0.9	1.5	1.8	1.5	1.5	1.5
Development education	0.6	0.8	1.1	1.1	1.0	1.2
Agency for Personal Service Overseas	2.6	7.0	10.5	10.7	10.6	10.8
Emergency Humanitarian Assistance	1.7	4.0	8.0	6.0	12.0	7.0
Rehabilitation	-	-	3.4	5.0	6.0	8.0
Refugees	-	-	2.7	1.1	11.0	9.0
Programme support	0.2	1.1	1.8	1.6	2.0	3.3
Democratisation/Human Rights	-	0.5	1.3	1.0	1.5	1.5
Information on Irish aid	-	-	0.1	0.1	0.1	0.2
Programme aid	-	-	-	-	-	6.2
Total bilateral aid	15.2	38.0	69.5	84.0	103.9	125.2

a = allocation

Sources: Department of Foreign Affairs (Ireland Aid), *Ireland's Official Development Assistance*,
various years and data supplied in June 2000

Expenditure under the headings of emergency humanitarian assistance and rehabilitation (reconstruction in post-conflict and post-emergency situations) increased significantly after 1994, reflecting the number of emergencies –natural and man-made – that affected developing countries, including sub-Saharan Africa, after that date. Expenditure under the heading of 'refugees' also increased significantly from the late 1990s. This heading relates to spending on people who seek refuge in Ireland, the first year's costs for whom may be counted as ODA under DAC rules (O'Neill, 1997, p. 204).

Links between Ireland Aid and NGOs

One feature of the aid programme that has remained a constant since it was first launched is its strong relationship with the Irish non-governmental organisations (NGOs) that work in development. The NGOs receive funding from Ireland Aid under four main headings. Five of the major Irish NGOs receive block grants. Second, they receive funding for projects under the NGO co-financing scheme. Together, these rose from less than IR£0.5m (around 16% of the bilateral budget) in the 1970s and early 1980s to over IR£2.5m (14%) in 1986 and to IR£6.4m (7.5%) in 1998. Third, Ireland Aid expends part of its emergency humanitarian and rehabilitation budget through the NGOs. If we add in the amounts spent through NGOs under these last two headings in 1998, the total comes to IR£20.7 million (25% of the bilateral budget and 15% of total ODA). The fourth link with the NGOs operates through the Agency for Personal Service Overseas. Part of Ireland Aid, it sponsors assignments by Irish people in developing countries. Since around half the assignees APSO helps to train and support are recruited by NGOs, it provides another significant link between the official aid programme and the NGOs.

The multilateral side of the Irish aid programme

Ireland joined the UN in 1955 and the World Bank in 1957. Apart from tiny amounts spent through the Overseas Trainee Fund (used mainly to train Zambian army officers and public administrators in the mid-sixties), all of what could be classified as official development assistance up to 1974 was spent through those two international channels. After joining the EEC (now EU) in 1973, however, the Commission rapidly replaced the World Bank as the main conduit of Ireland's multilateral ODA payments. And, of course, as the bilateral programme was built up, the multilateral side itself began to fall as a proportion of total ODA expenditure (Table 3). With the exception of discretionary payments to UN agencies such as UNDP, UNHCR, UNICEF and WHO, as well as replenishments to the World Bank's soft-loan affiliate IDA, the amounts payable on the multilateral side are mandatory and assessed by the individual organisations to which Ireland belongs. In the case of the EU, Ireland contributes to the European Development Fund (EDF), which finances the Lomé Convention and the newer Cotonou Convention between the EU and African Caribbean and Pacific (ACP) countries, and the development co-operation part of the EU budget which is spent by the Commission on food aid, humanitarian emergency assistance, and aid to non-ACP developing countries. Contributions to the EDF are paid

*Table 3: growth of the multilateral aid programme in the
1990s and allocation 2000 (IR£m)*

	1992	1994	1996	1998	1999	2000[a]
European Union	17.2	25.1	25.5	34.5	42.2	42.5
EU Budget (Development						
Co-operation)	10.3	17.2	21.4	26.7	30.0	33.8
EDF (Lomé Convention)	6.9	7.9	4.1	7.8	12.2	8.7
World Bank/IMF Group	4.4	4.2	4.9	5.3	16.4	9.8
IDA	3.3	4.1	4.4	4.9	4.8	7.3
IBRD	1.0	-	-	-		
IFC	0.1	0.1	0.1	-	-	-
Trust Fund/IMF HIPC						
and ESAF/PRGF	-	-	-	-	10.6	1.3
Global Environment Facility	-	-	0.4	0.4	1.0	1.0
Multilateral Investment						
Guarantee Agency	-	-	-	-	-	0.2
United Nations	2.6	6.4	10.1	13.0	12.8	17.1
UN Agencies	0.8	4.5	6.5	8.4	8.3	11.9
Food Aid Convention	0.6	0.6	0.6	0.8	0.9	1.2
IFAD	-	-	-	0.2	0.2	-
FAO Schemes	0.1	-	0.2	0.4	0.4	0.6
World Food Programme	-	-	1.0	1.1	1.1	1.3
UNIDO	0.1	0.1	0.2	0.2	0.1	0.1
Miscellaneous	1.0	1.2	1.6	1.9	1.8	2.0
Total multilateral aid	24.2	35.7	40.5	52.8	71.4	69.4

a = allocation

Sources: Department of Foreign Affairs, *Ireland's Official Development Assistance,* various years,
and data supplied in June 2000

through Ireland Aid while the budget contribution, as well as
payments to the World Bank group, are channelled through the
Department of Finance. The latter department also provides
Ireland's advisor to the World Bank and its alternate executive
director to the IMF.

Up until recently, debate on the multilateral side of
Ireland's aid programme was rather muted. To be sure, Irish
NGOs and academics, just like those in other countries, have
often criticised the lending activities of the World Bank and
IMF, especially in relation to structural adjustment loans and
facilities, whose conditionalities in the 1980s and early 1990s
were often perceived to have negative implications for social
spending and for the poor. But there was little comment on
Ireland's contributions to these organisations because payments
to them, apart from IDA, were mandatory. However, when the
government announced its decision to contribute to the IMF's
Enhanced Structural Adjustment Facility (ESAF) in 1994,

criticisms were voiced by Irish NGOs and payments were deferred. Four years later, however, although all of Ireland's aid is provided in the form of grants and therefore no developing country is indebted to it, Ireland decided to become involved in World Bank and IMF debt-relief programmes for the world's highly-indebted poor countries (HIPC), a group to which five of its priority countries (Ethiopia, Mozambique, Tanzania, Uganda, and Zambia) belong.

Ireland's role in debt relief

The World Bank and IMF launched the Heavily Indebted Poor Countries (HIPC) initiative in 1996 with the objective of assisting HIPC countries that pursue economic and social reform to reduce their debt overhang. Following criticisms from a number of NGOs and others in the international community, the scheme was modified in 1999 to make the debt servicing cuts 'deeper, broader and faster' (World Bank, 1999). The 'enhanced HIPC' also provides for stronger links between debt relief and poverty reduction. This link is to be achieved by using resources released from debt servicing for support of poverty reduction strategies. These strategies, in turn, are to be elaborated in a poverty reduction strategy paper (PRSP) which is supposed to be designed by the government of the HIPC country in consultation with civil society actors including the poor.

Reflecting the new objectives and procedures, the IMF established the poverty reduction and growth facility (PRGF) in September 1999. The PRGF replaced the enhanced structural adjustment facility (ESAF) which, as already noted, had been set up as a concessional lending facility more than a decade earlier but which had come under sustained criticism from development NGOs because of its negative impacts on spending in the social sectors and therefore on the poorest people in developing countries. The PRGF and the HIPC initiative are designed to function in tandem. Ireland has become involved in the trust funds set up by the World Bank and IMF for both of them as a result of a decision made by the Ministers for Finance and Foreign Affairs.

The Ministers jointly announced a debt relief package valued at IR£31.5 million in September 1998 with a two-pronged approach – part of the contribution was to be made through the World Bank/IMF HIPC Trust Fund and the IMF's ESAF (now PRGF) and part to be contributed bilaterally to some of

Ireland's priority countries. The elements of the package were: IR£15m to be paid to the World Bank and IMF under the HIPC initiative (most of which is effectively funded by reflows from the European Investment Bank); IR£7m to ESAF/PRGF (from the Central Fund); and IR£9.5m bilaterally to two of the priority countries, Mozambique and Tanzania (from Ireland Aid's budget). As Table 3 shows, IR£10.6 million was paid into the ESAF/PRGF and HIPC Trust Funds in 1999. An additional IR£4 million – which does not appear in Table 3 – was also paid into the IMF's HIPC Trust Fund (through a complex transfer out of member states' balances built up within the IMF for contingency purposes but no longer considered necessary for that purpose: Ireland's Central Bank, in common with those of other industrialised countries, agreed that its balances could be kept by the IMF and transferred into its HIPC Trust Fund).

The issue of policy coherence

An important issue for an official aid programme is its place within the overall range of government policies and whether other sectoral policies (in particular, those relating to trade, agriculture, environment and health) are coherent with it – or work against its objectives. The 1996 White Paper on Foreign Policy acknowledges that there are 'inextricable links between development co-operation and other pillars of foreign policy, notably human rights, conflict prevention and resolution, and commercial and financial policies' (Ireland, 1996, para 9.89). In addition to the co-operation that takes place on a government-to-government basis, the White Paper states that coherence involves close co-ordination within and between the various divisions of the DFA, as well as consultation between different government departments on the various policy issues which affect development. Until 1996, such consultations were carried out, for the most part, on an ad-hoc basis although there was an inter-departmental committee on development co-operation that concerned itself with the ODA budget.

At the EU level, development co-operation policy is decided in the Foreign Affairs Council which is responsible for all aspects of the EU's external relations. Trade is a matter of Union competence. The 133 Committee, which deals with commercial issues including trade, meets almost every week in Brussels. During the week before its meetings, a '133 co-ordinating committee' meets in the Department of Enterprise,

Trade and Employment – since ETE is the lead department on
trade issues – to co-ordinate the Irish position for the Brussels
meetings. Consultation takes place with other interested
departments (principally Finance, Foreign Affairs, Agriculture
and Food (DAF), and Environment) in order to arrive at a
common Irish position in advance of the Brussels meetings. The
DFA's role at these meetings is to put forward its views on those
trade issues that have implications for development policy. In the
same way, where development co-operation policy may have
implications for trade policy, then DFA – as the lead department
on development issues – invites officials from ETE to meet with
them to discuss the issue. Similarly, where development co-
operation policy has implications for agricultural policy, the DFA
again takes the lead and invites officials from DAF to discuss the
matter with them. In the case where agriculture is the lead player
but the issue has implications for development co-peration
policy (for example, its brief in relation to the Food and
Agriculture Organisation), DAF invites DFA officials to share
their views with them. These consultations enable each
department to ventilate its views and are designed to promote
coherence of policy at national level and in its presentation in
Brussels and at other international fora.

Also of relevance to policy coherence in relation to
development co-peration programmes, are the 'three Cs' set out
by the European Commission in its 1996 Green Paper entitled
*Relations between the EU and the ACP Countries on the Eve of the
Twenty-First Century*. These are respectively complementarity
(between the aid programme of the Commission and those of
the member states); co-ordination (between all these
programmes inside developing countries); and coherence
(among policies at both EU and member states levels).

A particularly interesting coherence issue, both at the EU
and Irish levels, was the 'Everything but Arms' proposal initiated
by the European Commission in October 2000 and agreed on 26
February 2001. This initiative proposes that the least-developed
countries should be given duty-free and quota-free access to the
EU market for all products except armaments. It will be
implemented very quickly, apart from transition periods for rice,
sugar and bananas. It represents a significant improvement on
access for 'essentially all products' agreed under the Cotonou
Convention. At the EU level, it has implications for policy
coherence as some member states ponder its impact on some of

their 'sensitive' sectors (for example, textiles in Portugal, rice and tomatoes in Italy, and beef in Ireland). However, at a wider global level, it will probably be difficult to resist because it could be the key to the launch of a new round of multilateral trade negotiations within the World Trade Organisation.

Finally, it is appropriate to note the forthright view that the Taoiseach expressed in his address to the United Nations Millennium Summit on 6 September 2000: 'A genuine commitment to fairness has implications for policy making in every area: in trade, investment and debt reduction as well as in health, labour, gender equality and a host of others. 'Coherence' may be an over-used word but it is an under-used approach. I am pleased that the Declaration we are about to adopt at this Summit has such a broad range of commitments. And the specificity of the language and the time scales mean that we can and will be held accountable for delivery. If we urge policy coherence and precise targets on the UN, we must be individually prepared to adopt the same disciplines.'(Ireland, 2000)

The DAC Peer Review of Ireland's aid programme

Ireland's aid programme received a very high rating in the peer review carried out by the DAC in 1999. That review summed up the evolution of the aid programme over the years as an 'impressive process through which Irish Aid (now Ireland Aid) has managed to accomplish such volume increases, while simultaneously strengthening the quality and operating professionalism of the programme' (OECD, 1999, 15). It added: 'By any comparative standard, this record of successfully combining volume growth with improving quality would unquestionably justify further increases in Irish Aid'. The report picked out for particular praise the programme's focus on poverty reduction, its recognition of the need for developing country (and local) ownership of the aid process, the way in which the programme puts the partnership approach into practice, as well its methods of delivery through area-based programmes and sector-wide approaches. The main recommendations of the review team were as follows.

- Ireland Aid should update its 1993 document *Ireland Aid: Consolidation and Growth* in order to give clear direction for future growth to the aid programme.

- To mark the twenty-fifth anniversary, Ireland should renew its commitment to promoting development and reducing poverty as priority goals for all government policy.

- Decisions on expansion of the programme should be based on development criteria and the scope for Irish impacts on poverty reduction.

- Ireland Aid should maintain and enhance its focused nature. Even a modest extension in the number of priority countries should be evaluated carefully.

- Ireland should pursue its consideration of joining the African Development Bank.

- Staffing, skill mixes and career perspectives must be reinforced and changed to maintain and enhance Ireland's contribution to development co-operation

- Reinforcing existing organisational structures is preferable in the short-term. In the longer-term, establishing an independent implementing agency is an appealing option from an operational point of view.

- Ireland Aid could do more to engender a culture of evaluation and a focus on monitoring and results. The evaluation of area-based programmes should be given greater emphasis (OECD, 1999, 22).

Issues on the agenda today

In an article published ten years after the launch of the bilateral aid programme (O'Neill, 1984, 259), I set out the issues for the 1980s as follows: publication of a White Paper on Development Co-operation; joining DAC; improving budgetary mechanisms including the possibility of a multi-annual rolling plan; improving administrative structures, including the possibility of establishing a state-sponsored executive agency for the aid programme (with policy-making remaining within the Department of Foreign Affairs); and amending the list of priority countries. Action has been taken on most of these issues. The White Paper on foreign policy (Ireland, 1996) which included a chapter on development co-operation, was published in 1996; a Strategy Plan (Ireland, 1993) was published in 1993 and Strategy Statements in 1997 and 1998 (DFA, 1997, 1998). Ireland joined DAC in 1986. The Department of Finance has recently approved a three-year budget for Ireland Aid in line with revision of overall budgetary procedures. The list of priority countries has been amended a number of times.

What issues should be on the agenda now – given the very large increases in spending implied by the commitment to reach the 0.7% of GNP target by the end of 2007? The list of priority countries is again under review. If it is expanded, and there are strong arguments for widening and deepening the programmes within the current priority countries before expanding the list of priority countries, presumably any potential addition would tend to be chosen from the current list of 'other countries' that have been assisted in recent years – with the possible addition of East Timor. Toward the end of 2000, a Development Co-operation Office was established there and a small 2-3 year programme will be launched in 2001 focused on governance issues, basic needs, and building up local capacity. It will be operated in close co-ordination with other donors, the World Bank, and the UN Transitional Authority.

It might also be appropriate to consider the pros and cons of bringing all multilateral spending under Ireland Aid. Another issue already on the agenda is a possibly larger role for the private business sector which, to date, has been involved only marginally in the aid programme. Another issue is debt relief. Should more priority countries be brought into the debt-relief scheme? And, what are the trade-offs between debt relief and other forms of aid? Finally, twenty-five years ago, APSO could send most of its enthusiastic young applicants on assignments overseas. Today, most need experience as well as relevant qualifications in order to be acceptable in developing countries. There is need to re-examine how best to involve young people – trained but with no work experience in developing countries – in the aid programme

The 1999 DAC review of Ireland's aid programme identified a number of options for channelling additional funding. These include:

- intensifying existing priority country programmes
- launching new priority country programmes
- starting different types of bilateral activities
- increasing funding for NGO schemes and special funds
- expanding contributions to multilateral agencies (OECD, 1999, 25).

The DAC review noted that various combinations of these options could be used. In its opinion, the policy statement of the

Department of Foreign Affairs, *Ireland Aid: Consolidation and Growth* (DFA, 1993), had provided excellent guidance for how Ireland's aid programme should expand during the period 1993 to 1997. However, in order to steer growth in the programme up to 2002 and beyond, Ireland should consider updating that document and spelling out how further expansion could be achieved.

In the view of the DAC review team, there is scope for Ireland to provide more aid under its priority country programme. Indeed, it rightly states that, although these countries absorb a significant proportion of Irish bilateral aid funds, Ireland is still a small donor in these countries and 'there is thus clearly room for Ireland to build on its strong base and become a less marginal actor in these countries' (OECD, 1999, 27). It points particularly to growth possibilities arising from the current expansion in SWAps and programme aid. Surprisingly, it doubts whether this would lead to 'rapid expansion' of disbursements.

The DAC team was rather cautious with regard to including new priority countries in the programme and advises that even a modest extension to new countries should be evaluated 'carefully'. However, it suggested that Ireland could intensify its programmes in other countries in Africa – it mentioned Eritrea, Malawi, Namibia, Rwanda and Zimbabwe – and upgrade its support to them as it had already done in Nigeria and South Africa, without giving them the status of full priority countries. It also suggested that, since all the existing priority countries are in eastern and southern Africa, there is already a good basis for developing regional programmes and providing support for regional institutions such as the Southern African Development Community (SADC).

The DAC team was also cautious with regard to the option of increasing substantially the amount of aid channelled through Irish NGOs, arguing that they already absorb 'a relatively large share' of the aid budget and, in addition, 'are generously supported by the Irish public and receive funding from other sources, such as the EU and United Nations agencies' (*op. cit.,* 18). It suggests, instead, that additional funding channelled through NGOs could be directed toward indigenous organisations in developing countries by expanding the In-Country Micro Project Scheme especially in the priority countries and in the 'other' countries assisted under the bilateral aid programme. It saw particular merit in reinforcing the development potential in these 'other bilateral' programmes by expanding activities through the Human Rights and Democratisation Programme in those countries.

There are several headings within the multilateral side of the aid programme under which the review team saw scope for expansion. It described Ireland's multilateral involvement as a 'lively and active engagement'. It noted the increasingly large number of UN agencies (thirty-nine in 1999) to which Ireland is making voluntary contributions and suggested that a more selective and targeted approach should be adopted if these contributions are to be expanded further. Interestingly, it advised that, 'as in its priority countries, Ireland might benefit from becoming less of a marginal player in some of the multilateral agencies it supports' (OECD, 1999). One specific suggestion made – indeed this is already under consideration – is that Ireland should join the African Development Bank (AfDB) which is described as meriting support because of its own reform programme. It claims that membership would be another means for Ireland to maintain and enhance the focused nature of its aid programme and to bring its experience from working in some of the poorest countries in Africa to discussions at the Bank. As regards increasing contributions to debt relief, the team notes that Ireland is looking carefully at current international initiatives aimed at deepening and broadening the scope of the HIPC initiative and speeding up disbursements and, while current debt relief efforts will contribute to resolving an urgent problem in the short term, 'they should not be expected to be a continuing growth area for the Ireland Aid programme' (OECD, 1999).

Ireland Aid had already been considering all of the options listed in the DAC review before the announcement of the pledge to meet the UN target. These included the widening of the programme to include another priority country and the deepening of programmes in existing priority countries and in the 'other bilateral' countries, and appropriate management structures for the programme. It is already providing some support for regional organisations in southern Africa. On the issue of funding for Irish NGOs, Minister of State Liz O'Donnell has already declared her intentions – and they differ from those of the DAC review team. Speaking in New York on 6 September 2000, she said: 'An expanded aid programme will also enable the government to commit considerably greater resources to the efforts of our own NGOs. In the coming year we will develop our relationship with the NGOs, placing our funding commitments on a new basis and preparing for a closer partnership in the context of a greatly expanded aid programme'.

On the multilateral side, Ireland Aid has been looking at the possibilities open to it to provide further debt relief under the HIPC initiative. The Department of Finance made provision for such increases under the terms of the Bretton Woods Agreements (Amendment) Act, 1999. Under these provisions, there is room for an additional IR£38 million (in addition to the IR£22 million already committed under the headings of the World Bank/IMF HIPC initiatives as well as ESAF/PRGF). However, for a variety of reasons, the maximum amount likely to be used would be around IR£9 million. Continuing criticism of the ESAF/PRGF make it unlikely that any further contributions will be made under that heading. As regards the IMF/HIPC Trust Fund, although there is provision for further amounts under this heading, they are currently redundant because the IMF has fully funded its current liability to the HIPC initiative. The ceiling for the World Bank HIPC Trust Fund was set at IR£20 million under the Bretton Woods Agreements (Amendment) Act. IR£8.1 million was paid by the Department of Finance in 1999 and further annual payments up to and including 2008 will bring the authorised total to IR£11 million. There is room for an additional possible IR£9 million to be provided under this heading. This, therefore, represents the effective amount that might be activated in the future – although no time frame has yet been specified. Another way in which further contributions to debt relief might be made would be out of the next replenishment round of IDA (IDA-13).

Ireland Aid is considering the possibility of joining the AfDB and other development banks. However, if it decides to join one only, the AfDB would seem to be the obvious choice. Indeed, given Ireland Aid's geographic focus on Africa, it is probably true to say that Ireland could be described as being conspicuous by its absence in the AfDB at this stage. Joining it could cost around IR£40 million in a once-off initial payment – but this would be spread over a few years. Joining the AfDB would certainly be a positive way of providing an expansionary boost to the Ireland Aid programme.

Following the September 2000 pledge at the Millennium Summit to reach the UN target by the end of 2007, it was announced that a major review of the Ireland Aid programme was to be launched toward the end of 2000. This review was under way in 2001 and included a comprehensive examination of all aspects of the programme, its context, content, general orientation, areas of concentration, management and staffing within Ireland Aid, as well as a review of agencies associated with the programme including the Agency for Personal Service Overseas (APSO) and the National Committee for Development Education (NCDE). It also examined the pros and cons of all the recommendations made by the DAC team. The group consulted widely with appropriate bodies including NGOs and social partners, the Ireland Aid Advisory Committee, APSO, NCDE, and the Joint Oireachtas Committee on Foreign Affairs.

Some concluding comments

The Ireland Aid programme has evolved over the years from a rather ad hoc collection of projects, largely managed by expatriates, into one that has a coherence in terms of objectives and approach and is much more strongly linked into the structures of partner countries. While poverty alleviation has always been a declared objective of Ireland Aid, all projects, as long as they were located in the poorest countries were assumed to be making a contribution, however indirect, toward this goal. This is no longer considered sufficient. Activities being supported by Ireland Aid in the priority countries today are focusing directly on poverty alleviation. And the concept of poverty that underlies this more direct approach, has itself undergone a fundamental reinterpretation – as has the concept of partnership. These ideas are not unique to Ireland Aid: they are part of the current orthodoxy in development thinking. What is remarkable is that they are now finding practical expression within the Ireland Aid programme in line with best practice among other donors.

Ireland Aid is concerned about aid dependence. Although some of its area-based programmes in the priority countries have been in operation for only five years or less, it is already planning 'exit strategies' in some areas. Ireland Aid is also concerned about sustainability, a concept it interprets in a multi-dimensional way (economic, social, environmental, institutional, organisational, and human). It confesses that the search for sustainability has so far produced very modest results in the very poorest countries (where two-thirds of Ireland's bilateral aid is spent). Both Ireland and its developing country partners will continue to grapple with the issue of trade-offs between sustainability and aid dependence in the years ahead.

Ireland Aid's programme has grown significantly in terms of size since 1974 and, with the commitment to reaching the UN target by the end of 2007, that growth promises to be very strong in the medium-term. As regards substance and approach, it now compares favourably with the other small EU donors. Ireland's aid programme forms a significant as well as an integral part of its overall foreign policy. It reflects well on the country and Irish people can take justifiable pride in it. The challenge now is to manage the expansion of the programme while retaining the integrity of its core objectives.

References

Department of Foreign Affairs (DFA) (1993), *Ireland Aid Consolidation and Growth: A Strategy Plan*, Dublin.

DFA (1996), *Challenges and opportunities abroad: White Paper on Foreign Policy*, Dublin.

DFA (1997), *Pursuing Ireland's External Interests: Strategy Statement of the Department of Foreign Affairs*, Dublin.

DFA (1998), *Promoting Ireland's Interests: Strategy Statement of the Department of Foreign Affairs*, Dublin.

DFA (various years), *Ireland's Official Development Assistance*, Dublin.

European Commission (1996), *Green Paper on Relations between the EU and the ACP Countries on the Eve of the Twenty-First Century*, Brussels.

Fitzgerald, Garret TD, Minister for Foreign Affairs (1973), *Parliamentary Debates, Dáil Éireann, Official Report*, Vol. 265, p. 767

Ireland (1996), Challenges and Opportunities Abroad: White Paper on Foreign Policy, Dublin.

Ireland (2000), Address by the Taoiseach, Bertie Ahern, TD, to the United Nations Millennium Summit, New York, http://www.irlgov.ie/taoiseach/press/current/06-09-2000.htm

O'Donnell, Liz TD, Minister of State at the Department of Foreign Affairs (1997), address to the National Committee for Development Education, Dublin, 18 July.

O'Donnell, Liz TD, Minister of State at the Department of Foreign Affairs (2000), 'O'Donnell Says Govt. Announcement On Overseas Aid Is "Historic Decision"', Press Release, Government Information Service, 6 September, 2000.

OECD/DAC (1972), *Twenty-five Years of Development Co-operation*, Paris: OECD.

OECD/DAC (1995), *Development Co-operation*, Paris: OECD, 1994 Report.

OECD/DAC (1999), *Ireland*. Development Co-operation Review Series, No. 35, Paris.

OECD/DAC. (2000), *News Release.* http://www.oecd.org/news_and_events

O'Keefe, Jim TD, Minister of State at the Department of Foreign Affairs (1981), address to Comhlamh, the Returned Development Workers Association, Cork, 8 October, p. 7.

O'Kennedy, Michael TD, Minister for Foreign Affairs (1979), address to Annual General Meeting of DEVCO, the State Agencies Development Co-operation Organisation, Dublin, 12 February, p. 2.

O'Neill, H. (1984), 'Ireland Aid: policy and performance' in Olav Stokke (ed), *European Development Assistance: Policies and Performance*, European Association of Development Research and Training Institutes, Tilburg, and Norwegian Institute for International Affairs, Oslo.

O'Neill, H. (1997), 'Ireland's Foreign Aid in 1996', *Irish Studies in International Affairs*, Vol. 7, pp. 191-207, Dublin: Royal Irish Academy.

O'Neill, H. (1999), 'Ireland's Foreign Aid in 1998', *Irish Studies in International Affairs,* Vol. 10, pp. 289-306, Dublin: Royal Irish Academy.

World Bank (1999), http://www.worldbank.org/hipc/about/hipcbr/ hipcbr.htm

List of Abbreviations

ACP	African, Caribbean and Pacific countries
AfDB	African Development Bank
APSO	Agency for Personal Service Overseas
DAC	Development Assistance Committee (of the OECD)
DEVCO	State Agencies Development Co-operation Organisation
DFA	Department of Foreign Affairs
EDF	European Development Fund
EEC	European Economic Community
EU	European Union
ESAF	Enhanced Structural Adjustment Facility
FAO	Food and Agriculture Organisation
FSU	Former Soviet Union
GNP	Gross National Product
HIPC	Highly-indebted Poor Country
IDA	International Development Association
IFAD	International Fund for Agricultural Development
IMF	International Monetary Fund
NGO	Non-governmental Organisation
NIEO	New International Economic Order

ODA	Official Development Assistance
OECD	Organisation for Economic Co-operation and Development
OPEC	Organisation of Petroleum Exporting Countries
PRGF	Poverty Reduction and Growth Facility
PRSP	Poverty Reduction Strategy Paper
SADC	Southern African Development Community
SWAps	Sector-wide Approaches
UN	United Nations
UNDP	United Nations Development Programme
UNHCR	United Nations High Commission for Refugees
UNICEF	United Nations Children's Fund
UNIDO	United Nations Industrial Development Organisation
US	United States
WHO	World Health Organisation

Chapter 4

The New Context of British-Irish Relations

Martin Mansergh

Since independence, there has been a steady broadening out of Irish foreign policy, much accelerated since we joined the EEC, now the European Union, in 1973. While at the present time the Northern Ireland peace process requires a high level of concentration and input from both the Taoiseach and the Minister for Foreign Affairs, the international backdrop for Ireland today consists of far more than just the totality of relationships within and between Ireland and Britain. Yet British-Irish relations have always been on the agenda of Irish foreign policy – either directly or as an indirect and powerful influence on other policy issues.

Professor Patrick Keatinge has been a leading pioneer of the study of Irish foreign policy as it broadened out during those early years and more recently as the agenda changed and further expanded. It seems appropriate now in this text, to take a long-term overview of Irish foreign policy through the lens of the dominant dynamic of British-Irish relations. The current peace process has helped develop new relationships between Britain and Ireland which are bound to have some impact on Irish foreign policy in the future. This chapter will take a chronological approach and look at British Irish relations in five distinct historical periods, that of the pre-independence era; the early years of the new state; Ireland's integration into Europe and, finally, the contemporary period.

Pre-independence

As the Downing Street Declaration of December 1993 noted in its opening paragraph, history has left a difficult and divisive legacy to overcome. To characterise British-Irish relations as 800 years of conflict is over-simplistic, and that point is often made tongue in cheek. The Middle Ages and the post-Reformation period should not be too readily assimilated. What worked best following the Norman invasion were the periods where there was a large degree of internal autonomy. But Ireland, like Scotland, was perceived as a potential source of political threat in the struggles for hegemony in these islands. This became especially acute after the Reformation, when English rulers suddenly realised how little real control they had established over Ireland in 400 years, and when, following their attempts to tighten it, the increasingly oppressed Irish Catholic population sought strategic alliances with continental powers, like Spain and France, and later Germany, who welcomed the opportunity for creating a diversion.

Following the new, more thorough, but still incomplete, conquest of Ireland in the sixteenth and seventeenth centuries, popular resentment continued to smoulder under a relatively placid surface at the country's neglect and second-class status, at thoroughgoing political, religious and economic discrimination, and at the dispossession and displacement suffered by the majority, treated and regarded by some of their rulers almost as if they were a native tribe of North America or Southern Africa.

Whereas Bishop Berkeley had counted it a blessing in the 1730s that Ireland did not have to concern itself with foreign affairs, the creation of new democratic states in France and America towards the end of the eighteenth century made patriot MPs like Sir Laurence Parsons and United Irishmen like Tone and the Emmet brothers feel strongly that Ireland was absent from the international stage, and that it should take its place among the nations, a phrase later borrowed for the title of one of Patrick Keatinge's books (Keatinge, 1978). The Union in 1800, concluded between venal parliamentary élites and not peoples, sought in the wake of the United Irish Rebellion of 1798 to pre-empt the development of an Irish national democracy and to anglicise Ireland (not to mention misguided evangelical efforts at proselytism). The Union succeeded in dividing again communities North and South that had momentarily threatened to come together. Ireland had its individual status and personality subsumed.

Thomas Davis, who sought to transform what was now a province into a nation once again, argued that Ireland needed a foreign policy to provide a counterweight to Britain. By 1880, when Parnell was the first Irish political leader to address the US House of Representatives in an approach to seek support for the land struggle and withstand renewed famine, Ireland was developing the beginnings of a foreign policy. The new world was being brought in to redress the balance of the old. Emigration had, to the immense chagrin of those who put their faith in the nostrums of political economy, transferred the Irish Question (in part) across the Atlantic. But we are apt to forget today how much Irish developments in the nineteenth century took place against a British backdrop at Westminster, or the degree to which Irish emigrants to Britain provided a workforce for the industrial revolution and associated construction work on roads and railways. Irish soldiers and sailors were a vital part of the army and navy that conquered an empire.

The whole Home Rule debate showed the hollowness of the equality promised at the time of the Act of Union, with the measure continually frustrated by passionate conservative and unionist resistance based on the premise that the Irish like other colonised peoples were unfit for self-government. The Summary attached to the Government of Ireland Act, 1920, threatened revolutionary Ireland with crown colony government (i.e. martial law), if it did not accept the limited devolution offered along with partition. While the Irish Free State had to content itself initially with a hedged-about freedom, intended to preclude an independent foreign policy, Britain held on to the more industrially advanced part of Ireland, and could be satisfied that a small, struggling Irish Free State with an ungrateful people would pose little military, political or economic threat to British interests.

The new state

Despite quite good relations between the Cosgrave government and the British governments of the 1920s, and a certain mellowness that finally settled in between Churchill and de Valera by the 1950s, Anglo-Irish relations were testy and prickly for the best part of four decades. The *amour-propre* of an imperial power did not take kindly to Irish secession from the United Kingdom, or the trouble this precedent caused elsewhere in the Empire. In the early 1930s, Nehru wrote at length about Ireland in letters from prison to his daughter Indira, both future prime ministers.

From an Irish perspective, Britain had imposed the Treaty under threat of war, had played a part in inciting civil war, and had demonstrated the depths of duplicity in the Boundary Commission on a par with the Treaty of Limerick. In the1930s, Britain tried to destabilise the de Valera government by the economic war, as he sought to dismantle the Treaty settlement in the Irish Free State. Covert pressures through restricting both food, military and other supplies were also applied by Churchill in the Second World War, who communicated to the British people a deep and abiding public resentment at Irish neutrality, regardless of the real and valuable co-operation that was taking place beneath the surface, or the voluntary enlistment of many individuals. Most fundamentally of all, there continued a constitutional conflict over the legitimacy of partition and Northern Ireland, a cause taken up violently by the IRA at regular intervals.

Partition was seen on the Irish side as a festering injustice. Irish Catholicism and mixed attitudes to a large flow of Irish immigrants also created prejudice in Britain. In political terms, Britain took little notice of Ireland in the 1950s. Paradoxically, at the time Ireland finally declared its complete independence as a Republic in 1949, 90% of its exports went to Britain, and Ireland remained part of the sterling area. The combination of political marginalisation and a high degree of economic dependence, along with the disproportion of size and population, did not make for an easy or compatible bilateral relationship. In his debate with Taoiseach Seán Lemass at the Oxford Union in 1959 on a united Ireland motion, the young lawyer Patrick Mayhew reproached Ireland with economic backwardness and political isolation, both things that Lemass would strive to correct. Much of Ireland's cultural justification for independence had rested on a rejection of English influence and an emphasis on the things that made Ireland different from Britain, especially an Irish language-based culture and Catholicism.

And then there was Europe

The1960s saw a definite thaw in relations as Ireland joined with Britain in applying for EEC entry, concluding the Anglo-Irish Free Trade Area Agreement in 1965 as a prelude and preparation. Harold Wilson, a prime minister representing a Liverpool constituency with a substantial Irish population, was interested in developing a friendlier relationship, and the return of the remains of Roger Casement, executed in August 1916, was a friendly symbolic gesture. The O'Neill and Lemass meetings took place with the active encouragement of the British prime minister.

The 1960s saw also the development of much greater national self-confidence, with the economy thriving for the first time since independence, and the feeling that the country was at last going places. With the new policy of welcoming foreign investment, which came mainly from the United States, replacing the outworn ethos of self-sufficiency, which had showed a valuable and important purpose for a while, exports began to diversify.

The onset of the Northern Troubles brought renewed strain to Anglo-Irish relations. In 1969, the official view of the British government was that the Irish government had no *locus standi* in relation to Northern Ireland, which was none of their business and, furthermore, an interference in their internal affairs. The breakdown of government in Northern Ireland gradually forced the British in practice to modify this and consult to a greater degree with the Irish government. But major political and security initiatives up to the fall of Stormont could take place, often with disastrous consequences, without any real or significant input from the Irish side. The absence of an effective constitutional channel for grievances contributed to the prolongation of violence. During this phase, even on a benign interpretation, British prime minister Ted Heath was disposed to treat Taoiseach Jack Lynch, as if he were very much a junior partner.

Joint entry into the European Community found Britain having to deal with Ireland (neither Éire nor the Irish Republic) for the first time as an equal partner in a wider multilateral setting. The growing influence of Irish-America meant that the Northern Irish issue began also to impinge on the Anglo-American 'special' relationship. The far-reaching Sunningdale initiative was co-sponsored by the two governments, but positions once more diverged when the British Labour government allowed the power-sharing Executive to collapse under the impact of the paramilitary organised Ulster Workers' Strike. It was not until 1980 that Britain and Ireland decided once more to approach the problem together by establishing a British-Irish framework, first of all on an east-west basis, subsequently on a north-south basis.

Meanwhile, in the European Community, Britain and Ireland followed markedly different paths, Ireland being very pro-European and joining the ERM in 1979 with some material help from the French and the Germans as well as loans from the EC, and being a strong defender of the CAP and Structural Funds, while Britain adopted a far more reserved, if not sceptical, approach. Rightly or wrongly, Anglo-Irish relations did not impinge significantly on Ireland's European policy or on Britain's either.

The early 1980s demonstrated the limitations of unilateral political initiatives, both James Prior's rolling devolution and the New Ireland Forum, or indeed of mainly intergovernmental ones, like the Anglo-Irish Agreement of 1985, which did not have cross-community support.

The reassertion of Irish neutrality during the Falklands War, when Ireland previously had a seat at the UN Security Council, characterised by Patrick Keatinge as 'a singular stance' (Keatinge, 1984), was an important episode, even though condemned by realpolitikers as deeply damaging to Anglo-Irish relations. Charles Haughey's government had hoped that Britain, acting as a persuader, might in a planned and agreed manner pave the way for eventual disengagement from Northern Ireland, a hope inspired by the negotiation, under the influence of Foreign Secretary Lord Carrington, of the independence of Zimbabwe, or a later agreed departure from Hong Kong, especially if the Irish government was more receptive to the strategic concerns of Britain during an era of renewed Cold War following the Soviet invasion of Afghanistan.

The Falklands dispute showed that Margaret Thatcher was intent, where she could, on proceeding in a quite opposite direction, with minimal regard to the sensitivities of any other sovereign government involved. The Haughey government, already like the SDLP at loggerheads with the Prior initiative, saw no reason, after the sinking of the Belgrano outside the exclusion zone, to follow tamely behind a far-flung and bloody neo-colonial adventure, when the original British seizure of the Falklands from a newly independent Argentina in 1833 had been a colonial venture of dubious legality. The Argentine junta in 1982, on the other hand, with its widespread abuse of human rights had few claims on international support. As in the case of Kuwait, eight years later, ambiguous diplomatic signals had encouraged seizure by a dictatorship, an act which closed down the chances of productive future negotiation, after all the effort and sacrifice of a reconquest.

Assumptions of the 1960s and 1970s that Irish neutrality would fade as European political integration progressed were also shaken by a pronounced hostility within Irish public opinion to Reaganite assertiveness in the nuclear arms race and US support for right-wing régimes in Central America, where there was a strong Irish missionary presence. It was Ireland's strategic significance, including Northern Ireland's, that largely faded, notwithstanding far-fetched theories amongst retired British military officers about either the danger of a European Cuba developing in Northern Ireland, or Soviet backfire bombers penetrating Irish airspace from the Atlantic. This weakened the case for any fundamental change of policy.

The end of the Cold War permitted Northern Secretary Peter Brooke to disclaim any selfish strategic interest on the part of Britain in Northern Ireland. Brooke's equal disclaimer of a selfish economic interest, with an annual subvention of three to four billion pounds, was so obvious that it scarcely needed to be said. The end of the Cold War worldwide encouraged the start of a decade of peace processes in many situations, where the East-West ideological conflict could be taken out of the equation. The Northern Ireland peace process followed the lead and example of South Africa and the Middle East, while taking stock of the peaceful revolutions in Central and Eastern Europe. The end of the Cold War also facilitated the other European neutrals who wished to apply for EU membership to do so – except of course Switzerland which chose not to.

Neutrality was a major issue in every European referendum from 1987 to 1998. Successive governments from 1987 sought to safeguard Ireland's neutral position within the EU, while going along with active participation in the development of peacekeeping as an auxiliary European task, complementary to NATO. In 1999, after much public debate, Ireland became one of the last European countries to join the flexible NATO-associated Partnership for Peace, defining itself as an Atlantic as well as a European nation in accordance with political and economic realities as well as heavy American involvement in the peace process. Apart altogether from the disappearance of any strategic significance, the gulf between Northern Ireland and the Republic in security policy terms has thus been somewhat reduced, particularly as the whole Western world is now much more focused on peacekeeping.

Skilful and purposeful negotiations in the late 1980s ensured that Ireland was included, along with the Mediterranean countries, as the recipient of a major increase in Structural and (later) Cohesion Funds, which helped transform the Irish economy, by dissolving the dichotomy between much-needed investment to tackle a serious and longstanding productive infrastructure deficit and the re-establishment of sound public finances, after a period when Irish public debt had rivalled Italy's and Belgium's at the top of the league. There was an absolute determination to meet the Maastricht criteria for membership of the single currency, and not to be discouraged by the hard currency rhetoric and patronising comments coming from the German government and the Bundesbank. Ironically, all of that was dissipated within a few months by the short-lived German Finance Minister Oskar Lafontaine, when he tried to bring a more traditional socialist perspective to bear on economic policy.

Over the last twenty-seven years, Ireland has stayed closer to the EU core than Britain. The experiment of British membership of the ERM ended in tears within a few years in September 1992. While Ireland had to devalue four months later, the devaluation of 1993 proved the starting point of the Celtic Tiger economy. Ireland signed up to the Maastricht Treaty and the Social Charter, where the British maintained a continuing reserve. Only in the case of the Schengen Treaty did the requirements of the common travel area supersede alignment with the core of the EU.

The extremely rapid growth of the Irish economy from 1993-4 to the present time has elevated Ireland out of the ranks of the poorer, peripheral EU countries and made it one of the runaway success stories of the European Union. It was agreed at Berlin that transfers to Ireland under the third round of Structural Funds up to 2006 would taper off, though the agricultural budget in both relative and absolute terms remains very important to Ireland. Moving towards the position of being a net contributor has led to a cooler appraisal of Ireland's interests. Economic policy based on social partnership provides our own blend of Anglo-American economic practice with European social solidarity and cohesion. But, as Ireland becomes a more significant player, it has attracted more critical attention. Britain, Ireland and Sweden stood out against the harmonisation of taxes other than by unanimity at the Nice Summit in December 2000, and it was one of the first times that Britain and

Ireland were on the same side on an issue of major importance to both, inside the EU. The Northern Ireland economy, saddled with an uncompetitive exchange rate compounded by certain aspects of British fiscal policy, has suffered from Britain's decision so far to remain out of the single currency, as is made visible by the border filling stations. The elimination of an exchange rate difference, when sterling joins the euro, in a way that will not reproduce for Ireland the unilateral dependence on sterling that existed in the past, will provide a substantial boost to North-South economic activity.

The peace process and Anglo-Irish relations today

The peace process has seen the most radical transformation of British-Irish relations. To achieve results, the two governments have had to work very closely together, not without some creative tension at certain points, but with increasing cordiality and sense of common purpose.

It was clear for a long time that a purely internal settlement would not suffice, because it would, even with power-sharing, confine nationalists to a position of minority disadvantage. It would ignore their links beyond Northern Ireland, whilst continuing to privilege unionist links with the rest of the United Kingdom. Hopes throughout the conflict for a spontaneous accommodation between constitutional parties on each side of the divide were never realised. It gradually became clear in the late 1980s that there might be a more direct path to peace, than pursuing the long shot of a negotiated settlement and hoping that popular support for it would then either deter paramilitary activity or facilitate a crackdown on it.

The peace process has involved both governments coming to grips with the underlying motivation of militant republicanism and militant loyalism. Only a radical political settlement was capable of bringing about peace. The Good Friday Agreement contains a whole series of radical initiatives; profound constitutional change; an Executive drawn from across the entire political spectrum from the DUP to Sinn Féin; active and ambitious North-South bodies; an East-West British-Irish Council drawing together all the devolved Executives of the UK with the two sovereign governments; a radical reform of policing; the release of all prisoners; and the decommissioning of paramilitary weapons. Every political initiative, not just of the last thirty years, but going back far beyond that, is distilled into the Agreement.

Negotiating the Agreement was a huge feat. Fully implementing it has been an equally daunting task. But, through it all, all sorts of unheard of things have been happening; unionist talks with Sinn Féin; republican leaders in Dublin Castle, Stormont, Chequers and Downing Street; unionists, loyalists and even the Rev Ian Paisley in Government Buildings in Dublin; a good working relationship between the unionist leadership and the Taoiseach. The Major government declined to be persuaders for unity. But all British governments are now persuaders for the Agreement.

Many oppositions have been dissolved. There is no longer a conflict of constitutional doctrine. The Irish conception of self-determination applied to the island as a whole has been reconciled with the unionist and British conception of Northern Ireland on its own having that right. Concurrent self-determination squares the circle. Conflicting claims over territory have gone, with the recognition that future status will be decided by the people and with the people. The one nation and the two nation theories have been squared, with a voluntarist conception of nationality, embracing all who value an Irish nationality, but leaving others, who do not, free to make their own decisions. North-South bodies are not just an expression of Irish identity; they fulfil a practical purpose. The spirit of democracy is in the process of displacing revolutionary violence.

For a long time after independence, there was a burning sense of incompleteness about Ireland as a state. This had principally to do with partition. It is very likely that it was against that background that its achievements were viewed as being against the odds, while many of its failures were projected onto partition. While partition was not the source of all ills, it certainly did handicap national development in many different ways.

But in the past ten years, due to a combination of the peace process and the Celtic Tiger economy, the psychological impact of Northern Ireland in the South has changed. Twenty-six county Ireland is now a striking economic success within the EU. For the first time, it has little to fear from comparisons with Northern Ireland. Greater North-South integration, while likely to be of benefit, is only tangential to continued success.

Potential engagement in Northern Ireland is a responsibility falling to the Irish government, not because of a selfish desire to pursue traditional aims, but to ensure peace, stability and reconciliation on the island, which, short, or long-term, is a vital national interest. If a united Ireland is to come in the future, it must come, as provided for in the Good Friday Agreement, peacefully, and by agreement and consent. Making the new dispensation work is justified in its own terms, irrespective of any ulterior development, and it should not be denigrated on the basis of what it is not. It provides a benign framework for future relations, whether or not constitutional change comes about at a future date.

The peace process has drawn the two governments more closely together than at any time in the past. Formal institutional expressions like the British-Irish Council or even the British-Irish Intergovernmental Council are secondary to the strength of the informal relationship, and the reflex on both sides of the need to work closely together, notwithstanding any differences of interest or standpoint on particular matters.

None of this presages a return of Ireland to the British sphere of influence or to some form of renewed political union, however loose. Having paid the costs of independence with many sacrifices along the way, Ireland is today enjoying the advantages, independence being the admission ticket to the councils of the nations. Ireland belongs to the numerous group of small to medium-sized countries, whereas Britain is among the larger ones though in terms of population rather than territory.

Partnership on both sides, recognising the unique relationship between the two islands, is only one part of much wider sets of relationships with Europe, with America, and with countries on other continents. Britain no longer overshadows Ireland to anything like the extent it did, even long after independence. Stabilisation and progress in implementing the new political settlement will remove most of what is contentious in relations between the two islands.

Bibliography

Keatinge, P. (1978), *A Place Among Nations: Issues of Foreign Policy*, IPA: Dublin.

Keatinge, P. (1984), *A Singular Stance: Irish Neutrality in the 1980s*, IPA: Dublin.

Chapter 5

Ireland at the United Nations
Noel Dorr

Introduction

In October 2000 Ireland was elected to one of two non-permanent seats on the UN Security Council assigned to the 'Western Europe and Other Group'. It served for a term extending over the two-year period 2001-2002.

The Security Council is the heart of the UN system. It has power to order sanctions or even armed action against an offending state; and its decisions are binding on all member states. The Council has five Permanent Members, each with a right of veto; and a rotating membership of ten other elected members, each of which serves a two-year term.

This is not the first time Ireland has held a seat on the Council – it did so for the two-year period 1981-1982; and, it served a one-year, split term in 1962. In recent years, election to membership of the Council has become extremely competitive and, in order to gain a seat on this occasion, it was necessary to conduct a prolonged and intensive lobbying campaign around the world. To those who know the UN however, more remarkable than the fact of election was the manner of its achievement against two other very strong candidates – Italy and Norway. The vote is by secret ballot among the UN membership as a whole.[1] Ireland was elected on the first count with 130 votes; Norway, with an initial 114 votes, took a seat on the fourth count; and Italy, which received 92 votes on the first count, was not elected.

Credit for this success is due to the Taoiseach, to government ministers and to Irish diplomats who conducted the campaign. The Permanent Representative in New York, Richard Ryan, and his team deserve special mention. But the vote also reflects a more general perception by other member states of the positions that Ireland has taken at the UN over many years.

For this reason it would be of interest to look back now over the whole period since Ireland joined the United Nations to see the kind of policies that it followed on the major issues that arose over that time.[2] To cover the whole period in any detail would, however, be outside the scope of the present chapter. Accordingly, I propose instead to look selectively at the early years of Ireland's UN membership, which are now generally seen as 'the golden age' for Ireland at the UN.[3] What kind of policies did Ireland follow at that time and is it right to take this, as commentators have done since, as the measure of the contribution which a small country like ours could, and should, make to the organisation, a measure by reference to which Ireland's record later as a UN member is seen to fall short? I will then consider how the world has changed since the mid-twentieth century, whether there is still a serious role for the UN and how a small country like Ireland might work to make it more effective and better able to address the problems of the new century.[4]

The United Nations developed out of the victorious alliance of the Second World War. The founding members were the states that participated in the San Francisco Conference of 1945. The conference was sponsored by four major powers – the United States of America, the United Kingdom, the Union of Soviet Socialist Republics and the Republic of China. They invited forty-two other countries that were at war as allies against the Axis powers on 1 March 1945. Four other countries were invited later. One other, Poland, was admitted on the day the United Nations Charter came into effect bringing the initial membership to fifty-one.[5] Ireland had remained neutral in the war – as many other small European states had tried to do with less success. In consequence it was not invited to the San Francisco Conference and it was not a founder member of the UN.

Application for membership

When the war ended in 1945 a residual bitterness about Ireland's neutrality meant that neither the US nor the British government were well-disposed to inviting Ireland to join the new organisation. The Taoiseach, Eamon de Valera, seems to have been satisfied by mid-1946 however, that the views of both countries had changed and that they would now support an Irish application.[6] Following a two-day Dáil debate at the end of July, Ireland applied to become a member on 2 August 1946.

It may seem strange at first sight that a country that had just managed to come successfully through the war as a neutral, non-belligerent, should opt so soon afterwards for membership of an international organisation based on the concept of collective security. In principle, collective security involves a commitment by all members of an organisation to act forcefully together against aggression, whether from outside or by one member against another; and Ireland, after all, had opted out of a war which could be said to have more nearly fitted the definition of a 'just war' than any in history.

To the Irish government of the time, however, and particularly to Eamon de Valera, the eventual decision to seek membership of the UN would have seemed fundamentally in line with long-standing Irish policies – even though at times in 1944 and 1945 de Valera had expressed scepticism about the concept of the new organisation.[7] All Irish governments since the foundation of the state have had in common a strong sense of the importance to small countries of justice and order in international life and have seen effective international organisations as the way to secure this.

Ireland had played a very active role in the League of Nations in the 1920s and 1930s and de Valera as President of the League Council in 1933 had delivered one of the more memorable and prescient warnings of the dangers that lay ahead if the member states did not act together to support the Covenant of the League. It was precisely the failure, as he saw it, of the major powers in the 1930s to live up to the commitment to collective security embodied in the Covenant that led him to declare early in 1939 that Ireland would seek to stay out of the war that he knew lay ahead. In the absence of an effective collective security system it was now for each state to look to its own direct interests; and Ireland's interest, in his view, dictated a policy of military neutrality for as long as that could be maintained.

Now however, the war had ended; and out of the rubble a new effort was being made to construct an effective international organisation based on the principle of collective security which the new Irish state had accepted in the 1920s when it joined the League and argued strongly for in the 1930s as a member of the League Council. In the UN, unlike the League, all major powers including the United States would be members and the prospects of success seemed correspondingly greater.

Article 4 of the UN Charter makes it clear that membership is open to 'all other peace-loving States'. Admission of new members is a matter for decision by the General Assembly on a recommendation by the Security Council. But because each of the five Permanent Members of the Council has a veto any one of them may block a proposal to admit a state to membership. In the event, Ireland's application was vetoed by the Soviet Union for reasons which probably included Ireland's neutrality in the war; its lack of diplomatic relations with the Soviet Union; and the perception that if admitted, it was likely to take a 'pro-Western' line in the Assembly. It was to be nine years more before Ireland was finally admitted to membership of the UN in late 1955 as part of a 'package deal' along with such other countries as Austria, Finland, Italy, Spain, Bulgaria and Jordan.

The General Assembly of the 1950s

The General Assembly at the time Ireland took its seat was very different from that of today. The Cold War was then at its height and votes in the Assembly were taken rather more seriously by the major powers than they have been for much of the intervening period. At times the Assembly became an arena for rhetorical combat between East and West, a stage on which what Conor Cruise O'Brien has called 'Sacred Drama',[8] which helps to avert bloodshed by substituting ritual for real conflict, could be acted out.

The fact that some of the more important member states were grouped into two rival blocs and the fact that at times they took rather seriously the rhetorical battles in the Assembly gave a handful of small and medium sized countries a real, though limited, opportunity to play a helpful role on occasion. Countries outside either alliance such as Sweden, and countries such as Poland and Canada which were alliance members but which were at times prepared to show a degree of independence, could help to soften the asperities of the Cold War as reflected in General Assembly debates and resolutions. These countries did not constitute an organised group or have any general agreement to act in concert but thought of themselves simply as 'good UN members'. Ireland as a new member readily identified itself with this approach.

A further notable difference between then and now was the virtual absence of sub-Saharan Africa from the General Assembly. The anti-colonial wave, Macmillan's 'wind of change', had not yet begun to gather force and at the time Ireland joined the UN, much of Africa was still under European colonial rule. Apart from South Africa, which, although criticised for its apartheid system, had not yet become a complete pariah, only two countries of sub-Saharan Africa, Ethiopia and Liberia, were UN members. More generally, there were far fewer countries from the developing world in the organisation at that time than there are today. The Bandung Conference, which marked the start of a self-conscious non-aligned movement, had just taken place but the concept of 'non-alignment' was still regarded with suspicion by states committed to the respective alliances on either side of the Cold War.

The approach of the Irish delegation

In these circumstances, Ireland as a newly admitted member state felt itself to be in something of a special position. It was a European state with friendly relations with its European neighbours. But it saw itself also as a submerged nation that had emerged to independence after a long struggle – in effect the first colony to shake off foreign domination in the twentieth century. When the opportunity arose it felt entitled by its own experience to speak out strongly against colonialism and in favour of self-determination.

After the relative isolation of the war years and some experience in the early 1950s in the more limited arena offered by the Council of Europe, there was a sense of exhilaration for the Irish delegation as it took its place in the General Assembly. Under the leadership of Liam Cosgrave as Minister for External Affairs in 1956 and under Frank Aiken in subsequent years, it found itself in a position to play a useful, and at times helpful, role on the wider international stage. A good deal has been written about the differing policy approaches of the two ministers. Under Liam Cosgrave, who was in office for only a single Assembly session, there was certainly a greater emphasis on what a memorandum to the cabinet on foreign policy by the

Taoiseach, John A. Costello, referred to as '[strengthening] the Christian civilisation of which Ireland [is] part'.[9] But looking back from the perspective of nearly half a century, one is more likely to be struck by the extent to which there was a continuity of approach and a persistent belief that a small country like Ireland could and should play a constructive role in the Assembly.

It is now widely believed that the four or five years which followed Ireland's admission to the UN – that is the period from 1956 to 1960 inclusive – were a kind of 'golden age' of Irish UN membership. There is a large measure of truth in this. It was due partly to the opportunities presented by the rather different character, composition and relative importance of the General Assembly at the time; and partly to the élan which the Irish delegation at the time brought to what was in effect Ireland's re-entry on the main international stage after the relative isolation of the war years. But it must also be said that some of the aura that attaches to those years is due to the fact that the activities of the delegation were extensively chronicled by one of those involved.

Personalities on the delegation

Conor Cruise O'Brien was a leading figure in the delegation and a principal advisor to the minister; he was activist and creative in his approach to the role that a delegation like Ireland's might play; and his elegant literary style was in evidence when he drafted speeches for the minister or for himself. But as a writer and historian of distinction he also had an opportunity to 'write the record' himself at a time when no other record was being written – or at least published; and his pen has helped to impart a kind of golden glow to the events in which he participated and, be it said, a sharp stab on occasion to those with whom he disagreed.

Liam Cosgrave, as minister, led the first delegation in 1956 to a fraught General Assembly session that debated the Suez crisis and the Soviet suppression of the Hungarian uprising. Understandably, however, since he led the delegation for more than a decade from 1957 onwards, it is the name of Frank Aiken in particular which is generally associated with that period.

Aiken was a taciturn man; a man of great and gritty integrity, conviction and stubbornness; somewhat puritan in outlook; at heart an engineer with an inventive cast of mind. He was willing to spend long periods at the General Assembly each year – far longer than any Irish Foreign Minister could possibly afford today. Unlike any other Foreign Minister he took the delegation seat in Committee as well as in Plenary and sat through debates there whenever one of the Committees of the General Assembly was dealing with a subject of concern to him. This made him a curious but respected figure to other delegations. The fact that he had been a revolutionary in his youth, now turned elder statesman, gave him a particular stature; and this, and the anti-colonial stance of the Irish delegation under his leadership, gave him a particular authority in the eyes of many smaller countries when he counselled, as he sometimes did, against 'armed struggle' to achieve liberation.

Aiken's almost Roman character and qualities were well-supported and complemented by the worldly-wise, sophisticated manner, the gravitas and the wide diplomatic experience of the Permanent Representative, Freddie Boland, and by the intellect, the literary talent and the activist instincts of a younger Conor Cruise O'Brien leading a number of other talented young Irish diplomats of the time. The interest of the minister in the work of the Assembly and the fact that it became a major focus for Irish foreign policy at that time meant that the Department of External Affairs assigned some of the best and the brightest young and middle-level officials to serve on the delegation in New York for the three-month session of the General Assembly in Autumn each year.

Issues in the General Assembly

The major issues that pre-occupied the delegation at the time can be traced through the booklets reproducing Frank Aiken's UN speeches which were published each year from 1957 until the mid-1960s. The topics included: disarmament; the representation of China in the UN; the situation in Tibet; the situation in the Congo; the need for support for the independence of the Secretary General; the Middle East; the financing of peacekeeping; and the Irish draft resolution calling for the negotiation of a treaty to prevent the spread of nuclear weapons. On all of these issues the Irish delegation under Aiken took what might fairly be called a constructive, and, at times, a creative approach. A brief account of two or three selected issues will help to illustrate this.

Apartheid and de-colonisation

The apartheid system of South Africa has now, happily, been dismantled; Namibia is independent; and colonialism, generally repudiated, is little more than a painful historic memory. In the Western-dominated UN General Assembly of the late 1950s however, it was not yet clear that things would go this way or that it was right for the UN, an organisation of sovereign states, to engage itself in a direct effort to bring both to an end. As many Western countries at that time saw it, the situation within South Africa, seen as a matter of human rights, was indeed deplorable but the General Assembly was inhibited in acting forcefully against it because of Article 2.7 of the Charter which bars the UN from intervening in matters which are 'essentially within the domestic jurisdiction of any State'. Colonialism, too, could be and was, defended. Some important European countries claimed that their colonies were in reality part of the metropolitan territory; others, at a minimum insisted that they could not withdraw 'precipitously' and 'without adequate preparation' from territories which they had governed in one way or another for a century or more.

The Irish delegation, reflecting attitudes shaped by a particular historic experience, took a firm position on both issues. It was active in seeking, with a small number of other countries, to have the issue of apartheid inscribed on the Assembly agenda, and it joined with them in sponsoring resolutions which, though they seem now in retrospect to have been restrained enough in tone were, judged by the temper of the Assembly at the time, highly critical of South Africa's policies. Aiken was particularly resolute in insisting on the complete illegality of South Africa's virtual annexation of Namibia, a territory for which it had been given responsibility as a 'sacred trust' under the mandate system of the League of Nations after the First World War.

In 1960 the delegation, under Aiken, also adopted a distinctive position on what came to be seen later as a landmark resolution – Resolution 1514 (XV). This 'Declaration on the Granting of Independence to Colonial Countries and Peoples' asserted flatly that 'all peoples have an inalienable right to complete freedom'; and it solemnly proclaimed 'the necessity of bringing to a speedy and unconditional end colonialism in all its forms and manifestations'. The draft resolution – particularly the key word 'unconditional' – was most unwelcome to many Western countries which saw it as 'propagandistic'. Aiken deserves considerable credit for his courage in voting and speaking for it in the circumstances of the time.

Nuclear non-proliferation: the 'Irish proposal'

The initiative by the Irish delegation from that period which is best remembered today is probably the courageous effort by Aiken from 1958 onwards to promote the idea of a treaty to curb the spread of nuclear weapons. This was one of those rare initiatives, like the idea of a conference on the Law of the Sea pursued in the mid-1960s by Malta, which if taken up and pressed with persistence and determination by a small member state can eventually open up a wholly new area for international negotiation and, eventually, international co-operation. At the outset, however, the general climate was none too favourable – indeed it might not be too much to say that some important countries that subsequently endorsed the concept were aghast when Aiken first put forward his draft resolution at the 1958 Assembly.

He did not achieve immediate success but he was wise enough to withdraw the resolution once he had achieved a vote on a paragraph stating the general principle, believing it more prudent to fight another day. He returned to the issue in each of the following years and eventually achieved the reward of his persistence when the Assembly adopted what came to be called 'the Irish Resolution' in 1961. Seven years later, after lengthy negotiation between the major powers, the Nuclear Non-Proliferation Treaty; which 'the Irish Resolution' had called for, was signed. Ireland was invited to be the first to sign the new treaty and, to mark the importance that it attributed to this positive outcome to the Irish initiative of 1957, it did so, not just in one but in all three capitals where the document was opened for signature. Aiken himself took the unusual step of travelling to Moscow to sign it there, even though Ireland did not have diplomatic relations with the Soviet Union at the time.

Peacekeeping: the Congo

Over this same period, the second half of the 1950s, the United Nations evolved the new concept of peacekeeping, inspired and guided by Dag Hammarskjold as Secretary General, Lester Pearson of Canada and others. Peacekeeping in its classic form interposes a thin blue line of lightly armed UN soldiers with the consent of the warring parties. Unlike the more robust concept of enforcement action, peacekeeping in this sense is not provided for explicitly in the Charter but arose from a creative development of some of its general principles.

It was to Aiken's credit that he accepted that the delegation's words in debates in the Assembly ought to be matched, when the need arose, by action – in this case by active participation in this new area. Ireland first joined a peacekeeping operation when it sent fifty officers from the defence forces to participate in an unarmed observer group in Lebanon (UNOGIL) in 1958. Two years later, in 1960, it broke new ground when it responded positively to a UN request and supplied a full battalion strength contingent to serve with ONUC, the UN peacekeeping force in the Congo.

On 1 July in that year, what was then the Belgian Congo (since Zaire and now, again, the Republic of Congo) had become an independent state. It was ill-prepared for independence under Belgian rule and the situation quickly deteriorated into something close to chaos. At the request of the new Congolese government, the UN Security Council, acting on a proposal by Hammarskjold, the Secretary General, decided to send a peacekeeping force. Ireland, and a number of other small and medium-sized UN member states were asked to supply contingents.

In sending this force to the Congo, the UN stepped into very deep waters; indeed, in view of subsequent events, one might even say into the heart of darkness. The newly established state began to fall apart amid accusations that foreign interference was promoting the secession of the mineral-rich province of Katanga through the use of mercenaries and seeking in other ways to ensure that colonial domination could be maintained indirectly even after nominal independence had been attained.

Never again until it took on a major role in Cambodia in 1992 did the UN become so deeply involved in the internal affairs of any member state; and never before or since has the UN itself come so close to disintegrating. As it was, it lost a respected Secretary General, when Dag Hammarskjold was killed in a plane crash on his way to Katanga in September 1961; it then faced a demand from the Soviet Union that the post of Secretary General be replaced by a 'troika' drawn from East, West and the Third World; and it ran into huge financial problems when some major countries, including the Soviet Union, refused to pay their assessed contributions.

Ireland too became deeply involved in the Congo. Nowadays the sending of Irish contingents to serve with the UN has become relatively common. At the time it was unprecedented and new legislation was required. The Congo was indeed a faraway country of which we knew nothing. Nevertheless in July 1960 the Irish government of the day readily agreed to the UN request to send a battalion of Irish soldiers to equatorial Africa. Wearing what was then the standard-issue heavy Irish 'bullswool' uniform they left Dublin for tropical Africa in US aircraft in July and early August 1960. This was the first time in the history of the Irish state that a unit of its forces bearing weapons for self-protection had served abroad. One battalion later grew to become two and at one point, up to 1,200 Irish troops – perhaps as much as one eighth of the defence forces at the time – were serving simultaneously in the Congo under an Irish General, Sean McKeown, who was appointed overall Force Commander for ONUC.

Before the operation ended in 1963 the Irish defence forces, for the first time in their history, had suffered losses in combat abroad – in the ambush in Niemba in 1960 and in the fighting in Elisabethville in Katanga against secessionist forces led by European mercenaries in the following years. Many Dubliners of an age to do so will remember the military funeral through the streets of the city of the eleven soldiers killed by tribesmen in the Niemba ambush in late 1960: the 'Dead March in Saul', a sombre counterpoint to the lively cheerful march of the battalion some months previously as it left for the Congo. It is important to record however that support in Ireland for Irish participation in UN peacekeeping remained strong. Even relatively substantial losses in a distant and rather obscure conflict did not lead to any serious pressure from public opinion for withdrawal of Irish troops. This contrasts, one might add, with what happened in some larger countries in recent years following military losses in peacekeeping in Africa.

1960: annus mirabilis

In retrospect, that year of 1960 can be seen as something of an *annus mirabilis* for Ireland as a member state of the UN. The Irish Permanent Representative to the UN in New York, Freddie Boland, had been elected President of the General Assembly in an election contested by two other strong candidates. The session over which he presided in the Autumn of 1960 was one of the most notable in the history of the UN: it brought together a galaxy of heads of state and government from around the world including Nikita Khruschev and Fidel Castro. Ireland had plunged fully into UN peacekeeping: it had a larger contingent serving abroad than at any time before or since; it had sustained its first, and tragically quite substantial, losses; and Ireland's General Sean McKeown was overall commander of the 20,000 UN peacekeeping force in the Congo. In early 1961 an Irish diplomat, Conor Cruise O'Brien, was appointed to a central position as the Special Representative of the UN Secretary General in Katanga. This was a post that O'Brien resigned from in controversial circumstances towards the end of that year following the death of Dag Hammarskold in a plane crash.[10] Ireland was certainly playing a role out of all proportion to its size in those years but *The Economist* allowed itself to be carried away by hyperbole when it began one of its leading articles entitled '*The Afro-Irish Assembly*' with a ringing statement that 'Ireland bestrides the UN like a Colossus'. *The Skibereen Eagle* could not have put it better.

Overall assessment of the early period

Is it valid to see these first five years of Ireland's UN membership as the golden age? Did the delegation, as is commonly believed, always take a courageously independent line and judge each issue solely on its merits?

It is certainly true that Ireland had a high reputation at the UN at that time and this was well-deserved. Under the leadership of Frank Aiken the delegation showed a considerable degree of independent thinking in its speeches and its voting in the General Assembly and this continued into the 1960s and beyond. But it would be an exaggeration to believe that, even in this earlier period, Ireland always judged issues entirely on their merits and took absolutely no account of national interest or of relations with important countries such as the USA. No government could afford to be so quixotic. This is not to say that it lacked courage when this was needed but, particularly in the latter part of the period when Sean Lemass took over as Taoiseach from Eamon de Valera, courage, on occasion at least, had to be tempered with prudence and realism.

The balance tipped a little more towards prudence on certain matters once the Irish government, under Lemass, decided to apply for full membership of what was then the European Communities, the EEC, in 1961. It was by no means a foregone conclusion that Ireland would be accepted as an applicant capable of taking on the role of a full member – after all it had been describing itself internationally as 'underdeveloped' only a short time previously. It was important therefore to maintain good relations with, and indeed to court, the six founding member states of the EEC. The stance of the Irish delegation in New York on such issues as the Algerian struggle for independence from France and the tension between Austria and Italy over the South Tyrol/Alto-Adige became a matter of concern to Lemass who feared that the result would be to antagonise countries such as France and Italy which were crucial to the success of Ireland's application for EEC membership.

Skelly in his study of the period[11] has shown that Lemass, like de Valera before him, followed quite closely what Ireland was doing at the UN on major issues. At the time however, as I recall it, it appeared as if Ireland had, in effect, two Foreign Ministers: Lemass as Taoiseach seemed to be Minister for Europe while Aiken, because of his stature within the government as one of the major figures in the War of Independence, close to de Valera, was largely given his head as Minister for the UN. While he did not speak out explicitly on the matter, I think it is fair to say that Aiken was more than dubious about the decision to apply for EEC membership and did not wish to be associated with it.

There is now a perception that even though Aiken remained minister through the decade of the 1960s there was a failure on the part of the Irish delegation to the UN General Assembly to show the same courage or independence as in the period up to the end of 1960. Certainly times and personalities changed – no delegation could hope to have more than one Conor Cruise O'Brien. But critics of that later period do not allow sufficiently for the fact that the General Assembly was changing rapidly at about this time. The membership grew dramatically during the 1960s, the decade of de-colonisation, and there was a large influx of new member states from Africa in particular. They soon took over the initiative on African issues, and on colonialism issues in general. This meant that it was no longer necessary for some sympathetic countries outside Africa such as Ireland to ask to have apartheid put on the agenda and to propose draft resolutions in regard to it. African countries were now in a position to speak for themselves and for their continent and they did so with increasing vigour and assertiveness.

The US and other Western member states had begun to take the Assembly less seriously and they were dubious about many of the proposals on the apartheid issue which were being pressed in the Assembly. Some still tended towards a 'strict constructionist' interpretation of Article 2.7 of the Charter which barred discussion of a state's 'internal affairs'; others, economically engaged with South Africa, did not consider demands for sanctions against it to be a good approach; and many were dubious about declaratory resolutions and about the competence or the capacity of the General Assembly to impose sanctions or to enforce them if they were to be imposed. Soviet bloc countries inevitably took advantage of the issue to embarrass 'the West' for its continuing economic relations with South Africa.

The new African members became increasingly frustrated at their inability, in the face of this kind of Western opposition, to secure action through declaratory resolutions of the General Assembly; and as they became more frustrated, the resolutions became stronger and more vehement in their condemnation of 'the major trading partners of South Africa' and in their calls for sanctions. On this and other issues, the General Assembly by the mid-1960s was thus more radical, and at the same time taken less seriously by Western countries than it had been in the early years of Ireland's membership.

In the meantime Conor Cruise O'Brien, who had maintained a judicious silence in the first years after he resigned in 1961, following controversy over his role and that of the UN in Katanga where he had been the Representative of the Secretary General, began to write more critically of Irish policy at the UN, particularly in regard to South Africa. Others, including the very effective Irish Anti-Apartheid Movement, supported this criticism and argued that Ireland was no longer showing the courage and independence that had characterised its stance in earlier years.

As the critics became more outspoken, Aiken, a man never given to active presentation of himself or his policies to the news media, became more taciturn. He was a man of courage and integrity but somewhat old-fashioned in his approach. It was simply not his style to engage in public debate on foreign policy issues and he gave no public answer to criticisms of Ireland's voting position on the apartheid issue. In the absence of any defence from the minister, who alone could defend policy publicly, the critics had it all their own way. The belief grew that Ireland was 'back-sliding' in a serious way from its past positions. Little account was taken of the fact that the General Assembly majority was now far more radical – and frustrated – than it had been in the late 1950s and that the resolutions which were being adopted were far stronger than anything that would have been proposed in the earlier period.

A dilemma can arise for a delegation when it is faced with a series of resolutions espousing a position which it shares in general but which do so in language which it finds difficult or impossible to accept in detail. The dilemma is even greater when, as sometimes happened on the apartheid issue, the sponsors of a resolution, with majority support, vote down any attempt to amend the proposal and refuse to allow separate votes on any of its paragraphs. This was the situation in the mid-1960s. African delegations, frustrated at the lack of response by the West, pressed ever stronger draft resolutions to a vote each year. The Irish delegation, stung by criticism at home which the minister was unwilling to answer, sometimes found ways to rationalise a vote for resolutions couched in terms that went well beyond anything which it could possibly have lived with in an earlier era.

Thus, although the Irish voting positions on apartheid issues became more radical at this time, the shift was nothing like as great as the overall shift in the temper of the Assembly. The result, paradoxically, was that even though Ireland was voting far more radically on apartheid than it would ever have done in the period up to 1960, the received opinion at home was, and still remains, that the decade of the 1960s marked a major deterioration and failure of courage and independence in its stance at the UN.

To deal in any detail with the later years would be well beyond the scope of this chapter but to overlook them entirely would leave it incomplete. At most it is possible to note some milestones. They include: Ireland's one-year term on the Security Council in 1962, now largely forgotten; Aiken's gallant but unsuccessful crusade in the mid-1960s to ensure that peacekeeping operations would be financed by mandatory assessment; the recourse by the Minister for Foreign Affairs, Patrick Hillery, to the Security Council in 1969 to ask for a peacekeeping force for Northern Ireland which, though it never got beyond the procedural issue of whether or not the issue should go on the agenda, helped nevertheless to defuse passions at home; the responsibility of speaking on behalf of the EC, now the EU, during Ireland's successive presidencies of the European Union; Ireland's terms on the UN Human Rights Commission in Geneva, culminating recently in an admirable, and admired, handling by the Irish Permanent Representative[12] of the delicate task of chairing the Commission; the appointment of Mary Robinson as UN Commissioner for Human Rights; Ireland's two-year term on the Security Council in 1981-82; and, throughout the whole period, its strong support for, and participation in, UN peacekeeping operations around the world.

The UN of the twenty-first century

Granted that the record of Ireland's membership for close to half a century is, overall, an honourable and respectable one, it might well be suggested at this stage that it is time for greater realism. The UN is worthy, it may be said, but essentially ineffectual; we should continue to play a part there but it can no longer be one of the central concerns of Irish foreign policy as it was in other times when the UN was virtually the only international forum where Irish policy concerns could find expression. On this view Ireland should look increasingly to its interests rather than to ideals which may have been appropriate to another, bygone era.

To say the least, this is a somewhat simplistic view. It is certainly the case that Ireland's international relations have broadened and deepened greatly over recent decades. The European Union is now, and will remain, absolutely central to Ireland's interests: membership of the Union permeates and influences every area of national life. Anglo-Irish relations must continue to be a particular focus of policy attention for government; and there are many other political, economic and cultural relationships that have now also become very important. Ireland's foreign relations are multifarious and no longer – if they ever were – one or two-dimensional. But realism, properly understood, and not just idealism, demands of countries like Ireland a continuing active involvement in the United Nations and the family of other organisations which has grown around it.

Since the United Nations was founded in 1945 – indeed since Ireland entered the organisation in late 1955 – the world has changed in many ways more than at any time in human history. Any brief description of 'the State of the Planet' today would show that as the new century opens the world faces an absolutely daunting range of problems which only much greater and more effective international co-operation can even begin to address. Consider some examples.

Over the last fifty years the population of the earth has nearly doubled. It is now about six billion and it will probably increase to ten billion by the middle of this new century. Humanity now dominates the earth as never before and it has the future of most living creatures, as well as the future of the planet itself, within its control.

To see this one need only reflect on the power of nuclear weapons. These weapons were developed in secret at the same time as planning was under way for the creation of the UN; and, in their early primitive form, they were used in 1945 just as the new organisation was being established. Thermo-nuclear weapons have been developed and stockpiled since then in numbers which could wipe out virtually all life on this, the only planet which we know to have life, and thus, perhaps, the only life in the universe. But, knowing this, we have nevertheless come to accept passively the demented logic which persists even after the end of the Cold War: that their retention by some states is a necessary 'deterrent' to their use by others; while those other states retain *their* weapons for exactly similar reasons. Today, despite arms agreements, nuclear and thermo-nuclear weapons exist in their thousands. Major countries still hold them on hair-trigger alert ready for instant use while other, less powerful countries work enviously to develop them.

We are distantly aware also from occasional references that in other laboratories scientists have been at work on diseases to see how, in new combinations, they might be made more deadly and more easily spread. Perhaps it is true, as they say, that this is done for defensive purposes only and solely in order to develop antidotes in case rogue states should use such diseases as a weapon, but past experience offers ample reason to be dubious about such assurances.

Even if these and other weapons of mass destruction are never used, humankind, by its sheer numbers and its effect on the fragile environmental envelope and the climate of the planet, has now become a threat to the survival of other species and perhaps to itself. It has already driven many other species to extinction, probably including some of whose existence it may not even have been aware before they disappeared forever.

'Globalisation' – a word that probably did not exist in 1945 – is an irresistible force at the beginning of the twenty-first century. Its tidal effects have transformed trade and manufacturing; the financial world; and news media, travel and communications. It has swept across cultural barriers and overwhelmed some traditional societies and economies. Indeed over the past half-century the world's individual economies are linked and interact to a degree that makes it legitimate to talk about 'the global economy'.

Capital investment and funds of all kinds now move around the world in amounts and with a degree of fluidity that far exceed the capacity of most governments to control. The world economy has grown enormously – the real gross national product of the world has more than quadrupled over half a century. By this measure, the world is richer and more productive of goods and services than in all of previous human history. Much of this production however seems to involve digging minerals out of the earth in one place and transforming and ultimately jettisoning them wastefully in another. But we are learning that resources as well as space to dispose of waste are limited. There is in any case a gross unfairness in the distribution of the wealth and the life opportunities available to humanity in different parts of the 'globalised' world.

One writer and historian, Paul Kennedy,[13] speaks of a 'vast demographic-technological fault line appearing across our planet'. As he puts it:

A population explosion on one part of the globe and a technology explosion on the other is not a good recipe for a stable international order.

Another writer, Mary Kaldor,[14] speaks of ;

... a new kind of global divide between those members of a global class who can speak English, have access to faxes, e-mail and satellite television, who use dollars or deutschmarks or credit cards, and who can travel freely, and those who are excluded from global processes, who live off what they can sell or barter or what they receive in humanitarian aid, whose movement is restricted by roadblocks, visas and the cost of travel, and who are prey to sieges, forced famines, landmines etc.

She sees this leading to a new kind of war which leads in some cases to the disintegration of the state into endemic violence with consequent danger to neighbouring states or to a whole region. Perhaps these descriptions are too apocalyptic. But there is more than enough in all of this to support the view that the world has changed rapidly and radically even since 1945 and that it faces many daunting problems at global level as the new century begins. And that new century, of course, already faces the challenges posed by the attacks on the United States of September 11, 2001.

What then of 'governance' in this twenty-first century world? How far has humanity developed a capacity to act globally to deal with global issues?

It is true that globalisation has swept over national boundaries and eroded national sovereignties. But for all the effects of these tidal forces, we live still in a world of states. In the mid-twentieth century when the UN was established, there were still dependent territories and vast areas under colonial rule. Today the territorial state, proclaiming itself sovereign, has become the universal form of social-political organisation on the planet.

If, as is the case, there is no single overall authority, how then are the conflicts of interest between some 190 states, each claiming to be sovereign, to be mediated; and how are actual armed conflicts to be averted or to be ended if they occur? How are the gross economic and social inequalities which cripple so many human lives to be redressed; and how are the so-called 'global commons' – environment, climate, oceans, resources and so on – to be conserved in the interest of humanity as a whole? These questions have now become acute, and it is important that we begin to realise this.

They are questions that cannot be left to one or two major powers, however important or however responsible, to resolve. Even if their own interests were not at stake, it would simply not be possible for them to do so. In the absence of any overall world authority – and the absence of any prospect of such an authority – it can only be done, if it can be done at all, through much greater international co-operation between states. And that, in turn, will depend on developing more effective multilateral organisations.

Fortunately, with all its faults and deficiencies, we have the United Nations, the first such universal organisation of states in human history. We have, too, a network of more specialised organisations and bodies which have grown up around it or which are linked, however loosely, to it; and we have the UN Charter which, over the latter part of the twentieth century, became universally recognised and accepted, even if not universally implemented, as the code of conduct for states in their relations with each other.

The UN is now more than fifty years old. It is remarkable that it has survived so long. It is idealised by some people, criticised or even anathemised by others; and seldom if ever utilised to its full potential. It is, at best, an imperfect organisation in an imperfect world. What is important is that it *is* a world organisation, the only universal organisation of states we have, or are likely to have, in a world that will remain a world of states for as far ahead as we can see.

The ethos and outlook that inform the UN Charter are essentially a creation and a projection of Western liberal internationalism. The Charter's principles are admirable but its basic structure presupposes a world of well-regulated states which co-operate for certain purposes; which have accepted that the Security Council should act on their behalf to avert or end conflict between states; and which do not interfere in each other's internal affairs. But liberal internationalism itself has gone through something of a crisis; and, in any case, the world in many ways does not measure up to the hopes and expectations to which it gave rise.

For one thing, the UN remains in principle an organisation of states. Many of the problems of today arise either below, or above, the level of the individual state; and, in some respects, despite the creative development of general principles set out in the Charter about human rights and social and economic development, this fundamental aspect of the structure of the UN means that it is not well adapted to dealing with such problems.

For another, many of the states whose representatives sit in the General Assembly and some who are elected to seats on the Security Council, are not democracies. Conor Cruise O'Brien takes a highly jaundiced view of this:

The United Nations is a gathering of representatives of states ... that is to say of persons who have in common ... the fact that they have the confidence for the time being of the apparatus of coercion and repression in certain named territories. Those Governments that can be changed by free and impartially conducted elections constitute a small and dwindling minority of the membership.[15]

Happily, today, in contrast to the 1960s when that was written, the number of elected governments has increased rather than dwindled. But it remains true that there are many UN member states that are not democracies in any sense, let alone liberal democracies. We may hope that democracy will spread further but we have to accept that the UN may never become the ideal universal organisation of democratic states that many of us would wish to see.

Concluding reflections: Ireland's future policy approach to the UN

So what is to be done? Short of a crusade to spread democracy, the precedents for which are not encouraging, we must take the world as it is and work to make it better. The need for the United Nations is greater than ever but the central question today is how to adapt it to deal with the 'globalisation' which is the dominant characteristic of the new world of the twenty-first century.

The UN Secretary General, Koffi Annan, in an important report to the UN member states in Spring 2000[16] pointed to what he called

> the crux of our problem today: while the post-war multilateral system made it possible for the new globalisation to emerge and flourish, globalisation in turn has progressively rendered its designs antiquated. Simply put, our post-war institutions were built for an international world, but we now live in a global world.

He goes on to say

> ... states need to develop a deeper awareness of their dual role in our global world. In addition to the separate responsibilities each state bears towards its own society, states are, collectively, the custodians of our common life on this planet – a life that the citizens of all countries share. Notwithstanding the institutional turmoil that is often associated with globalisation there exists no other entity that competes with, or can substitute for, the state. Successfully managing globalisation, therefore requires – first and foremost – that states act in a manner consistent with their dual role.

Without exaggerating what a small member state can do, I would suggest that Ireland's approach to the United Nations today should be to work as far as possible with other member states to create a better understanding of this 'dual role' and to try to ensure that it is given expression in practice. This means continuing to play an active role in the UN and working with other like-minded countries to adapt its institutions to the realities of the new world which has emerged over the half century since the organisation was established.

Today, in contrast to the 1950s and 1960s, Ireland is no longer a small, free-floating UN member state, respected yes, but with little influence beyond whatever is earned by a speech or by its single vote. Since 1973 it has been a member of the EEC, now the EU, and thus a member of one of the most significant groups in the UN, a group which on many issues is seen as their principal interlocutor by the countries of the Non-Aligned Movement who want the EU to act as a counterweight to the dominant influence of the United States.

In recent years, as the EU Common Foreign and Security Policy has been developed further through successive Treaties, the EU member states have sought to take a common position on a great number of issues and increasingly the member state which holds the presidency speaks with a single voice on behalf of all fifteen. One effect of this is that there is less opportunity to state a distinctive Irish position on many issues. Ireland's input comes instead during internal EU co-ordination meetings held to arrive at a common position. To balance this limitation however, there is the positive point that Ireland, small as it is, is seen as important by other countries in the UN because of the influence it may exert when the common EU position is being established. This perception of Ireland as a country of some influence and importance is further enhanced by the fact that, at intervals, like each other EU member state, it takes on the role of Presidency of the Union, and thus the responsibility for stating the common EU position.

This increasing commitment to work towards common EU positions does tend to subsume the positions of individual EU member states on some issues. It could, therefore, inhibit Ireland to some degree from making its own distinctive contribution. But there is still a good deal of scope for an active Irish role at the UN. This was in evidence over the past few years in such areas as the chairing during a year of some fraught sessions of the UN Commission on Human Rights in Geneva. It was in evidence too in the General Assembly in New York where the Irish delegation took the lead in bringing together a group of countries to sponsor an important initiative on nuclear disarmament issues which echoed many of the concerns of the earlier Aiken non-proliferation initiative.

Over the years 2001 and 2002 the opportunity to express distinctive Irish concerns will arise most obviously in the Security Council where Ireland holds a seat for those two years. Without going counter to whatever common EU positions it may help to establish, it will also want, as a Council member, to be responsive to the constituency which voted it into the seat by such a resounding margin. It is likely therefore that it will have distinctive views of its own to add in regard to various issues which may come before the Council during that time including Middle Eastern and African issues. There are also wider thematic and conceptual questions which the UN now faces. These include the problems of sanctions; issues in relation to peacekeeping and so-called peace enforcement; and the particular dilemma identified by the Secretary General which results from the tension between, on the one hand, the rule of not intervening in the internal affairs of a state and, on the other, the moral imperative of acting when there is gross and systematic violation of rights amounting to genocide within a member state.

It would not do to exaggerate the role that Ireland might play, on or off the Security Council, but it does seem fair to say that a creative Irish contribution on these and other issues would accord well with its past record since it was admitted to UN membership in the mid-1950s. Through that whole period it has always been conscious of the importance of the United Nations especially to smaller and weaker member states and ready to support proposals or initiatives to make it more effective. I would suggest that, for any Irish government, that will continue to be a worthwhile policy objective and one which will be more necessary than ever in this new century.

Notes

[1] Some smaller, poorer member states, in arrears with their assessed contributions, were unable to vote. The number of states actually voting was 173 out of the total membership of some 186. This makes the vote received by Ireland on the first count all the more noteworthy.

[2] There is, so far as I know, no general survey of this kind covering the whole period although Joseph Skelly in his book, *Irish Diplomacy at the United Nations 1945-*

1965: National Interests and the International Order (Dublin: Irish Academic Press (1997)), has provided a detailed and invaluable study of the early years.

[3] My account of the earlier years is based largely on personal recollection. I was assigned to the UN Section when I joined the Department of Foreign Affairs in early 1960 and I worked there during the 1960 Session of the UN General Assembly. I went to New York in the Autumn of 1961 as a junior member of the Irish delegation to the General Assembly of that year (arriving in New York on the day Dag Hammarskjold was killed in an air crash) and I attended many subsequent Assembly sessions.

[4] The first part of the present chapter is a slightly revised version of part of a paper delivered at a conference held by the National Committee for International Affairs of the Royal Irish Academy in 1995. The paper was published in the Committee's journal, *Irish Studies in International Affairs* Vol. 7 (1996).

[5] See Goodrich and Hambro (1949), *Charter of the United Nations: commentary and documents* (Boston: World Peace Foundation, p.11) and also *Basic Facts about the United Nations* (United Nations: New York (1998), pp. 287-291).

[6] See the interesting account given by Professor Ronan Fanning in his paper 'The Anglo-American alliance and the Irish application for membership of the United Nations', *Irish Studies in International Affairs*, vol. 2, no. 2 1986 pp. 35-61. Professor Fanning quotes as a 'prescient analysis of de Valera's position' an internal US State Department memorandum of 29 April 1946 which noted that he would 'in no event apply for membership without the advance assurance that it will be approved, for he would not dare risk a rebuff'.

[7] Fanning (1986) p. 36 quotes from a speech in November 1944 in which de Valera said 'what is being substituted (for the League of Nations) is a dictatorship of the great powers'. In a Dáil speech on 26 June 1946 de Valera compared the United Nations unfavourably with the League (Fanning p. 52). Nevertheless, 'Once (British and American) support was assured he acted quickly and decisively' (p. 58). I am speculating here that even though he expressed scepticism as late as June 1946 (in part perhaps, as Fanning suggests, because of his rooted suspicion of the activities of David Gray, the US Minister in Dublin at the time) there was nevertheless, in a longer-term perspective, a fundamental consistency in de Valera's thinking about the principle of collective security and in his view that Ireland should support it. His trenchant speeches in the League and the alacrity with which he acted in July 1946 once he was assured of US and UK backing tend to support this view. This view is supported strongly by Joseph Skelly in his paper 'Ireland, the Department of External Affairs and the United Nations 1946-55: a New Look' which appeared in *Irish Studies in International Affairs*, Vol. 7 1996. In that paper Skelly says (p. 69) 'Behind his mask of public indifference, de Valera strongly endorsed Ireland's entry into the United Nations. In fact, the decision to seek UN membership marked his reassertion of an Irish commitment to international organisations and involvement in international affairs temporarily interrupted by war-time neutrality'.

[8] O'Brien, Conor Cruise, with drawings by Topolski, Feliks (1968), *The United Nations: Sacred Drama* (New York: Simon and Schuster).

[9] See Skelly, *op.cit.*, p. 32.

[10] See Conor Cruise O'Brien (1962), *To Katanga and Back: a UN case history* (New York: The Universal Library edition).

[11] Skelly, *op.cit.*, pp. 170-171.

[12] Ambassador Anne Anderson chaired the UN Human Rights Commission in 1999-2000.

[13] Kennedy, Paul (1993), *Preparing for the Twenty-first Century*, (London: Harper Collins).

[14] Kaldor, Mary (1999), *New and Old Wars: organised violence in a global era* (Cambridge and Oxford: Polity Press p. 4).

[15] O'Brien, C.C. (1968), *Sacred Drama, op.cit.* (p. 285).

[16] *We the Peoples: the role of the United Nations in the twenty-first century,* Millennium Report of the Secretary General of the United Nations.

Chapter 6

International Relations as Poetry

Bill McSweeney

W hen the editors wrote inviting me to contribute to their celebration of Patrick Keatinge's work, my eye was drawn to the last paragraph: 'An exceptional scholar ... a true blazer of trails ... an inveterate idealist'.

Exceptional? Without doubt. Blazer of trails? In the field of Irish foreign policy Patrick was John the Baptist. But 'inveterate idealist'? Is this the same man who warned generations of Trinity undergraduates to leave their bleeding hearts outside the examinations hall and admonished his doctoral students that he was interested in their detached analysis, not their emotions? As a self-respecting realist, might he not be more offended than flattered by the editors' appellation?

Some realist scholars are ambiguous on the role of ideals in international relations (IR). Hans Morgenthau's early writings display the same antipathy to the intrusion of normative judgment into the academic sphere that his student Henry Kissinger would later show in diplomatic history or Kenneth Waltz in his foundational work on neo-realism. But Morgenthau's insistence on the primacy of national interest in driving foreign policy did not exclude ideals as a dimension of interest, and his later writings leave little doubt on that score. On the other hand, we could scour the works of Kissinger and Waltz and find no blemish in their steely commitment to a real material world unmoved by lofty considerations of ethics, severe in its response to state leaders who might think otherwise. For them, if not for Morgenthau, an idealist academic is an oxymoron.

Patrick Keatinge is more Morgenthau than Waltz. Most of his work on Irish foreign policy displays Morgenthau's conviction that history, not science, is the primary source of explanation of international events. He once characterised himself as an 'historian manqué'. His strictures on idealism were clearly intended to dissuade the lazy student from disguising moral judgments as factual observation, wishful thinking as objective analysis. This is a far cry from rejecting the relevance of ethics to the conduct of states. If Patrick prefered to think of himself as a 'realist,' that is less to do with a Waltzian notion of a material reality independent of human choice than a well-placed distaste for ideologues.

Most of Patrick's academic work has been preoccupied with the nature and dynamics of Irish entry and integration into the European Union. It was here that he met vociferous opposition to his positive view of Ireland's long-term interests. This opposition centred mainly on the question of Irish neutrality, and his impatience with the ideological character of the arguments advanced in its favour helped to feed the notion that he was an unreconstructed realist, out of touch with emerging trends in IR theory. In fact his writing on the subject during the 1980s and early 1990s illustrate far better than that of his critics the place of ideals in rigorous academic analysis. Although he loved the 'realist' tag, the enemy was not ideals, but ideologues.

This was impressed on me when Patrick was appointed to serve as Trinity College representative on the committee negotiating the new MPhil programme in peace studies in the Irish School of Ecumenics, where I taught, in 1988. Confronting a proposal that emphasised the place of ethics in international affairs in every course, this 'realist' from the discipline of political science might have been perceived at best as the devil's advocate, at worst as the devil himself come to demolish the pretensions of well-intentioned but naive colleagues. At that time – still in the Cold War – peace studies was a novelty for Ireland, and was still struggling for respectability in academic circles in the UK. Even in its home in the Scandinavian countries, it was junior partner to the more prestigious institutes of international relations, at pains to display its analytical rigour but lacking a theoretical base to square this with its inalienable moral impulse. The impolite would have it labelled 'Peacenik Studies'.

No doubt Professor Keatinge's background made him party to this sceptical assessment of the new approach to his subject of international relations. But if it was the devil at the negotiating table, he was in conciliatory mood, more concerned to construct than to demolish, to strengthen the case for the new programme rather than undermine it. The survival and success of the MPhil programme owe much to the active support of a scholar who saw in the early drafts of peace studies more than the prejudice of his home discipline would allow.

In honour of Professor Keatinge, and in deference to the editors' description of his inveterate virtue, it seemed appropriate then to discuss the question of idealism in IR theory, using the problems of the peace researcher as a starting-point. Two worlds collide in the contemporary academic debate, neither yielding to the other in terms of being realistic. They are not different perspectives on, or ways of viewing, the same complex entity, each complementing the other and adding to a cumulative store of knowledge. These are different worlds, incommensurable entities, constructed out of quite incompatible ideas about the nature of social action. One world is hard, objective, amenable to quantification and operational definition – in the essentials no different from the physical order addressed by natural scientists; the other is fluid, messy, built of normative standards and human choice, an integral part of the relations which comprise the wider social order. I shall argue the case for the latter, and end with a discussion of its implications for scholars in the field of International Relations and their moral vocation and responsibility.

Which is the real world?

The problem of finding a theoretical base to marry ethical concern with academic criteria of analysis emerged more openly with the end of the Cold War structures in which peace studies was born, and which had provided cover for peace researchers from the labour of justifying their academic credentials. Throughout the East-West confrontation, peace studies was largely parasitic on the scientific reputation of strategic studies. If the latter purported to explain on the basis of one set of empirical observations, peace researchers repeated the exercise with another set, disputed the observations, or focused on disarmament negotiations and proposals, using the same model of explanation that the strategic studies community could understand and evaluate. But the collapse of communism left peace research exposed to renewed uncertainty about its credentials.

The conviction in mainstream IR circles that there is a real world 'out there' which shuts out all consideration of the world as it ought to be is so strong that – until recently – it infected teachers in peace studies with a powerful self-doubt. Were they living in the real world? Were they engaged in academic research or moral advocacy? Political science for Brownies?

The allure of the realist school of international relations is partly grounded in its monopoly of the term itself, which it has colonised. No one aspires to being unrealistic. Douglas Hurd, former British Foreign Secretary, made the point bluntly in referring to the Soviet invasion of Hungary in 1956: 'Idealism said "liberate the Hungarians". Realism said "avoid a Third World War"' (Hurd, 1997). (Of course, what is considered 'real' in this sense depends on where we choose to start the story.) The implication that an objective force, independent of human choice, determines the course of international events, is clear. As leading neo-realist John Mearsheimer expressed it, '... the system forces states to behave according to the dictates of realism, or risk destruction' (Mearsheimer, 1995, p.91).

A more significant factor attracting us to the realist approach is the explanatory power that it promises, but never delivers. The awesome reputation of natural science as the only source of valid knowledge, and the prestige it offers to practitioners inducted into its arcane jargon and methods, easily seduce the student into constructing the social world in the image of the natural, susceptible to manipulation in the laboratory. Classical realism attracted Morgenthau, less because it could explain scientifically – he was a sceptic on that score – than because it emphasised what he regarded as the objective facts of human nature revealed in the behaviour of states throughout history. Like his mentor, the theologian Reinhold Niebuhr, Morgenthau believed that politics among nations was driven by the imperative of self-interest, not by ideals (Morgenthau, 1948). Where the former located the problem explicitly in an Augustinian interpretation of original sin, Morgenthau contented himself with the facts of history as he saw them, without questioning the assumption behind them.

The same assumption underlies the move from classical to neo-realism and the elaboration of a science of international politics by Kenneth Waltz (Waltz, 1979). The sway of his model of understanding over the community of international scholars can hardly be exaggerated. Finally, the topic of relations between states had come of age. Just as Durkheim established the autonomy of sociology a century earlier with his discovery of the collective consciousness as its peculiar object of inquiry, so Waltz invented the science of international relations, arguing that states exist within their own autonomous structure of anarchy, and their behaviour can be explained as its effect. 'Neo-realism establishes the autonomy of international politics and thus makes theory about it possible' (Waltz, 1990). By studying the properties of anarchy, it was thought, we can explain objectively the conditions that drive states to war or peace, alliance or balance. A pithy description of this anarchy which governs state behaviour is given by another follower of the new science: ... it's a jungle out there. 'Anarchy is the rule; order, justice, and morality are the exceptions' (Gilpin, 1986, p. 61).

On this reading, the international order, with anarchy as its stable condition, is a thing, an object external to and independent of the choice and volition of the state actors. It is an arena of incorrigible egoism where actors who attempt to co-operate are punished by the ineluctable forces of their environment. Long-term co-operation, through the merging of self-interest with the interests of others, is the norm within the domestic realm, where the state exercises the monopoly of force as a foundation to the rule of law. But in the international world of the realists, such cooperation is impossible, and behaviour suggesting otherwise must be interpreted as a strategy of self-interest. The metaphor of the jungle is intended to convey the peculiar dynamics of an autonomous world to which every actor must submit, and for the existence of which no actor can be held responsible.

This objectivity and autonomy of the international is the necessary condition for the elaboration of a science of the political. By surveying the empirical evidence, and observing the obvious regularities in the pursuit of self-interest through wars and alliances in history, the political scientist can construct a kind of laboratory in which the laws that govern the behaviour of states can be inferred. Apart from the assertion that self-help is the nature of every state and anarchy the nature of the condition in which it lives, however, no laws have been discovered which would explain international events according to the model of natural science.

If it was just a matter of waiting patiently for the new science of international relations to come up with an explanation

which satisfied its own canons of scientific inquiry, in place of
the historical descriptions, conjectures, or truisms, which make
up the IR literature, the potential gain might justify the
suspension of judgment. But there is profound reason to judge
that no such goal can ever be attained. Firstly, it is clear that the
autonomy of the international sphere vis-a-vis the rest of the
social order cannot be sustained. Secondly, the nature of all
social action is such that it can never be assumed to be stable
and, thus, susceptible to the measurement techniques and
replicability required for scientific explanation.*

The domestic analogy

On the first point, the radical disjunction which Waltz and his
followers postulated between the arena of the domestic and that
of the international is not substantiated by argument nor
adequately supported by evidence. Few IR scholars today continue
to sustain the claim that states are the irreducible units of
behaviour in determining the outcome of relations with other
states. Apart from the obvious impact of globalisation on the
thesis that states, and only states, are the influential actors in global
politics, the interpenetration of domestic and transnational issues
with state power and decision-making has for decades undermined
the myth of the domestic/international divide. It is not only the
state that makes things happen in the world outside it.

The autonomy of the international was taken to mean,
furthermore, that a different dynamic, a different ordering of
causal influence, operated to determine the relations between
states – different from that which functioned in the relations
between persons in the domestic sphere. The collectivity of the
state, it was assumed, was moved to act on different principles to
those governing the actions of persons. Persons have feelings,
purposes, intentions – all characteristics that do not yield to the
kind of control and manipulation required for scientific inquiry.

States do not have feelings, to be sure. But our
understanding of international affairs would be impossible
without ascribing purpose and intention to the collectivities
engaged in them. Even the most resolute disciples of neo-
realism are forced to factor intentions into the analysis of
foreign policy. In the field of security studies, for example, it is
not just the material capabilities of states that allow scholars to

---

*   An extensive discussion of this and other points of this chapter can be found
in McSweeney (1999).

infer the existence of threat, but the evidence that such capabilities are intentionally directed to threatening behaviour. Canada, for that reason, is one of the most secure nations on earth, despite having as neighbour the biggest nuclear arsenal in the world.

States may not be persons, but if we are to make sense of them their policies must be seen as intentional, purposive acts, and as the collective output of persons who interact in some measure with persons in other states. Inferring the intention underlying a state's foreign policy is certainly complex and requires the application of special research methods developed for that purpose, but the object of inquiry is the same as that which presents itself in the domestic sphere: the interaction of human beings. It is an error to suppose that states are *more* complex than individuals, as if the intentions of individuals engaged in social interaction were simple, stable, easier to infer. The macro-micro distinction in the social sciences, if it is taken to refer to complexity and structure at the macro level, simplicity and lack of structure at the micro, is fallacious. A child interacting with others in the playground presents a problem of analysis as complex as the superpowers confronting each other in the Cold War; the truth about a case of marital breakdown is as elusive as the most complex relations between institutions and states.

Waltz and his followers derive the autonomy of the international from little more than the conviction that international events *must* be explicable in scientific terms. Recently a rival school of thought, rightly sceptical of the aspirations of neo-realism, but equally enamoured of the idea that there is no fundamental disunity between the natural and the social order, has ruffled the feathers of neo-realism and sought to replace it with the even more reductionist approach of rational choice theory (Bueno De Mesquita, 1999; Waltz, 1999).

There is another possibility. What if the object of inquiry – the social order as a whole, with the international as a subset of that wider reality – has not yielded to scientific methods of explanation because it is not the kind of entity that can be reduced to numbers and quantitative analysis? Natural science may rightly be seen as the supreme source of knowledge, but it is not much use if applied to an object which is *discontinuous* with the natural order and which must be reduced to distortion in order to conform to the narrow demands of the laboratory.

Breaking the habit

As stated, the world of neo-realism derives from a particular interpretation of the behavioural regularities that we empirically – and correctly – observe in it. Because of the dismal repetitiveness of state behaviour of a kind appropriate to the metaphor of the jungle, it is easy to infer that states are constrained by something jungle-like in the ether – call it 'structure'. This is correct, but not very enlightening. We all know this from intuition of the constraints of history on our personal behaviour. We know that marital breakdown cannot simply be rectified by the volition of either party – by a mere act of will – but is constrained by the habits of a lifetime of marriage, obscuring judgment and inhibiting the actions necessary to break the habit. We also know from experience that it is *habit* that constrains, not god or some material force external to the actors, and that habits can be changed.

In this other real world, anarchy is a habit, embedded in human practices, not a fixed, constant force outside the sphere of humans. As a habit, it is no more or less inhibiting in principle than the other habits of social life which, although they constrain us, also allow us to know how to get on in marriage, business, academic life and the other institutions in society. By understanding 'structure' as habit, we draw attention to the fact – again obvious – that habits can be changed. They arise from human choice, not from nature. We draw upon habitual practices in order to make social life possible. Without habit, without an habitual structure to our lives, we would not be able to function in society.

Society is made possible by the illusion in which we all conspire that the habits created by human practices are not habits at all; they are not our fragile creations subject to constant re-evaluation, but hard objective facts external to us. This reification, or objectification, of human practices is a necessary condition for the routine of daily life and for the stability of our national and international institutions.

The illusion of objectivity is real. Even when we are emancipated from this illusion and see that concepts such as sovereignty, state, anarchy, marriage, feudalism, democracy, have no existence outside the human choices in which they originate and on which they depend for constant reaffirmation – even then we are confronted by the burden of history inhibiting social change. It must be accepted by all who feel intuitively repelled by the deterministic thrust of realism, and drawn by moral impulse to the search for alternative institutions and structures, that the international order does constitute a reality which places severe constraints on the power of states, communities, and individuals to change them in line with more acceptable ethical principles. Knowing that the thing-like quality of the social order is an illusion does not in itself give us the power to change it. But it is a necessary condition.

Which is the real world? Is it that of the structural determinist convinced that the regularity of state behaviour points to the existence of a fixed, constant, structure of international relations that causes that behaviour, in the manner that energy causes movement in a billiard ball? This is the 'real' world of Waltz, Mearsheimer and Gilpin, for whom the metaphor of the jungle aptly describes the nature – not the habits – of the creatures and of their environment. From their perspective, it is difficult to explain the fact of social change in general, of the end of the Cold War, and the emergence of long-term co-operation in pursuit of long-term common interests in a few regions of the world, including the European Union.

In my view there is no necessary connection between behavioural regularity in habit-forming human beings and the physical regularity that occurs in the material world. If states live in a jungle, it is for the same reason that couples live in loveless marriages: the burden of habit, the weight of history, and the illusion that there is no alternative to what god and nature have ordained. The knowledge that it is we who accomplish the regularities of our own behaviour in the social world, unlike the laws of nature that determine the pattern of behaviour in matter, is the starting-point of an adequate theory of international relations. It is the first step in emancipating people from the temptation to fatalism and recovering the power of ideals as an agency of change.

This is the *real* real world, the untidy mess of human choices and illusions that present themselves as objects like nature, but without surrendering their reality as human. Nothing causes social action in the manner that cause and effect function in the material world. Habits are the product as well as the source of behaviour. To use the more conventional terminology, social structure is both the effect and the cause of social action, just as the structure of language is both the effect and the cause of the action of speech. Causality in the social order − in which cause is not antecedent to, or independent of, effect − is incompatible with the conditions of the natural order that Waltz and the neo-realists mistakenly assumed in international relations. Social structure − including the structure of anarchy − is caused and affected by behaviour in the same moment of social action. This is why an explanatory science of international relations is impossible, even if it must be affirmed that rigorous empirical observation and analysis must be the foundation of research in this world of IR, as in history.

If the thrust of the argument so far has been to deny to the student of international relations the tidy, stable world of the neo-realist and the explanatory power it promises, what is the IR scholar to do, apart from keeping illusions alive and the machinery of academic life ticking over? If the disciplinary vocation of the specialist in international affairs is not that of the scientist, what is it?

The vocation of the IR scholar

The international is not autonomous − it is part of the social order, subject to the same rules, demanding of the observer the same respect for its peculiar character. Relations between states and relations between people present different problems of method, but they are ontologically the same reality. Three different disciplines come together in contemporary social theory to analyse this reality and to offer an understanding of what is going on in the world of social action − philosophy, history, and sociology. In the literature of modern social theory, more extensively represented in British and continental writings than in the United States, it is the label 'sociology' which stands for the new approach, in which the work of Giddens, Foucault, Bauman, Bourdieu, have been the most influential.

This is not to suggest that sociologists in general have abandoned their own scientific pretensions of the early post-war period and embraced the new approach to social theorising in a mass act of repentance and conversion. It is probably true to say that quantitative research à la natural science still looms largest in the professional journals. But the move among theorists to the acceptance of a discontinuity of the natural and social orders and its consequences for analysis is widespread enough to warrant the claim that sociology is the core discipline of the new perspective on social theory. It is also the case that modern social theory is self-consciously interdisciplinary in its reliance on the philosophy of language and on the centrality of history in exploring the meaning of social action.

Ever since Durkheim in the nineteenth century, sociology has been forced to confront the problem of the nature – the ontology – of the social order and the concomitant problem of explaining social reality. In much IR theory today, Durkheim is erroneously invoked as progenitor of the new thinking about international relations against the deterministic approach of Waltz (Wendt, 1999; Ruggie, 1998). This misjudgement derives from the view that Durkheim's emphasis on ideas, norms, and rules – cognitive factors generally – constitutes a break with the material structure in Waltz. It marks a difference, undoubtedly, but a superficial one. Durkheim's stress on ideas as the mediating element between social structure and social action made no difference to his understanding of the nature of causality in the social order. He is the supreme positivist, seeing social behaviour as the determined, almost mechanical, outcome of structure, leaving human agents as the puppets of an unseen hand of the 'collective consciousness', exactly as Waltz leaves states as the playthings of anarchy.

The struggle to understand the relationship between agent and structure in order to make sense of social change, and of the evident malleability of social institutions, continued with the noted American sociologist, Talcott Parsons. Is human behaviour to be understood only from the inside, from within its context – in which case it cannot be explained as the effect of an independent, antecedent factor – or as the consequence of an external force? Parsons left the problem where Durkheim had bequeathed it. The imperative of finding a scientific model overrode doubts about its appropriateness and drove the discipline into the cul-de-sac of the 1950s, with much hype and money chasing a promise that sociology could never deliver.

Finally in the 1970s, the influence of Wittgenstein, Garfinkel, Goffman and others encouraged the emergence of a more sober attempt to resolve the century-old dilemma of how to respect the fluid, unruly character of human choice without abandoning the idea of structure and the constraints on choice that it imposes. There is no way of dissolving the tension between human creativity and structural constraint into one or the other as the determining factor. Inquiry into social action reveals the constant presence of both; at times more constraint reinforcing stability, in some instances more space for the exercise of choice on the part of individuals, groups, or communities in favour of change. How we analyse events like the end of the Cold War – or the end of a marriage – depends on an empirical investigation which begins from the principle that agency and structure are engaged recursively in all social processes, not from the principle that structure is the independent and determining variable and that the event in question is essentially no different from an event in the natural order.

What, then, is the vocation of the IR scholar, no longer burdened by the hubris of neo-realism and the scientistic ethos it promotes? The idea of a vocation suggests a value-oriented discipline over and above the value of advancing knowledge for its own sake, implying a knowledge that is detached from its application to some human purpose. Even natural scientists today recognise that there can be no clean line which detaches scientists from human purpose and science from its moral impact on society. It is clear from the argument above that the engagement of the theorist with the facts, the observer with the observed, is grounded in the nature of social action – whether the theorist recognises it or not. A way of characterising the vocation of the social theorist is given in a recent article by Zygmunt Bauman, from which the title of this paper is drawn (Bauman, 2000).

Bauman likens sociology to poetry, seeing in both the responsibility to uncover 'yet-hidden human possibilities', to break down 'the walls of the obvious and self-evident, of that prevailing ideological fashion of the day whose commonality is taken for the proof of its sense'. For him the trick of great art (and of sociology) is 'to be inside and outside at the same time, to combine intimacy with the critical look of an outsider, involvement with detachment...'

Following Max Scheler, Bauman distinguishes between fate and destiny, between the real world which history has given to us, under the conditions of which we must live our lives in the present, and the conditions which will govern our living in the future – our destiny. To assume that life as we find it sets the boundaries of life as it must be in the future is to confound fate with destiny: fatalism.

It is unrealistic not to recognise the political realities that place limits on the possibilities for change and revision of the institutions that govern our lives. Moralism is the disease of those who perceive no limits to wish-fulfilment when the limits are observable from close, sometimes even casual, analysis of the social order and the distribution of power within it. But 'political reality' is a highly-charged term, easily sliding from its meaning as 'fate' to the illusion of 'destiny'; from its empirically-defensible sense of an existing set of institutional arrangements derived from a history of human choice, to the indefensible sense of a force in nature impervious to change and unyielding to attempts to transform it.

This slide from reality to fatalism arises from the illusion that makes normal social life possible. The basic institutions that govern the international order and our everyday lives could not function if they were subject to the constant revision which their malleability and fragility invite. Normality requires that they be invested with a facticity, or objectivity, which belies their origin. Analytical rigour requires that the student of social life should recognise this pseudo-objectivity for what it is, and should expose the error in the neo-realist attempt to ratify an illusory world and to build a science on a chimera of evidence.

A discipline specialising in the analysis of the social order is one called to separate reality from fantasy, 'to *emancipate* destiny from fate,' in Bauman's terms. The emancipatory thrust of sociology is to liberate ourselves from what must be in the future. The IR scholar has no less a vocation: to make publicly available the knowledge that institutions are choices made in the past, the awareness of which is a necessary condition of exercising the power to change them.

Professor Keatinge may wince at the title of this paper written in his honour and wonder at the attribution to him of a 'vocation', when he always prided himself on being a realist. But for this former student at least, it is the highest compliment that he saw in history rather than science the way to uncover the stories of international relations, 'to be inside and outside at the same time, to combine intimacy with the critical look of an outsider, involvement with detachment ...' He sought to emancipate his students from ideology and to inculcate in them, and in generations of diplomats, an ideal of international co-operation and moral responsibility in the formulation and management of Irish foreign policy. That he did so with modesty and wit was no mean extra.

References

Bauman, Zygmunt (2000), 'On writing sociology', *Theory, Culture and Society*, vol. 17 no. 1, pp. 79-90.

Bueno De Mesquita, Bruce et al (1999), 'Formal methods, formal complaints: debating the role of rational choice in security studies', *International Security*, vol 24, no 2 pp.56-130.

Gilpin, R. (1986), 'The Richness of the Tradition of Political Realism', in Keohane R.O. (ed.), *Neorealism and its Critics*, New York, Columbia UP.

Hurd, D. (1997), BBC radio interview 15 October 1997, and amply illustrated in his memoirs, *The Search for Peace*, New York, Little Brown.

McSweeney, B. (1999), *Security, Identity and Interests: A Sociology of International Relations*, Cambridge, Cambridge University Press.

Mearsheimer, J. (1995), 'A Realist Reply', *International Security*, vol. 20, no.1.

Morgenthau, H. (1948), *Politics Among Nations*, New York, Knopf.

Ruggie, John (1998), *Constructing the World Polity*, London, Routledge.

Walt, Stephen M. (1999), 'Rigor or rigor mortis?', *International Security*, vol. 23, no. 4, pp. 5-48.

Waltz, K. (1979), *Theory of International Politics*, Reading, MA, Addison-Wesley.

Waltz, K. (1990), 'Realist thought and realist theory', *Journal of International Affairs*, vol. 44, no. 1.

Wendt, Alexander (1999), *Social Theory of International Politics*, Cambridge, Cambridge University Press.

Chapter 7

Culture and Exile:
The Global Irish[*]

Declan Kiberd and Michael D. Higgins

James Joyce had his Dedalus write that the shortest way to Tara, the epicentre of ancient Gaelic Ireland, was through Holyhead, the port of disembarkation for Irish emigrants to Britain. This was more than just a characteristic witticism about the difficulty of reviving cultural traditions; it was a recognition that Irish people discover themselves to be such only on the streets of some foreign country. Before emigrating, a person might be known as a Kerry woman or a Wicklow man. In the precincts of London or Boston, however, such persons learnt what it means to be Irish, for nobody ever knows what his or her country is like until he or she has been out of it, experiencing the life of another for the purpose of contrast and comparison. Given that no people can ever fully define itself from within, exile is indeed the cradle of nationality. It was, after all, Germanic tribes who named and thus helped to invent the notion of 'France'. Likewise the people of England, and later the people of America – as well as those Irish exiles who moved among them – contributed massively to the invention and refinement of the idea of 'Ireland'.

This has interesting implications. 'Irishness' is often like 'Jewishness' – it is whatever other people say it is. To be Irish in such a context is simply to be called Irish, and to know what that means you generally have to ask the English or, failing that, the Americans. But, last of all, you ask the stay-at-home Irish who

* An earlier version of this chapter was published in *New Hibernian Review*, Autumn 1997, and arose from a lecture delivered by Michael D. Higgins TD at the launch of that journal in February 1997 at the Centre for Irish Studies at the University of St Thomas, Minnesota, USA.

tend to love the 'little platoon' from which they came and to give primary affection to townland or county – so much so that the novelist John McGahern wryly observed that Ireland is an island composed of thirty-two separate, self-governing republics. Jamaicans often report the same sentiments: that in earlier years their loyalty and self-image is wholly bound up with Jamaica, and that it is only on the streets of Camden Town or in the grandstands of The Oval cricket ground in south London that they learn what it is to be 'West Indian'.

The making of the Irish, like the making of C.L.R James' West Indians, seems to presuppose the sort of dialogue which happens among exiles. Only through contact with the art of other countries would a modern Irish culture be reshaped. So wrote Oscar Wilde in the belief that only when large numbers of Irish people spoke and wrote in English, and perhaps French and German as well as Irish, could this happen. The truly great periods of literary expression, he held, have manifested themselves at those points where cultures converge and cross-fertilise. Wilde made these arguments in his capacity as an emigrant. Though often berated by recent historians for their fanaticism and simple-mindedness, the Irish exiles of the nineteenth century were well aware of the hybrid sources of their own nationalism.

Irish nationalism has often been charged with stifling individuality, and the claim has much justice when applied to the introverted decades of mid-twentieth-century Ireland; but, more generally, the earlier nationalism declared itself part of a project dedicated to expanding the expressive freedom of Irish individuals, to the birth of what W.B. Yeats once called 'a new species of man'. Exile was always implicated in the search for individual freedom. Some writers went overseas in order to achieve that necessary distance which allowed them to recast earlier experiences with the sort of detachment required by art. A whole tradition of Irish writing from Joyce to Edna O'Brien falls into that category. In earlier, as well as more recent periods, many artists felt themselves repressed even suffocated by local conditions: whether the culprit was British rule, censorship by puritanical nationalists or by a philistine clergy, or the common bourgeois distrust of a bohemian lifestyle, they felt freer to become themselves in foreign places. For spirits such as these Frank O'Connor spoke, in joking that 'an Irish person's private life begins at Holyhead'. The shortest way to

Tara might also be the shortest way to modern art. No wonder that in the autumn of 1939 Samuel Beckett shocked his family by saying that he would prefer to live in France at war than in Ireland at peace.

What these men said, in effect, was that Bohemia is the artist's only homeland, and Bohemia by very definition is filled with nomads and exiles. From Dante's *Divine Comedy* to Günter Grass' *The Tin Drum*, some of the greatest works of literature have been written by exiles who wished by an act of imagination to define the components of that place from which they had been estranged. It was this 'note of banishment' which Joyce detected in the least likely of artists, that very William Shakespeare who had been celebrated by Victorian critics for his rootedness in the commonsensical world of rural England. Shakespeare's move from Stratford to London was, for Joyce, an action as momentous in its day as his own migration from Dublin to Paris, and so he read the whole canon, and not solely *The Tempest*, as an ongoing narrative of exile and loss: 'The note of banishment, banishment from the heart, banishment from home, sounds uninterruptedly from *The Two Gentlemen of Verona* onward until Prospero breaks his staff, buries it certain fathoms in the earth and drowns his book'. Art will always undertake to restore a world lost under the brute evictions of history; music, dance, dreams, literature are what fill the vacuum when an eviction has occurred. Those American jazz musicians, cabaret dancers and writers who sought to redefine the values of their own republic while living in another, the France of the 1920s, were also attempting to recreate the conscience of a race.

The Irish experience is not unique, therefore. What is remarkable is the sheer longevity and intensity of the exilic tradition. For this people, writing has always been a writing down, a fall from the world of energised orality, and so perhaps a form of exile from a happier world. The book-as-physical-object has been a bringer of trouble as well as illumination. It was waved by Christian missionaries announcing the end of the pagan days of wine, ale and fireside feasts; and brandished later by the occupying forces from the neighbouring island, hell-bent on replacing one form of Christianity with another far more calibrated to the literalist demands of a single book. Even the earliest saints had trouble with books. As far back as the sixth century, Colmcille was condemned never to set foot again on native soil after a controversy which began, simply enough, when he transcribed without permission the contents of a sacred text. The story of the saint's exile, and his eventual surreptitious return, became one of the master-narratives of Irish tradition, to be repeated in some mode in virtually every generation. Thirteen centuries later the *Jail Journal*, written by the patriot John Mitchel during his transportation to Tasmania in the 1850s, became a defining document of modern Irish nationhood.

What of those who stayed home? They also were massively transformed by all of these experiences. The comfort which they enjoyed might call itself a culture without always recognising that it too was an after-effect of migration. Those emigrants who left solved two pressing problems: their own and their people's. By moving out, they often secured the chances of greater material comfort not only for themselves but also for those who remained. Had they stayed, some would doubtless have been creative contributors, but many for want of employment would have been a drain on the public kitty. Ireland today would look a lot more like an underdeveloped country if the one in two who left since 1841 had remained. And places like North America and Australia might not be quite so interesting or so prosperous.

The same logic can be applied against a wider backdrop. What would have happened if all who left Italy, rural France, Poland and Scandinavia for the Americas and Australia had stayed put? Without these migrations, argues the historian Samir Amin, Europe would have been compelled to launch its industrial and agricultural revolutions against just the kind of demographic background which has retarded such developments in the Third World in the last century. It is often forgotten that 'the number of people of European ancestry living outside of Europe is currently twice the size of the population of the migrants' country of origin'. Had they never left, Europe might look very different and so might many other places. Europe, in short, might look a little more like the Third World and the Third World might look a little more like Europe.

Wherever European migrants went, they took with them something which those who remained on native ground seldom bothered to shoulder: an idea of Europe. If Ireland was invented in great part by the English, and France by Germanic borderers, Europe itself is in many ways a cultural construction of outsiders and émigrés. The 'mind of Europe' has been described by Americans like T.S. Eliot and Ezra Pound far more convincingly and more confidently than by many internal authors, and described so that they could lay claim to it. Today, in the midst of a radical critique of Eurocentrism on many campuses in the world, it is ironic that while the European Union has difficulty in shaping a clear cultural policy, much less a cultural self-definition, the Americans, Africans and Asians have far less difficulty in describing the concept.

How true a picture of the home countries did exiles and their descendants carry in their minds and hearts? They are usually accused of being arrant sentimentalists, and in truth the exile's world often does not seem over determined. Consider the English in Africa or India. To the natives they invariably gave the impression of a people at play, wearing white suits and taking tea in the jungle at four o'clock, not noticing the midday sun, impersonating just the sort of English people they felt they ought to be. And never could be. For it was usually the case that they were in India or Africa precisely because they were either more creative and enterprising or less moral and reliable than their cousins back home. Their exile was a mark of their refusal or inability to conform to those normative modes, yet out in the equatorial landscape they were desperately trying to imitate those types they could never hope to be. The personality, thus illustrated, became a vast simplification of the English national character; but, because it was relatively simple, it could be imitated by the colonisers and later contested by the natives.

If this was true of the predicament of the English in Africa or India, it may also have been true in a somewhat similar fashion of the behaviour of the Irish in England. Aware of the image of the stage Paddy, they played up to the role in order the better to know themselves, assuming an identity in order to prove it on their pulses. As early as 1818 the poet John Keats observed that the Irish 'are sensible of the character they hold in England and act accordingly to Englishmen'. The immigrants conformed to the stereotype, if only because it made an initial relationship possible. Coming from a near-Neolithic life in remote fastnesses of the West of Ireland, many new arrivals found it easier to don the mask of the Paddy than to shape a complex urban identity all at once. The modifications to the image could come later: at the outset, the policy of the immigrant was 'Mask, and it shall be given you'. The stereotype permitted some contact with the English, but only a rudimentary form of relationship which could be controlled and regulated at will.

In such ways modern Irish personality and culture was reshaped, in the words of Benedict Anderson 'like a white-on-black photographic negative' capturing the mixed, hybrid experience of the Irish in England, North America and Australia. The longing for the sod of Sligo earth felt in a London street by the young Yeats was one manifestation of this phenomenon; the American novels of John Boyle O'Reilly were another and Australian ballads about Ned Kelly the outlaw another still. All fed forces of an emergent nationalism. By the close of the nineteenth century, a group of activists decided to return and print a photograph from the negative exposure 'in the dark room of political struggle'. Concomitantly, the centre of gravity in Irish cultural activity was to be shifted back to Dublin from London and New York. Henceforth writers would look for publication at home first: in the words of Yeats 'all day I'd looked in the face/What I had hoped 'twould be/To write for my own race …'. Yeats believed that the creation of an Irish national literature necessarily involved the gathering of a national audience, for 'does not the greatest poetry always require a people to listen to it?' This writing process would be fraught with frustrations and disappointments. For one thing, people did not always welcome the art thus offered. If writers in the nineteenth century had sometimes misrepresented Ireland for the amusement of a 'superior' overseas audience, Yeats found that the honest attempt to express rather than exploit his country could cause problems at home. He soon came to conclude that the artist is usually an internal exile. Thinking of the rejection by riot of Synge's *Playboy of the Western World* in 1907, Yeats bleakly observed that whenever a country produced a man of genius, he was never like the country's idea of itself. The signs of that strain may be discerned even in the biography of Yeats: though acclaimed as the national poet, he managed to spend more years of his life outside Ireland than in.

For many artists the act of writing was not only a measure of their estrangement from official versions of Ireland, but also a measure of that Ireland's estrangement from its past. Unlike other emigrant groups bound for the New World, the Irish did not learn English on arrival in North America or Australia. Uniquely, they chose to abandon their native tongue and to learn English in the homeland. Within little more than a generation, most changed languages, with the result predicted by Friedrich Engels in a letter to Karl Marx: they had begun to feel like strangers in their own country, whose very maps and place-names, now couched in a foreign language, estranged then from their inheritance. In our own time, John Montague has compared a landscape marked by vestigial Gaelic place-names to a manuscript in a lost language:

> All around us shards of a lost tradition,
> The whole countryside a manuscript,
> We had lost the skill to read,
> A part of our past disinherited,
> But fumbled like a blind man,
> Along the fingertips of instinct.

Why did the Irish in Ireland choose to learn English? Many explanations have been given: to prepare their children for emigration, to master the language of modern commerce, to do well in school studies conducted through English. The famines of the mid-nineteenth century and subsequent migrations hit the Irish-speaking districts hardest, but over and above these explanations were others still. Perhaps the greatest paradox is that English became the language of Irish separatism, the one in which the nationalist case was put. If Benedict Anderson is right in saying that print-language creates a nationalism, and not a particular language per se, then English was the ideal medium through which the abstract bonding of people into a unified movement could be achieved. Newspapers, ballad-sheets, handbills, pamphlets – print, the very technology that undermined nationalism was available in the English rather than the Irish language. Moreover, if you were a rebel who wished to write a threatening letter to a landlord or to defend yourself in court, knowledge of English was essential. When they addressed large, mainly Irish-speaking, crowds, even those fluent in the Irish like Daniel O'Connell chose to speak in the language of London for much the same reason as Arab protesters in Baghdad today hold up placards in English rather than Arabic - in hopes that their sentiments would be received, understood and even acted out by hesitant well-wishers of the imperial power. Also, given the fact that colonialism has always worked off a demarcation between coloniser and colonised, and that in Ireland the people looked just like the Planters, it may well have secretly suited the English over the centuries to leave most of the natives Irish speaking. In that context, the sudden desire of tens of thousands to learn English might reasonably be seen as, at least in some cases, motivated by a desire to thwart a cultural version of the colour-bar. Yet, acceptance of English as the major medium of Irish nationalism seemed to undermine the very basis of the separatist claim, for if the distinctive Gaelic culture was rapidly evaporating, then the Irish Question could be treated as one more economic than political in nature.

It was as if the Irish had moved too far too fast in cultural terms. To give up a language and learn another would perforce become one of the defining experiences of modernity for many persons in the twentieth century, but for hundreds of thousands of Irish this happened in the nineteenth. Far from being a backward race, the Irish have been for almost one hundred and fifty years one of the most future-oriented peoples of the world. To have begun life in a windswept valley of west Mayo and to have ended it in Hammersmith or Hell's Kitchen was to have experienced the deracination and reorientation that would be for so many millions the central 'progress' of the twentieth century. Not necessarily modern by nature, the Irish were among the first to be caught in a modern predicament. If at times they evinced a nostalgia for a lost Gaelic past, they did so as the natural human response to being hurtled into the future at such breakneck speed. Those who suffer from giddiness or motion sickness may take some comfort in the rear-view mirror, but to infer that they are fixated in the past would be untrue. Yet this, of course, is a widely held belief, and one best exemplified by the British Airways pilot who told his passengers in the early 1970s 'We are now approaching Belfast Airport – please put your watches back three hundred years'. Far closer to the truth is the novelist William Trevor's observation that, whenever he arrives in Britain, he is impressed by thoughts of its glorious past, whereas on setting foot again in Ireland he is struck by the thought that 'This place will be very interesting in fifty years' time'.

For such a people, modernisation has been not so much an option as a *donné*. The sense of being denied a familiar context and being asked instead to improvise a set of values in a terrifyingly open space is the deeper subject of John Montague's lines, but it also characterises the world occupied by Beckett's tramps. On the stage they must invent a set of instant traditions: 'Yesterday … In my opinion … I was here … yesterday …'. And they must also imagine a detailed landscape, filled with subtle hints as to how they might behave, when what actually confronts them is a blasted, nearly empty setting. Their condition is rather like that of those ancient Gaelic bards whose self-image and training led them to expect far better things than they encountered: 'You should have been a poet', and then 'I was, once. Isn't it obvious?' Within the world of the arts, that also is one of the defining elements of modernity: the plight of the dandy, the courtier now deprived of his court who must attempt to retain poise amidst a world of disintegration, when all that sustains him is the memory of a style. Yet two centuries before Baudelaire and three before Beckett and Benjamin, this was the heroic task of that 'Hercules without work', the ruined Gaelic bard, who might appear in his own eyes as an exquisite aristocrat entitled to the ancient rights of a poet, but would be read by the new arbiters of elegance as a simple and silly beggar.

This typology of Irish culture has one strange quality: it is both modern and anti-modern at one and the same time; or, to put it another way, it is never more modernising in practical purpose than when it appears most nostalgic in its official self-description. The Easter Rising of 1916 might be cited as a characteristic example: it is now lamented by fashionable revisionist historians as foolish military misadventure, an attempt by men in revolt against modern life to return to a Gaelic Ireland. In one sense nothing could have been more romantic than the symbolic choice of Easter and springtime for an attempt by poets and playwrights to bring back the Celtic world. Yet, the date made pragmatic, even more than poetic, sense since it was a public holiday, leaving the colonial administration off-guard and vulnerable as the police and military spent their day at the races.

That same mixture of the poetic and pragmatic, the past and the future, may be found in the Proclamation of the Irish Republic by the rebels. It began with the phrase 'Irishmen and Irishwomen', thereby including women in the body politic at a time when they still lacked the vote, but when suffragism was at its height. Over fifty women fought as soldiers in the Rising – on the Irish side of course – and one woman, Hanna Sheehy Skeffington, was appointed to the inner cabinet of five ministers should the provisional government come into administrative being. She would have been the first female government minister in the world. Yet, the opening sentence of the Proclamation, in which Ireland was imaged as a woman summoning her children to the flag, was as old as the oldest Gaelic poetry. So the ambivalences persisted: the Rising was home-grown, but unthinkable without the help of 'gallant allies overseas', not to mention the example of other republics like France and the United States, nor indeed the *dulce et decorum* rhetoric of the Great War. Like so much else in modern Ireland, it too was an effect of the emigrant experience.

The rebel leader Patrick Pearse might summon the Gaelic hero Cúchulainn to his side, but he did so to validate his futuristic, social-democratic dream of a welfare state promised by the Proclamation, one which would 'cherish all the children of the nation equally'. As a vision, that had as much in common with Rosa Luxembourg as with Cathleen Ní Houlihan. The Irish modernist who shaped it knew how to have things both ways. After all, he was the man who had studied the educational methods of Maria Montessori in continental Europe and who then imported them to Ireland with the blithe assurance that amounted to little more than a return to the sort of fosterage systems practised in ancient Ireland. Pearse realised that if he had something new and intimidating to offer, it was wisest to present it as a reassuring restoration. History could in this way take on the contours of science fiction and the past become the future, projected back onto it.

Small wonder then that in the same period surrounding the Easter Rising, Joyce was learning how to wrap *Ulysses*, arguably the most subversive narrative of his age, in the structure of one of Europe's oldest stories, Homer's *Odyssey*. Although Irish modernism was both modern and counter-modern in the same gesture, it was modernity which ultimately set the agenda and terms: far from being fixated on the past, people like Pearse and Joyce relished their power over it, their capacity to make it answer current and future needs. This was one way of coping with the wrenching dislocations of modern life, the 'both/and' philosophy refused all 'either/or' options favoured by the analytic philosophers of England and North America and, instead, chose to see past and future as complementary rather than opposed categories. This philosophy was really an effect of translation, of a culture being 'carried over' from one code to another, while refusing to surrender whatever was good in either, however discrepant those elements might seem to the analytic mind. Its wisdom was close to that of the old Connemara folktale teller who, when asked by an American anthropologist if she really believed in the Fairies of whom she had told so many stories, thought long and hard before answering 'I do not, sir, but they are there anyway'.

This attempt by the Irish mind to live in both the old and the new worlds at the same time explains the awesome formal complexity of much of its twentieth-century culture. It accounts for the willingness of artists to take extreme liberties with the forms of English literature, to improvise, as Jorge Luis Borges observed, 'without superstition' and without undue deference to that imported tradition. Borges likened the freedoms taken by Latin American artists with Spanish literature to Irish experiments with English form: if freedom could not be won in them it would have to be won from them. The same forces underlay Joyce's unprecedented blend of the magical and the realist narrative modes in *Ulysses* which allowed the mythical and mundane to co-exist as the same order of event. Joyce's modernism was as much an anticipation of Marquez and Rushdie as of Mann and Eliot. He used myth as a means of criticising the limits of European realism as a chronicle of bourgeois life; and he simultaneously used realism to expose the limits of ancient myth-making. Central to Joyce's project was the conviction that more was gained than lost in the act of translating Homer into the terms of contemporary life.

A central tenet of postcolonial writing – that the more translated a person or text may be, the richer they become – is implicit in much literature of the Irish renaissance. That new species of man dreamed up by Yeats was intent on a perpetual *becoming*, his art a process rather than a product, his identity less a secure possession than a way of travelling through the world. The image of the migrant, the tramp or traveller recurs through the work of Yeats, Synge, Joyce and Beckett not only because displacement is the condition of the uprooted intellectual but more especially because such a figure is adaptive. Of such characters one might say what Rushdie observes of postcolonial exiles in *Imaginary Homelands*:

> They are a people who root themselves in ideas rather than in places, in memories as much as immaterial things; people who have been obliged to define themselves because they are so defined as others – by their otherness, people in whose deepest selves strange fusions occur, unprecedented unions between what they are and where they find themselves.

The migrant is not simply transformed into a hybrid by such travels; she or he thereby creates a wholly new art by virtue of multiple location. If Connemara comes to Chicago under such conditions, then Chicago may also be found in Connemara.

Being a small vulnerable island, Ireland is largely an after-effect of outside forces. If it had never existed, the English would have invented it, as a site of dreams, fears and fantasies. For centuries Ireland functioned as a sort of English unconscious, a zone in which visiting English could encounter whatever, whether noble or base, they had denied in themselves. What was true of economic and political forces, however, may also have been true of images: those suppressed at the imperial centre may have erupted on the peripheries. Thus it came to pass that the project for renovating the Irish consciousness led by Yeats and Joyce, had the ancillary aim of 'saving England', unfreezing the imperial mind and art from its self-induced rigidity. The radical readings of the plays of Shakespeare by Yeats and Joyce were just one instance of this process at work: the belief, shared by Marx and James Connolly, that a blow against empire in Dublin might put into question the deference of the English working class towards its lords and masters, was another.

Writers of such sterling quality are always helpful in the birth of a nation. All too often, alas, they themselves become the first victims of the new nation-state. Just as the Puritan reaction followed hard upon Shakespeare's epic invention of England in his dramas, so in Ireland censorship of the artist was instituted within a decade of independence. This was, indubitably less lethal in its effect that the Puritan ban on theatre in the London of the 1640s and far less damaging that the policies pursued by many newly freed African states in the 1960s, but the censorship was debilitating all the same, because it denied many artists not alone an audience but a livelihood in Ireland. Even more sapping, perhaps, was the change in the use which large sections of the public now had for literature: from being an element of the visionary, it was degraded to the mere tool of passing state examinations. Those African students who wrote to Chinua Achebe complaining that his novel *Things Fall Apart* lacked only a decent set of model questions-and-answers at the end might have had one or two counterparts in Ireland.

Yet the paradox underlying all this remained clear: literature in the eyes of politicians and church leaders was still a force sufficiently powerful and subversive to deserve control and even outright banning. By censoring so much of the best modern writing, the authorities between the 1930s and later 1960s maintained it at the level of an heroic opposition, endowing it with a conspiratorial glamour long after it had begun to loose that status in other countries. The exiled writers liked to joke that they returned every few years simply in order to remind themselves what a terrible place the country was. Beckett may have spoken for more than himself when he wrote in *All That Fall* that, while it was suicide to be abroad, to stay at home was to court a lingering dissolution. Yet, the agenda of the Irish renaissance was still upheld most notably by Beckett, who saw literature as an act of perpetual translation, of necessary translation, as he sought to escape the 'wit and wordplay' excesses routinely expected of an Irish author in English. Instead he burrowed down into his learner's French, seeking not just *le mot juste* but a true point of underdevelopment: Beckett's aim was to use its works with all the literal-minded carefulness of a newly arrived immigrant or 'guestworker'.

Beckett was just one of many who discovered that they could be truer to themselves in an acquired language: if Wilde had discovered the meaning of being Irish in England, Beckett found a similar freedom in French, on the understanding that whenever a man dons a mask his face relaxes sufficiently to reveal some truth. Yet, the freedom which Beckett found in French – escape from the pressure of an Anglo-American audience wanting traditional 'blarney' – was found by other artists, such as Brendan Behan and Eoin Ó Tuairisc, in the Irish language. In it they could express what might otherwise have been exploited in English. Such writers could, indeed, forget the whole question of Irishness and Englishness, for writing in Irish meant that they no longer needed to worry whether what they composed was Irish or not. Hence, the remarkable pursuit of the 'international theme' in texts as different as Ó Tuairisc's *Aifreann na Marbh* ('The Mass of the Dead') or Caitlín Maude's *Dán Grá Vietnam* ('Vietnam Love Song').

To emphasise the analogies between Irish arts and those of Borges, Rushdie and Marquez is not to suggest that analogies with the Euromodernism of Proust, Mann and T.S. Eliot are less secure. What makes the Irish case interesting is that it is at once postimperial and postcolonial, a land which contributed to the making of empires as well as to their undoing. If the Willy Brandt Commission was correct to suggest that the key relationship of the new century will be that between North and South, there is a sense in which that confrontation is enacted in many Irish texts of the last decade, from *Dancing at Lughnasa* to *The Commitments*, or those songs which married the technique of the Blues to the modes of Gaelic music. This was an overdue reversal of the tendency which, back in the 1920s, led Langston Hughes and certain artists of the Harlem Renaissance to incorporate the example of Sean O'Casey and J.M. Synge. In some respects, the use made of the inherited art forms of Europe by Irish artists has been reminiscent of that made by those black men and women who picked up the musical instruments of their masters and by sheer audacity of improvisation invented jazz.

Some of the recent 'hybridisation' of Irish culture arises from a somewhat unlikely source: the religious consciousness of the people. Colmcille was one of the first Irish missionaries to a wider world, those holy preachers who radiated out across the continent of Europe founding monasteries from Lindesfarne to Bobbio. Ever since, young people have travelled vast distances to preach the Christian gospel. Although Ireland, unlike many of its west European counterparts, never attempted to found political colonies, many persons tried to found a 'spiritual empire', which reached a sort of missionary peak in the mid-twentieth century in the emerging countries of Africa, Asia and Latin America. Returning from these places, priests, nuns, and development workers continue to make their own comparisons between their postcolonial culture and those of the 'Third World,' and many have brought back a liberation theology and democratic notions of reform with them.

If Ireland at the outset of the last century was a model for the decolonising world, then, at the end of it, its people had a great deal to learn from Africa, Asia and Latin America. Out of the entire experience has evolved a rich literature. Roddy Doyle's international bestseller *Paddy Clarke Ha Ha Ha* contains a hilarious description of what Irish children were once taught about Father Damien and his leper colony, but a more tender treatment of the missionary theme may be found in Brian Friel's *Dancing at Lughnasa*. This shows how an elderly priest, having returned from central Africa to his native Donegal, finds the harvest rituals of both places hopelessly confused in his own mind. A number of Irish writers would probably endorse the claim made by a character in Doyle's novel *The Commitments* that 'the Irish are the niggers of Europe'. Indeed, President Mary Robinson reversed the formula and complicated it with memories of the Great Hunger when she visited a famine-stricken Somalia and told her hosts that they were 'the Irish of Africa'. Nobody wishes to overstate these points of contact – except perhaps the *Daily Telegraph* editorialist who wrote in February 1987 that 'the only thing keeping Ireland out of the Third World is the weather' – for clearly the analogies have more to do with the Irish past than the present. Today, Ireland is an unambiguously First World nation but it is one with a Third World memory. So, it is not surprising that Black artists have taken up the challenge of Langston Hughes to study Irish models: the West Indian poet Derek Walcott has explored points of contact between Ireland and his native Caribbean in the epic *Omeros*, having been introduced to the work of James Joyce by a Christian Brother from County Cork who taught at his secondary school in St Lucia. If *Ulysses* demonstrated how the life of one seafaring people of the Mediterranean could be mapped onto Ireland, *Omeros* successfully Caribbeanises both Joyce and Homer.

The writing produced by persons of Irish background in other countries is now a vast repository of the national experience. In its widest definition it might be taken to include Eugene O'Neill's *Long Day's Journey into Night*, of which O'Neill himself said it simply transplanted an Irish family saga to North America. Many, at home as well as abroad, have followed Eugene O'Neill in treating the family as a metaphor for the Irish condition: even de Valéra's Constitution of 1937 did that. A surprising number of noted American authors have Irish roots. That their number is surprising owes much to a certain reservation among some about being identified as being Irish at all. In part this reticence recalls the bad old days of the nineteenth century, when signs were hung in Boston shops saying 'No Irish Need Apply', with the result that immigrants preferred to enter middle America as silently and as smoothly as possible. In even greater part, however, it arises from disinclination within families to wash dirty linen in public. When Mary Gordon tried to describe the cultural life of her community in some detail, she found herself attacked at family weddings and funerals by relations who accused her of betraying the tribe to its enemies. Hence, someone like Scott Fitzgerald occluded the Catholic and Irish sources of many of his stories, even as he proclaimed his conflicted feelings about his father from the rooftops.

Each major English-speaking country bears traces of Irish migrations. In Australia, the ballads about Ned Kelly became a rallying point for the celebration of the frontier ethic with its cheerful improvisations and scepticism of established legal procedure. A contemporary novelist like Tom Keneally has explored the links between the Australian Republican Movement, of which he has been chairman, and the contribution of earlier generations of Irish immigrants to the identity of the rugged new land. His autobiographical writings, from the early *Three Cheers for a Paraclete* to *Homebush Boy*, could be transposed with little strain to Ireland of the same period.

Those who left Ireland in the wake of the famine could seldom hope to return, but one of the most fascinating developments in recent cultural life is the contrasting phenomenon of the 'part-time-exile'. The speed of travel means that artists can now live each year in two very different countries, as if for the price of living in one. Such poets as Paul Muldoon, Seamus Heaney and Eavan Boland divide their time between life on the American campus and life back in Ireland. Equally, novelists like Joseph O'Connor and William Trevor have developed the kind of narrative which is spliced between Ireland and another country. O'Connor's *Desperadoes* describes the search by two separated Irish parents for a son missing in Nicaragua; and Trevor's *Felicia's Journey* cuts between rural Ireland and urban England. Even in drama, that sort of hybridity is not only reported but practised at the level of form: Janet Noble's wonderful play *Away Alone* – written, incredibly, before she set foot in Ireland – marries the techniques of Sean O'Casey to those of Sam Shepard in exploring the lives of immigrant youths in the New York of the 1980s.

All of these developments reflect a more open, ecumenical definition of the Irish. They are no longer seen as the people of the twenty-six counties of the Republic nor even of the thirty-two republics of the island but rather as encompassing all those anywhere who feel that they may belong. In her inaugural address on becoming President of Ireland in 1990, Mary Robinson reached out to that community and quoted a poem by her friend Eavan Boland on 'The Emigrant Irish':

> Like oil lamps, we put them out the back –
> of our houses, of our minds. We had lights
> better than, newer than and then
> a time came, this time and now
> we need them. Their dread, makeshift example …

Chapter 8

Ireland and Europe

Miriam Hederman-O'Brien

W hat is the nature of the relationship between Ireland and Europe and what affects Ireland as part of Europe? History and geography, culture and religion, economics and trade are all potential points of departure from which to explore such issues. Each of these aspects, however, deserves the presentation of an expert and more lengthy treatment than is available in a single chapter.

The nature and impetus of the change that has occurred over the last century in both Ireland and the whole of Europe is intriguing. It provokes a series of speculations that may be introspective and which may never produce adequate answers. Those speculations mark the beginning of a journey that will last indefinitely because the process continues even as the discussion rages. Given the current preoccupation with decades, centuries and millennia, consideration of change itself, rather than the recording of times or dates, is probably a better path to the understanding of ourselves and our history.

The following modest attempt to consider some of the changes that have occurred in Ireland and in Europe, particularly during the recent period when both entities have become increasingly inter-related, looks at our perceptions of who and what we are and what we want to do. 'Europe' is not confined to the European Union but membership of that Union has brought Ireland into the European family from which she had heretofore felt largely excluded. The EU therefore figures prominently in any Irish-European scenario.

This chapter raises some of the intangible factors which drive many of the developments analysed by others throughout the volume. The dynamic which drives the EU within the wider Europe depends on a vision of what kind of society some Europeans want to achieve. The momentum to transform Ireland into a modern, 'progressive' state is coloured by a vision of *what kind of society* is anticipated when the transformation has been achieved. The traditional question 'where do you think you're going?' is entirely appropriate for Ireland and Europe at this time. But to know the answer we must look a little at where we are coming from.

Europe

As the centre of the universe tends to be wherever the historian or geographer is situated, it is not surprising that those Europeans who have related the story of Europe through the ages have regarded the rest of the world as the backdrop to their own continent. However naïve and egocentric this view of life may appear, it explains the way in which change has been analysed and understood. It has also contributed to a certain self-interest in the commentators' assessment of developments which they considered significant and worthy of note. And the note-takers colour our view of the past and our understanding of the present.

Physical, political and social environments alter and affect the way people live and think. Europeans remain fascinated by their place in the world and convinced of the importance of their particular view of life. Indeed, Europe's contemplation of its own history, philosophy, culture and activities has led to some of the most prolific industries of modern times. Enthusiasm for publication, in every form, is now shared by the cultures of the Americas and other regions which have some of their roots in Europe. There is no shortage of historical, political or philosophical arguments to explain why Europe is as it is. Neither is there significant agreement among the experts on the current reality, nor on the reason for its existence nor on its likely future. 'What is Europe and who is European?' Many answers have been put forward but few of them advance our understanding much further.

Physical realities, on the contrary, are less open to challenge. The boundaries of Europe to the north, south and west have been constant for centuries. The eastern border, however, has varied over time and still reminds us that Europe is an extremity of the landmass of Eurasia. The political maps of the continent reflect the ebb and flow of war and power and follow the alliances that were made over the years. The seas, the mountains and the rivers remain, even when their names have been changed. The nature of Europe has been shaped by the waves of invasion and migration that have swept across it. Europe, in its turn, has impinged on the history of other continents as its peoples invaded and migrated to the east, the west and the south.

War and political, religious and commercial conflict have marked the history of Europe. In this respect, it is interesting to see the extent to which the current map of Europe has come to resemble that of the early part of the last century. The emperors and most of the kings may have gone but so has the Iron Curtain. Some old nations, which had lost their autonomy, have reappeared. The most significant innovation is the outline of the European Union.

The two world wars of the twentieth century marked a qualitative change in the nature and extent of war. These wars originated in Europe and each left a large swathe of the continent, and of the world, devastated in its wake. The resolve that such conflict should never recur was to inspire the creation of what was to become the European Union. The elaborate administrative, legal and political structures and the social dimension which underpin the Union all flow from that resolve. This is not a bland comment, made to honour the past, but a fundamental statement of the raison d'être of the EU. To ignore this reality is to misunderstand the dynamic of the EU, however wayward the direction of that body may appear to be from time to time.

The Europe of 1949 (when the Council of Europe was created) had to cope with the environment of post-war destruction and of a potential military confrontation between the United States and the Soviet Union. Subsequent steps to deal with fragile economies and a Cold War, which could easily turn hot, were to lead to a gradual extension of the areas of closer co-operation in Western Europe. These extensions were erratic. Some, such as the creation of the European Coal and Steel Community (ECSC) in 1951 were regarded as representing radical progress. But this was followed by the rejection of a European Political and Defence Community some three years later by the same six member states – a move considered a retrograde move as far as integration was concerned. After this political set-back, economic collaboration was chosen as the standard bearer for the next step towards co-operative progress. With movement forwards and backwards and a widening of membership, which promises to accelerate significantly in the near future, the tempo and nature of the changes in European co-operation may have varied but the general direction was somehow maintained.

Within forty years of the creation of the Council of Europe, the context in which Europe operated had changed completely. In 1989 the Soviet bloc crumbled and disappeared. The 'Balkan Question', which had been regarded as consigned to history, was to kindle not one war but several. In the continent of Europe, significantly perhaps, Germany was again one state.

One of the most significant developments within Europe has been the extent to which the original goals of the founding fathers of the ECSC in 1951 have become relevant again. They are now being propounded by countries outside the EU. Economic strength has been shown to be inadequate to deal with the security issues of the continent or with the fears of the citizens of EU member states. The limitations of the political structures have been exacerbated by national failures and weaknesses of political leaders and parties in many member states. It is clear that solutions will have to be found, as Schuman advocated fifty years ago, in the political and social arena. Europe will not satisfy its people with progress solely relating to agriculture, to trade, or to investment.

Ireland

The earliest maps of Europe show an oddly shaped Ireland, surrounded by menacing seas. It probably figured more widely in the sea-charts of Scandinavia than in the maps of Rome. It was the island beyond Britain as far as mainland Europe was concerned.

The history of Ireland, as an entity apart from the main landmass, has also been affected by geography and the movement of populations. Island people are moulded by the sea, just as river people are dominated by the great water arteries of the world, and mountain and valley people are influenced by their own terrain. The location and climate of a country affect not only living conditions and economic activity but also shape the culture of the inhabitants. So Ireland, as an island situated on the continent's western perimeter, has always been part of European geography, mobility, history and culture.

Independence from the United Kingdom for the greater part of the island was the most significant political change which occurred in Ireland in the twentieth century. Much of Ireland's experience of modern European history had occurred almost incidentally when it was involved, as part of wider conflicts, in its relationship with its neighbour England. When England expanded to become Great Britain and the United Kingdom of Great Britain and Ireland, any distinctive Irish role in Europe was virtually extinguished. At the same time, and as a result of the same development, any significant European influence on Ireland became restricted to the realm of ideas. Indeed, even the realm of ideas was filtered, over time, through the strong influence of British law, education, language, administration and social mores. In many ways, North America became a more influential force than Europe in Irish affairs until the nineteen seventies. The relationship between North America and Europe in general is mirrored in the ties that still exist between Ireland and the United States and Canada but such ties are not of the same nature as the close inter-linkages which now operate within the member states of the EU.

One of the characteristics of post-colonial states is the extent to which their former masters continue to dictate economic and commercial life and, more unexpectedly perhaps, their conventions, taste and cultural activity for many years after military and political control have been relinquished. Ireland manifested much of the post-colonial mentality well into the nineteen sixties.

The extent to which every Irish issue was coloured by the British stance on the matter was a feature of Ireland's search for economic and cultural viability during the first forty years of its independence. In some areas, such as agricultural trade, British interests were so powerful that London dictated the outcome for Irish producers. However frustrating it must have been to the successful leaders of independence, the experience of the economic war showed that a sovereign Irish government was not able to operate a totally independent and effective economic policy on a long-term basis. Sovereignty did not guarantee economic independence and without economic power, political freedom of movement was severely curtailed. In other areas, because of the situation in Northern Ireland, automatic opposition to British foreign policy was considered essential. The combination of economic dependence and defiant assertion of independent opposition undermined efforts to establish coherent Irish policies that would be credible to the rest of the world.

In the early years after Irish Independence an uneasy tension existed in commercial, social and cultural affairs. British ideas and goods were often considered intrinsically superior to anything produced in Ireland (or elsewhere) while, at the same time, anything emanating from Britain was instantly opposed. To confuse the atmosphere further, many people switched from one attitude to the other as the occasion, in their view, required. Diehards were firmly pro or anti British but most of the population, including many of the political leaders, were ambivalent about the effects of continuing British influence. The relationship between Ireland and Britain was virtually a permanent preoccupation for the Irish until issues arising from membership of the European Communities put new and important items on the political and economic agenda. As Patrick Keatinge put it, membership of the European Communities held out the promise of a counterweight against exclusive British influence on Irish economic and political issues (Keatinge, 1973).

One of the most interesting changes which has occurred in relations between the United Kingdom and Ireland over the past twenty-five years or so has been the reduction of this tension and its replacement by a more normal ebb and flow of agreement and disagreement as between neighbours. The developing experience of Ireland and the United Kingdom, as members of the European Communities/Union was new for both states. In the context of Northern Ireland, it can be argued that membership of the EU has been a benign factor. It has contributed a range of political and economic supports available to all the jurisdictions involved. The increased prosperity of Ireland, due to a large extent to the benefits of membership, has produced viable options that would never have been considered had the original economic imbalance between the two parts of the island remained.

Ireland has also seen significant changes in the areas of economics, law and social affairs and in the cultural life of its people. 'Brussels' has become the substitute for 'London' to some degree in the lexicon of those who wish to shift blame elsewhere for unpopular decisions. But it is now impossible for Irish politicians or administrators to avoid complete responsibility for European as well as national policy. The openness of the European Commission, at least in comparison with most national bureaucracies, and constant lobbying by every sector of economic and social life have affected public awareness of the allocation of praise and blame. It is now known, even if it is not particularly welcomed in some instances, that decisions must achieve an equilibrium across the European community. Indeed, the wide range of beneficial social and economic effects that have flowed to Irish people from membership of the European communities make it more difficult to continue to cast the EU in the role of Goliath to a national government's David.

The process of transition

The Marshall Plan, which injected new life and economic energy into post-war Europe (and into Ireland), was an initiative that has been greatly praised but never exactly duplicated. The combination of massive financial aid from the US and an agreed co-operative multi-national response by European recipients proved to be a dynamic agent for improvement. The drive towards collaboration altered the scale and structure of a range of economic activities including agriculture, industry and services. The thrust of such co-operation was obviously strongest in the six original member states of the ECSC but all the European countries involved were affected and gained considerable benefit. The development of new technologies, the increase in international trade and the consolidation of some of the biggest multi-national companies, particularly from the sixties onwards, accelerated the rate at which economic and social change took place.

It was difficult for traditional policy-makers, particularly in larger states that had enjoyed considerable economic autonomy in the past, to respond adequately to a position where their freedom of action was gravely curtailed by forces outside the control of their government.

Small and economically weaker states are naturally more realistic about the extent to which they control their own destiny. In this context, the political and social aspects of the Communities which succeeded the ECSC made economic sense to countries in a position to join. Preparation for and subsequent membership of the European Communities provided first the incentive and then the means with which to break the cycle of economic dependence and deprivation for Ireland. It is a common experience that it is easier to get people and organisations to change for an external reason and to meet a deadline than to reform because it is the right course to take.

The question which now interests outsiders, particularly those coming from countries struggling with problems similar to those which characterised Ireland prior to 1973, noted above, is: how was it done? What is the recipe for moving out of poverty? How can emigration and unemployment be reversed? What drives the exercise? And what is the price that must be paid?

The provision of investment is a first requirement. But the correct view of where and how to use resources is fundamental to success. Ireland invested heavily in the infrastructure of the state and education was considered a vital element in that infrastructure. But others invested as much or proportionately more, without equally dramatic improvements, so what made the difference? Ireland opened its borders to trade, first with the UK and then with the EEC, reversing the policy of protecting its native industry which had served it well in the early days of independence and during the period from 1939 to1945. This was necessary but it was also painful. The courtship of foreign industry to fill the gap left by an absence of an adequate home-grown structure was undertaken to bring skill, access to markets and modernisation into the economy. It was driven by the need to make the Irish economy competitive. It was also designed to bring financial investment and employment.

The adaptation to Irish conditions of a more European-style 'consensus' approach to industrial relations and economic/social policy, which resulted in a series of national agreements on pay and conditions, was significant. This change was not only useful in itself but it altered the over-adversarial approach that had undermined many earlier Irish programmes for economic and social transformation. The ground had been prepared by the creation and work of the National Economic and Social Council (NESC), a forum established in 1973 to promote a fundamental range of objectives and consisting of representatives of the social partners. These included trade unions, employers, farmers, government departments and independents from the voluntary and private sectors. The reports published by the NESC covered a wide range of issues relating to the economy and brought a new analytical approach to previously contentious discussions. This can be seen in the report for instance on social policies published in 1981 (NESC, 1981) and the almost annual reports on economic and social policies published during the 1980s.

The cultural change, represented by the NESC, to a greater level of agreement on social and economic progress between protagonists was supported by the existence of the social-policy dimension of the European Communities and encouraged by the experience of representation in European bodies which embraced trade unions, employers and, in some instances, the voluntary sector. As successive European Treaties were agreed they extended, however unevenly, the practice of consultation and co-operation between different sectors of the European economy.

Changing aspects of identity

The increase in Irish national self-confidence, which is so striking on reading the press of the past forty years, began almost imperceptibly. The voluntary organisations that had laboured throughout the lean years of the nineteen forties and nineteen fifties had emphasised what would, today, be called self-fulfilment, i.e. access to the opportunity to use talent and acquire skill. Extension of formal education at second and third levels to increasing numbers of the population was a prerequisite to releasing natural reserves of talent on a greater scale than any amount of voluntary effort could effect. Opportunities were created and many took full advantage of whatever was on offer, at home or abroad.

Religion, which played such an important role in Irish history, has been part of the change that took place in a turbulent period in both Europe and Ireland. The 'counter-counter-reformation', represented by Vatican II, had a seismic effect on the Roman Catholic Church. The subsequent secularisation of many aspects of Irish society had an even more profound impact. The extent of the change in the relationship between the people and leaders of the Catholic Church in Ireland has been considerable but the full nature of the change in religious culture is not yet clear. Whyte commented on this as follows: 'the ability of Irish Catholics to remain loyal to the Church on some matters and not on others is an interesting characteristic, and it is to be hoped that some day and investigator will seek an explanation for it' (Whyte, 1980 p.12). The alteration in religious observance and attitudes which is observed during the nineteen nineties is not the first that has taken place in Ireland. Its ultimate results will be clearer when the next generation assumes power and responsibility. The residual effects, both good and bad, of earlier relationships of church and state muddy the current scenario.

The arts in Ireland were also affected by a stirring of confidence and a surge in activity during the final decades of the century. The continuing decrease in the common use of the Irish language was not accompanied by any obvious loss of a sense of national identity. The numbers in the camps of those who valued all things Irish and deplored any dilution of their Gaelic heritage and those who appeared to want to divest themselves of every aspect of that heritage declined. The middle ground, in which new growth flourished, increased. Theatre, poetry and the visual arts began to attract a wide patronage again. Traditional Irish music adapted and popularised itself. Television, which has been credited with some of the most significant changes in public attitudes, has managed to open some wonderful new horizons and some utterly banal vulgarity to Irish viewers.

The Irish identity has been deeply influenced by the numbers of Irish living in the English-speaking world. On the one hand this gave those who lived in Ireland access to a far greater stage than they would otherwise have enjoyed. On the other, it tended to diminish their interest in developments in non-English speaking areas and, indeed, to lead to a quite common misapprehension in Europe and elsewhere that Irish people speaking English were actually British. Membership of the European Communities has been a crucial part of self-identity for the English-speaking Irish. They have had the added advantage of being able to retain access to North America, Australia, New Zealand and part of Africa and Asia.

This discussion leads us to consider where we are going and in particular the significant current challenges facing Ireland: the challenge of poverty and the challenge of prosperity.

The challenge of poverty

Poverty, like prosperity, is measured in relative terms. To consider its impact it is necessary to evaluate the price exacted by lack of resources for a range of human and social needs. This price is being paid today and constitutes a moral failure shared by those who misuse resources and those who refuse to share them.

Some of the most fundamental changes that have taken place in Europe have been inspired by the need to eliminate war and poverty. The devastation left in 1945 meant widespread poverty for the population. Not only had cities and towns to be rebuilt but industry, which had been diverted into the war effort on both sides, had to be reconstructed and agriculture re-established. The effects of the sanctions imposed on Germany after 1918 created severe deprivation and also helped to fuel the rise of the Nazi Party. The social imbalance throughout Europe in the inter-war years generated support for fascism and for dictatorship and communism of several shades. The leaders of the movement to create a 'new Europe' therefore insisted that its construction would include a new social equilibrium and a new and expanded view of economic activity.

In Ireland too the experience of poverty exacted a heavy price. When Irish society during the first fifty years of the Irish state is portrayed, two very different approaches are common. One is to present it as repressive, unenterprising, poor in every respect and generally miserable. The other is to depict it as a world in which the virtues of respect, frugality, and neighbourly concern more than compensated for shortages of material goods. The reality of course was more complex. Evidence can be, and has been, produced to justify both interpretations.

One of the most obvious results of economic poverty in Ireland was the constant haemorrhage of young people through involuntary emigration. The numbers might vary from year to year but they were always far too high. Many bright and enterprising people left, as did many of the slow and the lazy. The misery of the parents who saw them go was as profound as the loneliness of the emigrants. The network of friends, relations and neighbours created Irish communities abroad. Ireland exported many of its 'problem' children as well as those with the most potential. Other countries therefore had to cope with our failures as guardians of all the children of the state, while they also benefited from our investment in education and human development.

Another effect of poverty was unemployment and under-employment. This of course fed into the emigration figures and exacted a high human cost on those who remained, unable to find paid work or working well below their capacity. How can one work harder or more productively when there is no demand for one's labour? No wonder the Irish were said to work so hard when they had left Ireland and were rewarded for their labour. Unemployment and emigration affected the social life of town and country. Sport and community associations lost members and leaders. The arts were affected because there was no money to support them.

Lack of resources contributed to an inadequate infrastructure. Difficult choices had to be made every year, in every budget, in every sector. Housing or hospitals, roads or new schools, support for investment or social welfare? The justification for any particular choice would not satisfy those who were not to be beneficiaries and had to continue to suffer from failure to address their particular problems. The political decision-making process remained opaque but retained the loyalty of the broad majority of the population. The problems that festered have only come to light in recent years.

One of the most important changes which the European Communities has produced is the creation of a structure which enables its member states, including Ireland, to draw on community funds and thereby address the serious issues underlying long-term poverty in a coherent way. The manner in which they do so, of course, depends a lot on national factors. The aspirations of the founding fathers have not yet been realised. The promised expansion of the EU to include countries with a higher level of comparative poverty than the existing members has brought these aspirations to the top of the agenda once again.

The challenge of prosperity

Europe as a whole and the EU in particular have become much more prosperous over the past decades. The creation of wealth, however, affects the physical and social environment of a community.

Modern economic development has been made largely at the expense of non-renewable natural resources. Transport and other aspects of the infrastructure of an economically successful economy have been developed by changing land-use, exploiting sources of power and generally discarding labour-intensive ways of producing goods.

It can be argued that the first price of creating prosperity has been a deterioration in the physical environment and that this price is now being paid in Europe and throughout the world.

The deterioration is not uniformly extensive and disastrous. It can be managed but it cannot be contained within national or even regional boundaries; hence the expectation that the EU will take a lead in reducing the most calamitous effects of unrestricted damage. The governments of the member states have committed the Union to vigorously pursue measures to support the maintenance of good environmental management worldwide. However, sectoral interests and publicly applied pressure, often in the name of those who fear loss of revenue or work, hinder and slow down the introduction of essential reforms.

Exploited and vulnerable economies currently pay for the prosperity of those that are economically advanced. And within Europe itself, poverty remains a problem, stubbornly persisting despite increasing affluence.

Because prosperity is rarely evenly spread, the nature of a state's distributional policy is affected when it becomes wealthy. If great wealth and consumption flourish alongside poverty and deprivation, the equilibrium of the community is undermined and its cohesion broken. Seriously unbalanced prosperity is an affront to social justice but it also has a negative effect on the capacity of society to maintain its prosperity into the future. Distributional problems have always been with us. Professor Joe Lee indicates some of the reasons for a change in their impact. These are the growth of television and radio since the nineteen seventies and the impetus this gave to consumerism; the increase in the number and aggressiveness of vested interests, 'expressing their demands more stridently, more self-righteously, and more avariciously, as they launched demand after demand ... from a growing but ineffectual state' (Lee, 1989, p. 648). To these could be added the heightening of the normal tension between different sectors of the economy as to who has contributed most to the creation of wealth and who should benefit most from its existence. Will consensus be maintained in Ireland in the face of growing wealth and increased prosperity for some?

Prosperity and stability have attracted many European countries to seek membership of the European Union. They have also attracted many immigrants, asylum-seekers and economic refugees. Whether or not such people are regarded as part of the 'price' depends largely on the policy-makers and the leaders of public opinion. In the Irish context, policy-makers have to take into account the effects of net immigration, whether of returning Irish or fellow-citizens of the European Union, or refugees and asylum seekers from outside the Union, or simply non-EU nationals who want to live and/or work in the country. This is the first time in the history of the Irish state that such an issue has impinged on the administration, on the economic and social forecasters or on the consciousness of ordinary citizens.

Which problems would we prefer?

Faced with the problems of high rates of economic growth, increasing demand for goods and services, single-figure rising inflation in exchange for the devastation, economic stagnation and double figure inflation of previous generations of Europeans, which choice do we think they would have made? Even the unrest now evident throughout many parts of the continent would probably be regarded as being substantially better than the experience of the nineteen thirties. The reasonable observer may worry whether the changes which are being effected at this time will lead to new and potentially disastrous crises in the future. But set out side by side there can be little doubt that the challenges of 2002 look more containable than those of eighty or even fifty years ago.

Developments in Ireland such as the spiralling rise in the price of housing (with the corresponding problem for average income first-time buyers) should not be seen as fundamental problems of a flourishing economy. They arise from a mismatch between supply and demand but they are not an inevitable product of prosperity. Neither is the labour shortage which has replaced unemployment, since this, too, can be addressed. These are indeed problems which could jeopardise future good fortune but they are soluble and not to be compared with the effects of global recession on a small open economy or a gigantic natural disaster on an emerging one. Neither are they necessarily a result of prosperity.

The issues of environmental damage and distributional policies, however, have the potential to make changes of a kind that may not be remedied for a long time – if ever. The environment has been subject to degradation by humans for as long as history and geography can record. Greed, ignorance and perversity have bedevilled the issue of sharing, which is what distribution is all about, since the history of humanity began. If Utopia were attainable it would have been achieved long since. In its absence we can at least attempt an acceptable substitute in which people can lead productive and decent lives. But the existing view that well-being involves infinitely increasing consumption and, by definition, production, has to be changed. Conspicuous consumption is still considered a mark of success or at least of wealth.

Another problem that has altered in its manifestation is fear of crime. War provides carte blanche for the commission of crime and the immediate after-math is seldom accompanied by a feeling of security on the part of ordinary citizens. Extreme poverty pushes people to desperate measures. However, prosperity manages to generate its own patterns of organised, highly technical and internationally organised crime. In the context of the European Union '(t)he late and slow enforcement processes, and the complexity which hinders the procedural security indispensable to any criminal prosecution process, makes it easier for criminals to operate with impunity. And the traditional methods of mutual assistance in criminal matters are becoming increasingly inadequate for coping with the new forms of crime' (European Steering Committee, 2000, p.4).

Concerns about the level of crime are undoubtedly affected by media coverage. It is therefore reasonable to argue that many crimes that went almost unnoticed, except by the victims and in the immediate community in which they occurred, in the past are now known to the entire nation. The nature and extent of crime, however, have been affected by changes in the global as well as the national economies. The growth of the drug trade now impacts on Irish towns and communities and is no longer confined to a giant metropolis in some other region or to communities which traditionally had to cope with this form of addiction.

But addiction itself, in the form of alcohol, was a curse of poverty as well as of prosperity, and has long flourished in Ireland – in bad times as well as in good. The contribution of prosperity to substance abuse and the crime and violence which attend it is that more money, more goods and greater wealth make it more profitable for criminals to organise and to exploit their 'clients'.

It is the size and scale of the profits which generate organised and efficient crime, including fraud, robbery, trafficking in human beings and a range of activities, involving the widespread sale and distribution of drugs and the laundering of profits made from such enterprises. So the fear that is expressed in the barometers of public opinion is real, even if most of the respondents will not come into direct contact with its cause.

We are not, as a general rule, given an option as to which problems we must face. We can, however, keep a sense of perspective in the face of near-hysteria. We can also, as did the people of the post-war era, use the means at hand to cope. And if the means are inadequate, we need to improve them or find new ways. After all, energy and invention are characteristics which we claim as part of the European cultural heritage.

Changes to come?

'The customs and the minds of men alter less rapidly than the vagaries of political ideological change' (Andric, 1995). This opening line of the introduction to one of the most powerful books of the twentieth century, is a reminder of the passions that lie beneath the bland 'global village' which seems to engulf us. Talk of European citizenship underlines how greatly we still vary in our interpretations both of 'Europe' and 'citizen'.

In the intellectual field, the schism that has occurred between the sciences and philosophy will have to be healed if European (and Irish) society is to utilise the enormous advances of the former for the good of the community. This dichotomy, which has emerged over several generations, is not in the interests of scientists nor of policy-makers and certainly is not likely to keep Europe in the forefront of social and economic progress.

Some group, as yet unidentified, will have to emerge as honest broker to interpret the changes that are taking place and affecting the people of Europe. Workers, consumers, parents and children, the old and the young, have to come to terms with changes in how they live, whether these changes occur in the areas of the physical or social environment. People are adaptable but they have been deceived and misled too often and are now sceptical of reassurances issued from any source. Government has been shown to be under obligation to commercial interests; academics have been revealed as less than totally rigorous; the media has become less diverse, less localised and less independent; scandals involving self-interest pursued for years by those in positions of power have been revealed in institutions regarded as above suspicion. But because humankind seems to need some form of authority and because democracy expects that authority to be in the interests of the people, we are faced with filling the empty seats of discredited leaders. The question remains, whom are we going to trust?

We can consider two images of the face of Europe. The first comes from the final chapter of that remarkable book already mentioned, a novel which covers three and a half centuries. 'The bridge remained as if under sentence of death, but none the less whole and untouched, between the two warring sides' (Andric, 1995, p.307). The other emerges from the press-cuttings of the European Commission and European Parliament offices where picture after picture appears of young people from all over the European continent visiting Brussels or Strasbourg or Luxembourg, looking for the reality of the new Europe, greater democracy, and a dynamic structure within which old enmities will be reconciled.

Credit has been claimed for good decisions and blame allocated for bad ones made by Ireland during its transition from poverty to prosperity. The element of luck, good fortune or providence should not be discounted. The opposite has dogged our history for long enough. The process of transition continues for Ireland, for Europe and for Ireland as part of Europe. Let us hope that fate will remain benevolent and that we will be allowed to take the responsibility of making our own luck.

References

Andric, I. (1995), *The Bridge Over the River Drina*, Harvell Press, London.

Keatinge, P. (1973), *The Formulation of Irish Foreign Policy*, IPA, Dublin.

Lee, J. (1989), *Ireland 1912-1985 – Politics and Society*, Cambridge University Press, Cambridge.

NESC (1981), *Irish Social Policies: Priorities for Future Development*, National Economic and Social Council, Report no 61, November.

Whyte, J.H. (1980), *Church and State in Modern Ireland 1923-1979* (second edition), Gill and Macmillan, Dublin.

European Steering Committee, 2000, 'Protecting European Citizens against International Crime', Notre Europe: Groupement d'Etudes et de Recherches, no.1, June.

Chapter 9

Breaking Ranks: the EU, the US and the Middle East*
Robert Fisk

According to President George Bush and his secretary of state, James Baker, the 1991 Middle East summit in Madrid was the start of a real 'peace process' in the Middle East. Here, at last, Palestinians and Israelis, Jordanians, Syrians and Egyptians would sit down together to resolve a conflict that had already lasted for forty-three years. And even though Yasser Arafat's Palestine Liberation Organisation was not allowed to represent itself, and the Israelis held a veto over who could represent the Palestinians, there seemed to be some hope of success. Israel came to the conference grudgingly, the Arab states came with deep foreboding. Neither Israelis nor Arabs had expected this initiative from Washington at the conclusion of the 1991 Gulf War. In a magnificent hall built upon the site of a Muslim fortress – from which the statue of a European king slaying a Muslim warrior had been thoughtfully removed on the order of Baker's press secretary – the delegates sat down together in mutual suspicion and animosity, of course, but around the edge of the same room.

Now although this was an American initiative, Washington wisely conducted each session as an exercise in international co-operation. The co-chairmen were the representatives of the dying Soviet Union as well as of the United States. The United Nations was represented. So was the European Union (then the European Community). No one could complain of superpower hegemony even if the Americans sat at the top of the table when Yitzhak Shamir of Israel and Faroukh el-Sharaa of Syria made their opening speeches.

---

* This chapter was completed for publication prior to the most recent crisis in the Middle East peace process and the 2002 Israeli occupation of parts of the territory of the Palestinian National Authority.

In the vast auditorium in which the delegations maintained their offices, however, I discovered a more brutal order of precedence. The US maintained a suite packed with State Department officials. The EU maintained two offices housing about twelve bureaucrats. When I visited the UN, its conference headquarters turned out to be a small, empty, white-painted office with a fax machine. Soviet headquarters also turned out to be a small, empty, white-painted office – without a fax machine.

Thus did world television audiences watch the last great act of American-Soviet peacemaking without any clues as to the physical realities that lay behind the appearance of Messers Bush and Gorbachev. For most of those delegations at Madrid, however, the most important reality was the confidential letter of invitation that each had received from James Baker. President Assad, for example, was persuaded to send his foreign minister to Madrid only because Baker specifically promised him that the peace negotiations would be based upon UN Security Council Resolutions 242, 338 and 425. These called for an Israeli withdrawal from occupied Arab land in return for the security of all states in the area, including Israel.

Thus all the Arab delegates, party to what the Americans liked to call the 'peace process', were persuaded that any peace would indeed be framed around these critical UN Resolutions. Washington had said so. The EU said so. And the EU did, indeed, support an American initiative that seemed, at least in James Baker's hands, to have about it a fresh and intuitive approach. Baker's public expression of frustration with Shamir's Likud government in Israel promised for so many Europeans, as well as Arabs, a departure from a policy which had always been heavily biased towards Israel. American-European military victory in the Gulf War was to be followed, it seemed, by American-European victory in the land that was once called Palestine.

It was the EU, we should remember, which had accepted long before the Americans and Israelis, that the PLO should be involved in the peace negotiations. At a time when President Jimmy Carter was being forced to rid himself of a secretary of state who had met privately with a PLO official, British and other European ambassadors around the Middle East were publicly meeting with Yasser Arafat's senior officials.

The EU: from Venice to Oslo

There is a long-standing story among PLO officials that many of the speeches made by Arafat between 1988 and 1992 were drafted by the then British ambassador to Tunis. We should not be surprised if this turned out to be true. It was, after all, the EU member states that had drafted the Venice Declaration in 1980 which specified that the PLO should be 'associated' with peace negotiations. 'Only if violence or the threat to use violence is renounced by all parties' the Declaration stated, 'can a climate of confidence in the region be created which is considered to be a fundamental element of a comprehensive settlement of the conflict'.[1]

When EU foreign ministers met in Paris in 1984, they reiterated the terms of the Venice agreement, adding their support to what they called the 'right of the Palestinian people to self-determination with all that this implies'. And the words 'with all that this implies' were underlined in the relevant document for emphasis in the official summit declaration.[2] The EU maintained its commitment to Middle East peace. In Brussels, in 1987, EU foreign ministers were demanding an improvement in living conditions of the Palestinians of the occupied West Bank and Gaza Strip. They granted aid to the population there and also gave preferential access to the EU for goods from the occupied territories.[3] The same year, EU declarations in Copenhagen and Bonn supported the peace initiatives of US secretary of state George Shultz and deplored what they referred to as Israel's 'repressive measures … which are in violation of international law and human rights'.[4]

A year later the EU was welcoming the Palestinian National Council's acceptance of UN Security Council Resolutions 242 and 338 – 425, of course, called for an Israeli withdrawal from Lebanon – as the basis for an international peace conference. Later that same year, the EU called on the US government to reconsider its decision not to grant an entry visa to Arafat to address the UN General Assembly.[5] The PLO's acceptance of these resolutions meant, for the EU at least, that Arafat had accepted the right of Israel to exist and had explicitly renounced 'terrorism'. Oddly, 'terrorism' always applied to Arab violence. Israeli violence was almost invariably referred to in the media as 'extremism' or 'activism'.

A glance at past EU policy towards the Middle East will therefore show consistency in the commitment towards peace in the region; a peace that would be firmly and irrevocably based on the Security Council resolutions that almost all Arab nations were prepared to accept. At no point was it suggested that these resolutions would take second place to a resolution of the conflict. Committed as much to the UN as to peace itself, perhaps, it never occurred to the EU leaders – who were prepared to put their money behind their commitment – that the resolutions would become a key to the door of peace rather than the basis of peace itself.

In September 1993, however, two years after the EU leaders thought they had understood the basis of the new Middle East peace, Yassir Arafat accepted a secret deal with Israel after prolonged and secret negotiations between Israeli and PLO officials in Oslo. At a ceremony on the White House lawn, which the public was urged to regard as representing the end of a hundred years of conflict between Arab and Jew,[6] the world was encouraged to believe that the Middle East had at last found salvation. While loosely based on Resolutions 242 and 338, the peace that was achieved – if that is the right word – did not accord with these resolutions. The PLO-Israeli peace was concluded only on the ultimate aspiration of Israeli withdrawal from occupied Arab lands. In the meantime, there would be Israeli 'redeployments'.

Interrogating the 'Peace' Accord

The 'peace' that was signed contained no international guarantees. Even more serious was the lack of any guarantees of human rights. Each year, it quickly transpired, would produce a test of the PLO's leadership. Arafat was elevated overnight from super-terrorist to super-statesman. But the conditions for a lasting peace were now a subject of huckstering. The future of occupied East Jerusalem, which was most assuredly occupied Arab land captured by Israel in the 1967 Middle East War, would be discussed only after five years. Withdrawal was turned into a discussion on redeployment. The Jewish settlements on that occupied land, which the EU had condemned as illegal with such consistency – as had the US until the Oslo agreement; the Declaration and Principles on Interim Self-Government Arrangements, signed on 13 September 1993 – were to be the subject of negotiation. The issue of the three million strong

Palestinian diaspora (those who had fled their homes in 1948 or their children and grandchildren who had clung to the UN General Assembly's December 1948 resolution which guaranteed a 'right of return') was to be debated only after five years. The very UN resolutions upon which EU policy in the Middle East was based, it now seemed, were no longer resolutions to which Israel must adhere. They became the subject of negotiations, of discussions and of bargaining. And when the Palestinians who were left out of these negotiations – the diaspora – objected, they were immediately vilified as enemies of peace.

What the Palestinian academic Edward Said has called the 'dictatorship of consensus'[7] and, elsewhere, 'the rise of democratically induced conformism'[8] had seized control of the television channels as well as of diplomats. The unwillingness of US journalists (sometimes amounting to paranoia) to question the most important foreign policy commitment of the US, meant that to doubt the wisdom of this, the most pro-Israeli of all US administrations in a generation, was seen as unpatriotic or, even worse, as anti-semitic. And, given the pro-Israeli bias of much of the British press and the habit of many British newspaper editors to accept the news values and judgements of US and British satellite television, this dangerous and corrosive practice took hold in Britain, and indeed, in Europe as a whole.

Edward Said's comments, however, were very much to the point. It is his thesis that in a vast and heterogenous society like the US, it is easy to stir up feelings of endangered patriotism and national insecurity. Appeals to tradition or to family values or to patriotic sentiment tend to be extremely intolerant of dissent. He might have added that in Europe too, especially where European nations are at war, dissent is too often regarded as treachery or betrayal. Minority views are regarded with the deepest suspicion for fear that a minority view might later become a majority view.

This, unfortunately, is part of the context of the new Middle East 'peace'. Since 1993, for example, to no public objection from the EU, US diplomats in the Middle East have been instructed to refer to the West Bank and Gaza, not as the occupied territories but as 'the disputed territories'. Here again is the diminution of Resolutions 242 and 338, resolutions that the EU still regards as sacrosanct. The West Bank is supposedly no longer occupied by a foreign army – which in Area C of the

Oslo agreement it is – and is open for negotiation. This implies that the 120,000 Jewish settlers living there on Arab land – this number excludes the vast Jewish settlements around occupied Arab East Jerusalem - may have some internationally legitimate right to the land. The CNN satellite channel was even to refer to Jewish settlers who had seized Palestinian land, and the Palestinians who owned it, as holding 'competing heritage claims'. UN resolutions, in other words, are no longer up for adherence. Rather they are up for negotiation – a privilege which is, of course, not available to others who decline to obey UN resolutions. The fact is that while Israeli troops have left certain urban areas of the West Bank, those same soldiers remain in the territories. Some of them maintain checkpoints that render it impossible to travel from Ramallah to Nablus, or back, without Israeli permission. And still, no Palestinian living in the occupied West Bank or Gaza is permitted to visit Arab East Jerusalem without permission. This was the current status quo more than seven years after a peace agreement that the majority of Palestinians and Arabs now regard as dead.

Similarly, the Israeli-Jordanian Treaty of Peace, signed on 26 October, 1994, specifically based on UN Resolutions 242 and 338, refers in its text to Palestinians solely in terms of UN assistance programmes for refugees and not to UN resolutions that would allow those Palestinians to return to the land they call Palestine.

EU member states generally welcomed the Israeli-Jordanian accord, ignoring the fact that it was greeted with silence by most of the Jordanian population. For, despite the creeping programme of the Middle East peace process, it remained a fact that the forces opposed to it were, in the words of the director of the Jerusalem Council on International Relations, Marwan Bishara, 'on the march and showing no signs of fatigue'.[9]

At least three million Palestinians in the diaspora were uneasy with this peace, many actively opposed to it. So were Jordanian labour unions and opposition members of parliament. So were all the Egyptian opposition parties and so was the Syrian government, and, as Bishara reminds us, so too were probably most of the Syrian population not to mention the Gulf Arabs.

Gulf Arabs, specifically those in Oman and Qatar, had shown some willingness to accept Israel. But the Saudis refused to give further support to a new Middle East economic banking system until they saw evidence of real progress towards a Palestinian state. Following the assassination of Yitzhak Rabin by an Israeli gunman in a Tel Aviv suburb in 1995, some editorial comments in the Arabic press reveal the mood among the Arab regimes. In most of the Middle East, such editorials could not be published without the consent of or at least the acquiescence from the governments concerned. Take for example *Al Raya* of Qatar which recalled that 'Rabin's hands were stained with dear and precious Arab blood and that thousands (of Arabs) met martyrdom at his hands throughout his long career'. *Al Khaleej* of the United Arab Emirates commented that 'Rabin could not be portrayed as a man of peace. The agreements he sought with the Palestinians … were all in the interests of Israel …' In *Al Arabi* of Egypt we found that 'He was not a hero but a professional killer. He was not a politician but a gang leader in fancy dress'. This is what the majority of Arab people believe. In the opposition *Al Wafd* newspaper in Cairo: 'It (the murder of Rabin) was … an accumulation of Israeli policies of extremism and violence'. The pro-government Egyptian newspaper *Al Ahram* wrote that Rabin's murder was 'the bitter result of a culture of violence upon which Israeli society is built'. And in *Al Qabas* of Kuwait, the nation for whom Europe as well as America went to war in 1991: 'The assassination of Rabin is a response to the blood of Arabs which stained his hands … we hope that other "heroes of peace" will be assassinated'.

Amid the massive, almost romantic, undoubtedly genuine sorrow with which the west greeted Rabin's assassination, these voices were not heard. Such editorials – and I quote from only a few of them – proliferated in the Arab world where Palestinians recalled that Rabin was a man who undertook the military operations that drove Palestinians from Lydda in 1948 and who called on his soldiers to 'break the bones' of Palestinian stone-throwers during the first intifada.

Another odd phenomenon which slipped our attention at the time of the 'peace' drive; why was it that the first Arab leaders to make peace with Israel after the Iraqi invasion of Kuwait were the only two leaders to have embraced Saddam Hussein following the invasion? Let us cast our minds back for a moment to the days before the Allied advance into Iraq. American and European diplomats alike had written off Arafat and the PLO. They were doomed, they said, for allying themselves with Saddam. And so too was King Hussein of

Jordan. American and European journalists asked themselves in print how long the Hashemite monarchy could survive after King Hussein had visited Baghdad to offer his sympathy to Iraq. So why was it that the two men condemned in 1990 and 1991 for flirting with Saddam were later the first Arab leaders to be praised for the quality of their peacemaking? I will suggest an answer: because the PLO and Jordan were weak enough to make peace with Israel. Because in order to make peace with a powerful Israel supported by the world's only superpower, it is necessary to be weak.

In parallel fashion, Syria – which had sent its troops to Saudi Arabia during the 1990 Gulf crisis albeit they had not much inclination to fight – was later vilified as a nation that wished to throw the prospects of peace away. When President Clinton visited Damascus in October 1994, US diplomats referred to President Hafez el-Assad's demands for the return of all the occupied Golan Heights in return for peace as 'the obstacle to peace'. In fact, Assad was merely adhering to that letter he had received from James Baker in 1991 which had convinced him that he could negotiate on the basis of, and only on the basis of, UN Resolutions 242 and 338. These had, as we know, called for an Israeli withdrawal from territories occupied in the 1967 war in return for peace and security. By sticking to this formula, Assad had become an 'obstacle to peace'. At no point was it suggested that the Israelis might be the 'obstacle to peace' by refusing to make a full withdrawal, as opposed to a staged withdrawal. So why was Assad singled out for our opprobrium? Because he wished to upset the 'peace process' or because he was still too strong to make peace with Israel?

Little wonder, then, that many Arabs came to regard the peace process not as an Arab-Israeli peace but as an Israeli-American steamroller that could not be resisted except at the price of diplomatic isolation. They began to grow accustomed to a new political order where merely to question 'peace' agreements became an act of potential risk. King Hussein warned his own political opponents inside Jordan not to betray their country by condemning the new Israeli-Jordanian peace agreement signed at Araba. Yet Jordanians did question it. They pointed, all too relevantly, to Article Two (6) of that treaty which appeared, at least on first reading, to lay to rest the King's nightmare - partly crated by Ariel Sharon – that the Palestinians of the West Bank might one day be pushed across the Jordan

river to turn Jordan into a Palestine. Article Two states that the
parties to the agreement 'believe that within their control,
involuntary movements of persons in such a way as to adversely
prejudice the security of either party should not be permitted'.
Palestinians in Jordan were the first to point out that the phrase
'within their control' might, however, permit a future right wing
Israeli government to drive Palestinians out of the West Bank on
the grounds that it was the Palestinians themselves who chose to
leave. This remains the official Israeli version of how the
Palestinians left what is now Israel in 1948.

A peace that is thought to be unjust will not be a lasting
peace. The collapse of the Camp David talks in the summer of
2000 was proof that the Oslo agreement failed to inspire the
trust of both parties and, indeed, that it failed to adhere to the
UN resolutions on which it was supposedly based. The
commencement of the Palestinians second intifada, fuelled by
resentment, frustration and a conviction that the Israelis and
Americans did not intend to allow the existence of a viable
Palestinian state, should have proved that any continuation of
an Oslo-style peace process was doomed. Arafat was not to
receive sovereignty over those areas of Arab Jerusalem captured
in 1967, but rather only control over certain areas that were a
sort of miniature version of the 'bantustan' already existing in
the West Bank. There would be no 'right of return'. Most of the
Jewish settlements built on occupied Arab land would stay.
Persuaded that what Arafat was offered – control over the
Haram al-Sharif in Jerusalem, a parcel of Israeli land next to the
Negev desert in return for the maintenance of most existing
Jewish settlements on Arab land and a few further withdrawals
on the West bank – were major Israeli 'concessions' which the
Palestinians had violently rejected, Israelis also believed Oslo to
be dead.

The EU – in search of a policy?

So where do we go from here? Hitherto, Europeans had given
their approval to each stage of the American process of
negotiations, happy to be remembered in a Middle East that
shares so much of its history with Europe, always willing to
come forward with funding for a future peace. The EU's
financial support had been largely, if not totally, uncritical. And
yet the knowledge of the weakness inherent in this new peace
was shared by EU diplomats and officials.

In 1995, for example, the EU funded an analysis of the recent Amman economic summit.[10] The summit was hailed by those who believed that economics rather than politics are the panacea for conflict. The *Washington Post* described the meeting of Arab, Israeli and American business men as a conference aimed at 'breathing life into a new version of the Middle East where countries make deals instead of war'.[11]

But business analysts took a somewhat gloomy view of the proceedings in their own assessment. One quoted William Ryrie, Vice President of Barings Holdings Company, as saying that 'the region cannot be said to be open in a very serious way'.[12] A Jordanian economic journalist concluded that the summit 'brought home to the region's leaders that the Middle East and North African region have to become more cohesive and stable, politically and economically, before the West will invest on a scale that will turn economic dreams into reality'.[13] The same publication noted that the Saudi trade and industry minister listed the conditions for co-operation with Israel in a regional economic institution as 'a just resolution of the issues of Jerusalem, Palestinian refugees and Jewish settlements.'[14] These were precisely those issues that had been postponed because they appeared (and subsequently proved to be) insoluble. Equity partnerships were 'much slower to come to fruition than many foresaw' while Israeli investors were unwilling to commit themselves to big investments 'in what is still seen as a politically unstable investment environment'. It was noted that there were 'deep misgivings' among Jordanians who felt that 'Israeli investment would be more acceptable to Jordanian and Palestinian business men if they felt that the benefits were really flowing in two directions'. Under agreements reached so far, the 'Palestinians are kept economically crippled and Israel can hide behind protectionist barriers'. This analysis concluded that the 'Middle East peace process still had some way to go .... but Israel is trying to reap the economic benefits now.[15]

Nor did the Israelis dispute this pessimism. An Israeli financial journalist concluded that much of the business discussed in Amman was still 'sometime in the future'. He added that 'the public seems to assume that the Israeli-Jordanian peace treaty and the ... accords with the Palestinians have sowed (sic) up the economic issues at stake. The truth is that the execution of these agreements is still stuck ... Every month of delay means more disillusionment and lost faith'.[16] Despite the pessimism that emerged from the Amman summit, however, the EU remained silent.

Indeed, it is very difficult for the EU to have a voice in the Middle East when it so obviously and significantly lacks a common foreign policy. It is very easy for the EU to substitute money for policy, to grant funds and assistance to the Palestinian authority and to Israel, to agree a new customs arrangement with Turkey. The EU and the US do, at least, agree on the importance of a secular state in Turkey; what is much more difficult to obtain is a return on its financial or political investment.

If the EU has supported US policy towards the Middle East – which, in Arab eyes often means US policy towards Israel – it's loyalty has been ill-rewarded. Take for example, the case of a non-Arab country, Iran. If we set aside Britain's own recently settled dispute with Iran over the 'fatwa' sentence against Salman Rushdie, we find the EU unhappily at odds with Washington over Tehran. In 1995, the US instituted an economic boycott of the Islamic republic which the EU was asked to support but chose, for obvious reasons, not to do so. Not only was the US campaign associated with an attempt to overthrow the regime – for which the CIA has been publicly given millions of dollars –– but it was also evidently part of an Israeli offensive against Iran. In fact, President Clinton announced the US's new measures at an American-Jewish meeting in New York. Yet within months, any European oil company doing business with Iran found itself liable in US law. European objections were overruled by Congress. Which is small reward for our support for America's Middle East 'peace process'.

Perhaps what we need is a closer realisation of what the Middle East, and the North African nations too, mean to us as Europeans. The US had identified national interest in the Middle East: cynics might identify them as Israel and oil, though not necessarily in that order. We too have interests although we have something infinitely more important. The nations of the Middle East are our neighbours. They will never be neighbours of the US. But they will always be neighbours of ours – and historic neighbours too.

Since the eleventh century, the conflict between Christianity and Islam has been our conflict and it may be worth asking why the people of the Middle East should ever trust us, given the murderous state of that relationship. In 1995, in almost total but understandable silence, we passed the 900th anniversary of Pope Urban's call for the First Crusade. In 1997 we passed the 80th anniversary of the Balfour Declaration when Britain promised to support Palestine – all of Palestine, not just the part that became Israel – as a homeland for the Jews. In 1995, with not a single commemoration, we passed the 75th anniversary of the Battle of the Maysaloun Pass in Lebanon when French troops fighting with tanks against Arab cavalry crushed the final Arab attempt to seek the independence that Britain had promised them in the First World War. Nineteen-ninety-five marked the fortieth anniversary of the end of the Holocaust in which Europeans tried to destroy the Jews of Europe, a crime of Europeans against Europeans but also, of course, against the people of an ancient Middle East faith. It would be dishonest not to remember another date in 1995, and a town called Srebrenica, where European soldiers failed to prevent the murder of thousands of innocents whom those same soldiers had been ordered to protect. And those thousands were Muslims, believers of another Middle Eastern faith, just as Judaism and Christianity are Middle Eastern faiths.

And yet, in many parts of the Middle East, the EU is still seen as an enlightened international community whose friendship will last longer than America's; whose interests are more intimate to the Middle East and whose relationship with the region – however tragic or evil it has been in the past – at least avoids the excesses of US policy. To a people whose understanding of mathematics and whose discovery of higher mathematics once astounded mediaeval Europe, America's scientific advancement and technology may constitute a threat as well as a wonder.

Not the least of the dangers attendant on current US policy in the region is the notion that by moving forward with its 'peace process', it is somehow countering what US academics and journalists like to call 'Islamic fundamentalism'. Indeed, one of the most frightening elements of American thinking towards the Middle East in recent years has been the ever more popular idea that it is fighting a war against what *Time* magazine once referred to on its cover as 'Islamic terror'. Israel, it must be said, had done nothing to dissuade the US from accepting this concept. When President Clinton visited the Knesset in Jerusalem in 1994, Yitzhak Rabin used the words 'Islamic terror' to define the West's enemies in the Middle East.

Of course when Israel's enemies, be they suicide bombers or gunmen, claim that they attack Israel in the name if Islam, it is understandable that many thousands of Israelis will believe that 'Islamic terror' is their enemy. But the two words are not mutually compatible and to ally one of the worlds' greatest religions to the concept of violence is extremely dangerous. Perhaps the US can contemplate a war against Islam, but Europe, with its own large Maghrebian, Turkish and Pakistani Muslim communities, certainly cannot afford to play any role in such a battle. Islam is also the religion of our neighbours from southern Russia to Turkey, Bosnia and Morocco and we can have no business participating in such a crusade.

But let us turn to the other element of US foreign policy in the Middle East which can also be so perilous to its allies: the dependence that American alliances tend to induce among its friends. This does not just refer to 'friendly' Arab nations like Egypt, that are now locked into a straightjacket of loyalty for fear of losing massive US subventions that save it from bankruptcy. It also applies to Israel. Ever since the foundation of their state, Israelis have been rightly concerned at the extent of their own dependency on the US. Israeli politicians of left and right have both noted the degree to which Israel must rely on America not just for its military and political protection, but also for its financial solvency. This situation cannot be expected to last forever. Israel may have been an unsinkable Middle East aircraft carrier against the Soviet Union, a bulwark of the American alliance against communism during the Cold War or even a standard-bearer against the dangerous illusions of 'Islamic terror' in the immediate aftermath of the Cold War. But whatever their worth, these are temporal roles. There may come a day when America's friendship cannot be taken for granted and when Israel does not exert such influence over the making of US foreign policy. And if that day comes, it is to Europe that many Israelis will look for a new form of alliance if not, given the wickedness of Europeans in the last century, with much confidence. Rather through a growing necessity.

The Barcelona process

It was at Barcelona in 1995 that the EU at last began to take a serious role in the new Middle East which, though not opposed to that of the US, insisted on its complimentarity rather than its subservience. For the Barcelona conference was not about dependence. It was about partnership – a key word that ran throughout the conference agenda. The meeting, it was stated, was not intended to replace the other activities and initiatives undertaken in the interests of the peace, stability and development of the region. This of course, was a careful though not fulsome bow towards the US. The document went on to support a 'just, comprehensive and lasting peace settlement in the Middle East based on the relevant UN Security Council resolutions and principles mentioned in the letter of invitation to the Madrid Middle East peace conference, including the principle of land for peace with all that this implies'.[17] Here, then, was the reminder of those original terms for peace contained in the James Baker invitations of 1991; terms that had become so diluted over the following two years.

Before Barcelona, there was a feeling that the EU would give money to the newly freed lands of Eastern Europe rather than to traditional former colonial friends. But the EU is trying to transform those friendships, from a system where Middle East and Maghreb states are assisted to one where they become 'assistants' to Western policy. At Barcelona, Europeans were talking not about the 'region' but about 'common interest'. The new Euro-Mediterranean partnership, which dispenses with the very term 'Middle East' since it reaches westwards towards Morocco and Algeria, also produced some political objectives. These included democracy, human rights and liberal economics: not the sort of aspirations likely to commend themselves to Arab regimes but worthy nonetheless and essential for the nature of the relationship. For the truth of the matter was that Europe could not, and still cannot, continue with its own internal development with unstable neighbours next door.

There were times when Anglo-French relations seemed to be straining the stability of EU policy towards the Middle East. In October 1996, French President Jacques Chirac toured the region on a visit that was well received by Arabs and deeply criticised by Israel with whose security police Chirac had tussled in Jerusalem. Condemning Jewish settlement building and the continued confiscation of Palestinian land, demanding that Israel live up to its promises under the Oslo agreement, Chirac went on to shore up France's traditional relations with Syria and Lebanon. The British foreign secretary, Malcolm Rifkind, criticised the visit as 'colourful, romantic and dramatic'. Chirac's foreign minister, Herve de Charette, responded that Rifkind's remarks revealed an 'old Franco-British jealousy'.[18]

The steady collapse of the Oslo accord was noted by the European Council when it met in Dublin in December of that year. It expressed its grave concern at 'the continuing deterioration in the peace process', calling on 'all parties to discourage violence'. It added that 'the settlement issue is eroding confidence in the peace process. Settlements contravene international law and are a major obstacle to peace'.[19]

If this was mild by comparison with Washington's far tamer criticism of Israel, it at least expressed a reality: that the 'peace process' was deteriorating. Yet within four years, and in the aftermath of the failure of the Camp David talks – and the start of the second intifada – the EU proved its impotence at the Euromed EU foreign ministers conference in Marseille on 15 November, 2000. There EU ministers called for both sides to bring violence to an end: as if both sides were equally armed and equally powerful. Palestinian delegate Nabil Shaath's appeal, supported by other Arab ministers, to condemn Israel for excessive use of force, went unheeded. The Syrians and their Lebanese surrogates refused to attend. The Middle East, it seemed, was now killing off the Barcelona process.

Israel and the US had no reason to fear the Marseille conference. When news came of the death of a German citizen, killed by an Israeli missile at Beit Jalla on the West Bank, German foreign minister Joschka Fischer accepted Israel's condolences and announced that Israel was to begin a 'profound investigation' into the death. A few hours later, Israeli foreign minister Shlomo Ben Ami denied that any such high level enquiry was taking place.

EU foreign ministers concluded that American pre-eminence was accepted in the search for peace in the Middle East, effectively ruling out any independent European peace-making efforts. President Chirac had said as much in an interview reported in the French weekly *Le Canard Enchaine* in October of that year. 'The Europeans don't count in these negotiations', he is reported to have said … 'we must not have any illusions. Clinton is running the whole thing. (Eygptian President) Mubarak and I, we are oiling the works but it can't go any further than that'.[20]

Conclusion

There are two developments that could provide the EU with a fresh opportunity to devise its own initiatives in the Middle East. Firstly, there is the growing realisation that US peacemaking – in so far as it drove the Oslo agreement – has failed. Secondly, a new administration has shown neither the inclination nor the interest in moving beyond the discredited terms of the old 'peace process'. True, EU foreign policy and interests are still so divided on the Middle East that a new initiative is unlikely in the immediate years ahead. But the EU could help both Israel and the Palestinians to refocus on the foundations of the peace that they started discussing in 1991: the provisions of Security Council Resolutions 242 and 338. Such an approach may not immediately commend itself to the Israelis, for whom the Oslo agreement would have maintained de facto Israeli sovereignty over all of Jerusalem and many of the Jewish settlements. But ever more repressive military measures to end the Palestinian intifada have failed. In 2001, Israelis voted for a government that would give them security. But without peace, security is impossible to sustain. In time, the benefits of UN resolutions may become more obvious. Israel wishes, for example, to keep East Jerusalem as a part of its 'eternal' capital. Yet many Israeli Jews remain fearful of going there. A Palestinian East Jerusalem, sanctified by a final peace treaty, would allow Israelis to visit East Jerusalem in safety. If UN resolutions were applied, could Europe not provide the bulk of any observer and peacekeeping force to guarantee implementation of these resolutions?

Of course, the problems are immense. The EU produced no settlement for Algeria. The EU's policy towards Iran remains, thankfully, independent of that of the US. Bosnia remains a symbol of our impotence and shame. The EU's failure there was only re-emphasised by its reliance on the US to wage war on the Serbs in 1999.

But at least the structure of a common policy on the Middle East could emerge and one that could be of benefit to both Arabs and Israelis alike. Both attended the Barcelona meeting and even participated in the Euromed Marseille conference at the height of the Israeli-Palestinian violence in 2000. Of course the EU will not oppose the US in the Middle East. But it could produce a policy of complimentarity, a constant reminder that the framework of Middle East peace lay in UN resolutions rather than in secret deals that contain no international guarantees. It may even produce some form of safety net when the elaborate construction of the 'peace process' is finally abandoned by the US.

Notes

1 Venice Declaration, 12-13 June, 1980.

2 European Community foreign minister's declaration, Paris, 27 March, 1984.

3 European Community foreign minister's declaration, Brussels, 23 February, 1987.

4 European Community foreign minister's declaration, Copenhagen, 13 July and Bonn, 8 February, 1988.

5 European Community statement on visa for Arafat, 30 November, 1988.

6 This was Yitshak Rabin's publicly stated statistic on the same lawn although no one chose to question it.

7 See Said, E. (1994), *The Politics of Dispossession: The Struggle for Palestinian Self-Determination, 1969-1994,* London: Chatto and Windus.

8 Said, E. (1994), 'American Contrasts', in *Al-Ahram Weekly,* Cairo, 17-23 February.

9 Bishara, M. (1995) 'Don't Throw Good Money After Bad', in *International Herald Tribune,* 20 October.

10 'Peace Economic' published by the Economist Intelligence Unit, supported by Peace-Media, a programme of the European Union, 1995.

11 Cited in *International Herald Tribute,* 30 October, 1995.

12 'Peace Economics', op. cit. 11.

13 *Ibid.* 12.

14 *Ibid.* 18.

15 *Ibid.* 26.

16 Cited in Bilan, M. (1996), 'The Aman Agenda', in *I ink,* Tel Aviv, January.

17 See Barcelona Declaration adopted at the Euro-Mediterranean Conference, 27-28 November, 1995.

18 See *Le Journal de Dimanche,* 27 October, 1996, for details.

19 See Declaration by the European Council on the Middle East Peace Process, Presidency Conclusions, Dublin 11 and 14 December, 1996.

20 See *Le Canard Enchaine,* November 15, 2000.

Chapter 10

The Quest for an Institute

Tony Brown

Introduction

In the concluding paragraphs of his 1973 publication, *The Formulation of Irish Foreign Policy*, Patrick Keatinge wrote of the new pressures on the makers of Irish foreign policy and on those implementing it in the new and complex setting of membership of the European Economic Community and made the point that

> in most areas of public life, policy making is aided ... by the measure of understanding and the systematic organisation of knowledge which is to be found in the study of and research into the relevant academic disciplines. That foreign policy is the sole exception to this has been in the past something of a curiosity; in the future it could be a crippling weakness. (Keatinge, 1973)

He went on to make the proposal that 'in addition to the commitment of the Irish university system to the study of international relations, the creation of a research institute in this field would provide a means of linking what might otherwise remain an unnecessarily theoretical academic pursuit to those individuals with a more practical and immediate interest in Irish foreign policy' (Keatinge, 1973). He saw such an institute providing public discussion of foreign policy with 'focus, depth and continuity ... which has hardly existed up to now' (Keatinge, 1973).

The story of the search for an Irish institute in the area of policy research on the country's international – and particularly European – relations covers the decades since the 1972 referendum on EEC membership. It is a story of individuals, initiatives and institutions and, inevitably, of compromises. It is also a story of the slow growth of a recognition that both Patrick Keatinge's critique of Ireland's capabilities in a critical policy area and his proposed solution were correct.

New challenges

In the latter part of the 1960s two issues emerged to confront Ireland's political and administrative system with great challenges. In Northern Ireland the civil rights movement had set in motion events which would dominate political life for the remainder of the century and which became increasingly international in nature, involving this country's relations with Great Britain, Europe and the USA. And, the decision to accede to the then European Economic Community meant that Ireland was no longer a peripheral island but a full participant in the historic project of European integration. Both of these developments called for an entirely new approach to policy formation and implementation, for new institutional arrangements and for serious attention to the analysis of key issues.

The conviction that the Ireland of 1973 needed a forum for discussion of policy options in the new circumstances of EEC membership was shared by a number of individuals from different backgrounds, including this author. I was then working as Special Adviser to the Tánaiste and Minister for Health and Social Welfare and had become immersed in the complexities of the emerging EEC Social Policy initiative, led with characteristic vigour by Commission Vice-President Patrick Hillery.

With few available resources in terms of ideas and options, ministers and officials found themselves in a new policy environment. Across the broad range of EEC competences, enlargement was stimulating fresh thinking in economic, social and other areas. From adjustment to the Common Agricultural Policy to the evolving debates on regional development and international trade, the incoming member states needed to develop structures for policy analysis and innovation. The heads of government of the enlarging EEC, meeting in Paris in late 1972, had launched the concept of a Social Europe with implications for such issues as equality, vocational training, training for handicapped persons and worker participation. All member states were challenged to contribute to the development of detailed policies within this political framework.

The Irish response to the social policy initiative is, of course, another story. It did, however, lead to such important institutional developments as the Combat Poverty Agency and the National Rehabilitation Board and to the stimulation of significant research work. The seminal efforts of individuals like Seamus O Cinnéide of Maynooth had put Ireland at the forefront of European thought and action against social exclusion. Irish political leadership, notably by the late Frank Cluskey, led to the establishment of the European Community programmes to combat poverty and to its major research component that continues to the present day. However useful these specific efforts may have proved, it was clear from the outset that the wider elements of European and international relations required a structured response.

The saga of the International Affairs Institute

On 26 June 1973, a meeting took place at the invitation of Brendan Clarke, then Communications Director of the ITGWU, to consider the establishment of an Irish Institute of International Affairs. Those present, at the ITGWU offices in Palmerston Park, Dublin, were Brendan Clarke, Mary Robinson, Frederick Boland, Sean MacBride and myself. On the basis of a paper circulated by Brendan Clarke, it was decided to draft an outline proposal and budget and rapidly to expand the group. And, with a significance that was not at the time appreciated, it was agreed that representations should be made to the Minister for Foreign Affairs on the question of a state subvention for the project.

The initial paper proposed an institute with the objectives of promoting informed public opinion, carrying out and publishing objective studies and liaison with the sources of study and information at home and abroad. It was to be a membership organisation, with start-up funding from the state and a continuing state subvention, but with the long-term intention of seeking finance from corporate sponsors and foundations.

The project gained momentum within weeks. The original group was rapidly expanded, although Sean MacBride did not continue to participate. Over the summer of 1973 work progressed on a number of fronts. An extensive Memorandum on the Objectives and Structure of the Institute was prepared under the direction of Brendan Clarke. Articles of Association were drafted by a group including Alexis Fitzgerald, Mary

Robinson and Patrick Keatinge, who was an early and active recruit. Another group, headed by Kieran Kennedy of the ESRI, commenced the preparation of a detailed budget, including consideration of staffing requirements. Contacts with the heads of the Irish universities led to the possibility of finding suitable, temporary accommodation in the Earlsfort Terrace premises of UCD.

An initial meeting took place with the Minister for Foreign Affairs, Dr Garret FitzGerald, who underlined the urgency of establishing an independent forum for research on international and European affairs and expressed strong support for the initiative. He argued that the institute should give priority to close links with the university system. The possibility of finding a basis for government funding, at least in the early stages of development, was discussed in some detail and sympathetically.

Brendan Clarke's memorandum began by underlining the fact that Ireland was unique in its failure to develop an institute for the study of international relations. The situation in a number of countries was summarised, with particular reference to funding, staffing and library resources. The pace of change in Ireland's international commitments was underscored together with the increased pressures on Irish civil servants and other representatives in a range of institutions and inter-governmental bodies. It was pointed out that there was no centre of thought in Ireland which could bring together 'for analysis and development, the concepts, the policies and the projections which various official and unofficial bodies separately promote in the world outside' (Clarke, 1973). The importance of interdisciplinary study was stressed, as was the need for the development of an authoritative body of scholarly work in international affairs.

The case for backing the project was given particular weight by reference to Patrick Keatinge's analysis of the needs of a modern Irish state in the conduct of its foreign policy

> The domestic environment in which Irish foreign policy is made remains at a fragmentary and relatively unstructured stage of its development. Irish political parties, and the parliamentary institutions through which they operate, have made even less impact on foreign policy than in most parliamentary democracies, and interest groups, while contributing to policy formulation, have not always

encouraged the evolution of coherent policy guidelines. Thus, apart from the sensitive area of Anglo-Irish relations, it is fair to say that the policy maker has, up to the nineteen seventies, been left largely to his own devices in meeting the challenge which the external environment represents. (Keatinge, 1973)

In a significant passage, the memorandum raised the relevance of what was described as the 'Chatham House Formula' referring to the working methods of the Royal Institute of International Affairs in London. This formula involved bringing together people from the public service, business, trade unions and other sectors of society in a dialogue with academic specialists. This was seen to be desirable to meet the perceived needs of the Irish policy community. An attempt was made to identify a research agenda for the institute, covering Irish-UK relations, EEC questions, the UN, the Third World, global economics, strategic issues and superpower relations and finally trans-national phenomena, including multinational corporations.

In November 1973, a critical meeting of the organising group took place at which key institutional decisions were finalised. A list of eighteen invited subscribers to the Memorandum and Articles of Association was agreed, with Dr Frederick Boland as chairman, Professor T. Desmond Williams as vice-chairman and Brendan Clarke as secretary. The group included representatives of the universities (UCD, UCC, UCG, TCD and NIHE Limerick), the main political parties and the Department of Foreign Affairs together with individual participants. The title of· the institute was 'Irish Institute of International Affairs (IIIA)/Foras Éireann le Gnothaí Idirnáisiúnta'. Efforts were quickly underway to finalise the legal, staffing and financial elements of an overall package capable of delivering the institute project.

Much had been done and many supporters of the IIIA had been recruited by the end of 1973. But events – Harold Macmillan's celebrated bane of the decision-maker – dealt a terminal blow to the initiative. The impact of the Yom Kippur War, and of the subsequent world oil crisis, on the finances of all European governments was severe and at least equally so in Ireland. Existing, and contemplated, spending plans were subjected to cuts and postponements across the board and the institute project became an unintended victim. In early 1974, it became clear that there was no prospect of government funding for the IIIA and, since this was deemed as essential in the start-up phase, the organisers found themselves effectively stranded. The generally bleak economic environment clearly made it impractical to seek private sector funding in place of the anticipated government support.

Enter the Academy

While the project was stalled – in itself a serious blow – the concept was by no means killed off. The core group of organisers remained closely in touch and looked for alternative roads forward. They were told that they were to be kept informed of developments and were given indications that alternatives might be identified within a reasonable time. The Minister for Foreign Affairs, Garret FitzGerald, retained his strong personal commitment, reinforced by the emerging European agenda and by the exigencies of the upcoming 1975 Irish presidency of the EEC Council of Ministers.

The decision of the EEC heads of government to ask the Belgian statesman, Leo Tindemans, to draw up a report on the future process of integration added new dimensions to debate among the member states. The leaders themselves resolved in 1974 to transform their periodic meetings into a more formal system, the European Council, the first such meeting taking place in Dublin in March 1975. The creation of a directly elected European Parliament underlined a new political imperative. The need for relevant, high quality intellectual back-up to national policy debate was evident.

Following the collapse of the initial effort, discussions began among interested individuals and, at an early moment, an institutional player took the stage – the Royal Irish Academy. Key individuals within the Academy discussed the institute idea with Garret FitzGerald and raised the possibility of using the historic and respected structures in Dawson Street as the focus for advancing the main elements of the project in a form which would have the necessary standing and which could mobilise participation in both academic and public service circles. The IIIA group was consulted and was given undertakings about its involvement in any RIA effort. Significantly, it was suggested that Patrick Keatinge would become secretary of the RIA body. It was understood that the RIA would envisage an appropriate mix of research, academic and publishing functions. Consideration of these questions continued through 1974.

In February 1975, the Council of the Royal Irish Academy made the formal decision to establish a National Committee for the Study of International Affairs, with Professor Patrick Lynch of UCD as convenor. This was seen as a significant advance and had broad support, including that of the original institute sponsors. It was to be given the public blessing of the Minister for Foreign Affairs in an Academy Discourse in June but, unhappily, events overtook aspirations. The RIA is obliged to inform the Department of Education, which is responsible for the Academy's funding, of any decision to set up a National Committee. News of the move into study of international affairs was not well received in Marlborough Street and an interminable delay ensued with some rather fraught correspondence between the two institutions on the rationale of studying international affairs.

For once, frustration led to positive action. The RIA Academy decided that their original decision was well founded and that, in the interest of swift action, an Academy Committee rather than a National Committee should first be launched. This was possible without further dialogue or disputation with the Department of Education and the Committee was launched in November 1975. This coincided with the delivery, somewhat belatedly, of the Discourse by the Minister for Foreign Affairs. Dr FitzGerald spoke on 'Irish Foreign Policy Within the Context of the EEC' and highlighted the need for Ireland ' to play a more active role than before in some fields and to influence in a limited, but nevertheless significant way, the evolving policies of the Community ...' (FitzGerald, 1975). He pointed to the real constraints on Irish foreign policy arising from the country's limited resources but underlined the achievements of even a small diplomatic staff in running a successful EEC presidency.

The Academy Committee was given a two-year period of office. It was also given a clear mandate to report back to the Council on: (a) the form and constitution of an entity which should be entrusted with responsibility for the future activities in the study of international affairs; (b) the framework for a programme of research; and (c) an estimate of the cost of a professional secretariat to support such a programme. A broad-based group of more than twenty persons was approached to serve on the Academy Committee. They included many of the IIIA organisers, among them Patrick Keatinge. The historian and former Secretary of the Department of Posts and

Telegraphs, Dr Leon O Broin, became the Committee's wise and energetic chairman.

In its two-year term of office, the Academy Committee carried out much valuable work and made a positive attempt to advance the quest for a structured forum for policy research in Ireland. A relatively superficial search of personal archives reveals a number of thoughtful and focused reports on key issues: organisation of the study of international affairs; the study of international affairs in Irish universities; and possible form and objects of an institute of international affairs. These – and a range of parallel inputs from individual members of the Committee – were discussed and debated

The Committee, with its strong university links, was able to bring together those academics with a real interest in pursuing the idea of systematic study of international affairs. Among those who contributed to the Committee's assessment of needs and opportunities were Patrick Keatinge (TCD), Tom Garvin (UCD) and Joe Lee (UCC).

Among the issues identified in the studies and deliberations of the Committee was that of fragmentation of resources. While several third-level institutions were offering courses in the various elements of international relations and individual academics were developing specialist knowledge in key areas, there was a perceived weakness arising from the need to reduce traditional disciplinary barriers, both within and between institutions. The study of international relations had to cross faculty boundaries, thus limiting the options for students. Given the limited resources available for this field of study the question was raised of the need for specially designated centres of inter-disciplinary study.

It was also noted that research output in international relations was minimal. This was seen to be very much a matter of inadequate resources since individual academics were overstretched in terms of teaching duties and lacked provision for paid sabbatical leave. In most cases, research came a poor third to the demands of class teaching and college administration.

A number of specific difficulties were identified and described overall as being the absence of essential facilities – research funding; specialist publication outlets; provision for interaction between academic researchers and practitioners; and specialised archive, library and reference facilities. These considerations led to the conclusion that attention should be directed to the creation of a specialist institute, within or without the university system. The example of the New Zealand Institute of International Affairs was advanced as a case study in both inter-disciplinary work among academics and inter-action between academics, researchers and the national foreign policy community.

Patrick Keatinge contributed to the Committee's deliberations by means of a well-focused survey and assessment of 'the organisation of the study of international affairs' in sixteen countries. This looked at research, teaching, and promotional supporting activities. The widespread existence of specialist institutes was noted and these were classified – big, general purpose; small, promotional; special aspect; and internationally based. The survey addressed key organisational features such as funding, staffing, facilities and publications.

All of this work was pulled together by a sub-committee that was requested to bring forward proposals for the future shape of an Irish institute. This was done in a paper produced in April 1976. The work of the original IIIA organisers was reflected in many of the details but a crucial element of the proposal was the suggestion that the concept be developed within the framework of the RIA. The alternative of an institute established as a separate legal entity was also put forward.

The paper proposed a relatively simple model for the institute with a Council; membership on a basis to be decided; a director, initially part-time; and finances to be sought from a number of sources, reflecting awareness of the flaw in the original IIIA scheme which relied too heavily on the availability of government cash. The importance of establishing a regular outlet for publication of research findings was also stressed. A draft budget suggested that the project could be launched for about £10,000 per year! In its final stage of development the annual budget would be in the region of £90,000 per year, with a full-time director and as many as eleven staff, including six research experts and a visiting senior research fellow.

The National Committee for the Study of International Affairs

Discussions within the RIA based on the deliberations of the Academy Committee led to a decision to follow the internal route. This time, the Council of the Academy was in a position to establish a National Committee for the Study of International Affairs on 21 February 1977. The Committee had sixteen members, with representatives from the six universities on the island and NIHE Limerick together with members from the Academy itself, ESRI, IPA, Confederation of Irish Industry, ICTU, An Foras Forbartha and the Department of Foreign Affairs. Dr Garret FitzGerald, who by this time had left office as Minister for Foreign Affairs, was invited to participate as an individual member. Three of the initial IIIA organisers – Brendan Clarke, Desmond Williams and Patrick Keatinge – were included. Dr Pierce Ryan, representing the Academy, was the first Chairman and Richard Sinnott, then with the ESRI, became secretary.

The RIA issued a statement in connection with the establishment of the National Committee:

> The purpose of the Committee is to create a forum in which those interested can discuss important questions relating to Irish participation in international affairs.
>
> Up to now, no obvious focus existed in this country for the various elements interested and involved in the study of international affairs. The universities and other third-level institutions provide valuable courses and are generating an academic background to Ireland's international relations. Our diplomatic representatives and personnel employed in international organisations constitute another valuable source of expertise. There is, however, a growing public interest, not necessarily purely academic, in the study of international affairs. This has been encouraged by our membership of the EEC and by the expansion of our diplomatic, trade and cultural links.
>
> As the Committee's work progresses, it is proposed that conferences and seminars will be held on topics of interest and that occasional papers will be published. It is also intended in due course to produce a Journal. (RIA, 1977)

The first Committee, in the period 1977-1979, firmly established itself as an active and forward-looking body which developed a strong work programme and gave due consideration to future expansion of activities. An inaugural annual conference took place in May 1978 on the theme 'An Irish Perspective on the Study of International Affairs' and a second was held in June

1979 on 'External Relations of the European Communities'. The Committee also organised a series of seminars at which papers were delivered to an invited audience. This initiative served two purposes: informing interested individuals on a variety of topics and providing a forum for the presentation of papers which could be considered for publication in a journal. In addition, the Committee has provided a suitable forum for round-table discussions with distinguished visitors from many countries and from international organisations. An annual forum for the presentation of papers by young academics has produced an amount of interesting work and given a useful opportunity to the next generation of experts in relevant fields of study.

The third annual Conference, in 1980, merits particular comment. I had become a member of the National Committee at the beginning of the year, in my capacity as international secretary of the Labour Party. I put forward the idea of a Conference devoted to a discussion of neutrality. This was a subject which for many years was regarded as a part of the political landscape but had never been seen as a matter for serious analysis. Nonetheless, interest in the concept – and its policy implications – was growing in both academic and political circles in the light of international and Cold War developments. The idea was accepted, and I was fortunate to be in a position to persuade the Finnish Social Democrat politician, Kalevi Sorsa (twice prime minister and several times foreign minister), to participate as a keynote speaker from a most interesting neutral country. The Conference, on 21 November 1980, was a considerable success with a large attendance, a number of very high quality papers and good discussion. However, hardly had the chairs in Jury's Hotel been stacked when controversy erupted. The entire venture was publicly denounced by no less a personage than Sean MacBride who, in an open letter, suggested that it had been planned conspiratorially by either, or both, British and American intelligence services to undermine Irish neutrality – 'more CIA than RIA' as one wit summed it up. This broadside, which provoked troubled debates in the senior reaches of the Academy, was one of a number of similar manifestations that led to a visiting academic writing a paper on the neutrality debate in this country under the title 'Almost Like Talking Dirty'.

Planning began at the very start for the production of a high quality journal to provide an outlet for scholarly contributions by academics, practitioners and other interested individuals. The first volume of *Irish Studies in International Affairs* was published in 1979 with the list of contributions including John Bowman on 'De Valera on Ulster 1919-1920: What he told America' and Patrick Keatinge on 'New Directions in Foreign Policy'. The journal has since been developed as an annual publication with a number of established features – publication of papers delivered to the annual conference and of a mixture of submitted and commissioned articles; review articles; and authoritative annual reviews of Ireland's foreign relations and Ireland's foreign aid activities. While the standard of contribution has reached and maintained a high level under editors such as Liam de Paor, Patrick Keatinge, P.F.Doran, John Bradley, Denis Driscoll and Michael Cox, the journal has never achieved a high circulation and tends to be confined to a limited audience including those academic institutions in correspondence with the RIA.

The National Committee became the focal point of a project of great significance in the study of Irish international relations when the idea was put forward by the Department of Foreign Affairs of publishing a multi-volume series of official documents on Irish foreign policy. The idea was proposed at a meeting of the National Committee in 1994 and enthusiastically endorsed. With the active support of the then Tánaiste and Minister for Foreign Affairs, Dick Spring TD, and of the Director of the National Archives, the project was approved by the RIA Council in 1995 and an editorial board was appointed, consisting of Professors Ronan Fanning (UCD), Dermot Keogh (UCC) and Eunan O'Halpin (DCU) with Dr. Michael Kennedy as executive editor. The 'basic aim is to make available, in an organised and accessible way, to people who may not be in a position easily to consult the National Archives, documents from the files of the Department which are considered important or useful for an understanding of Irish foreign policy' (RIA, 1995). The first two volumes, covering the periods 1919-1922 and 1923-1926 and running to 1100 pages of text, have already appeared under the imprint of the Academy.

While the National Committee did revisit the institute theme more than once this idea has faded into the background as its programme of seminars, conferences and publications became formalised and built up their own relevance and quality standards. The National Committee is today looking forward to its own silver jubilee in 2002 and has established its special place in the architecture of Irish foreign policy studies.

Whatever happened to the idea of an institute?

It was not until the referendum on the Single European Act in 1987 that the idea of an international affairs institute re-surfaced. Over the years following the setting up of the RIA Committee the originators of the IIIA concept moved on to other commitments and the routine involvements of many interested individuals increased as political, academic and business life became more complex and demanding. But, in the eyes of some, the underlying requirement had not gone away.

From the initial EEC referendum in 1972 until the negotiation and ratification of the Single European Act, Ireland's participation in the evolving European integration project had been carried forward by the momentum of economic policies and programmes. Agricultural subsidies and regional funding provided an apparently sufficient rationale for involvement and a relatively uncomplicated policy agenda. The prolonged period of European stagnation that was the outcome of the two oil crises was finally overcome by the arrival in Brussels of the Delors Commission in 1985 and the Iberian enlargement of 1986.

The Single European Act was the first substantial revision of the founding treaties. It confirmed the existence of the European Council as an institution and made a number of amendments seen as necessary to facilitate the '1992 Project' – the completion of the Single Market. These included the extension of Qualified Majority Voting in the Council and an enhanced legislative role for the European Parliament. And, most significantly for this country, it provided for the formalisation of the procedures known as European Political Co-operation, the forerunner of today's Common Foreign and Security Policy. The SEA was initially seen by the Irish government of the day, headed by Garret FitzGerald as Taoiseach, as largely technical and within the terms of the original constitutional amendment providing for EEC membership. The government therefore initially proposed that the Oireachtas would ratify the SEA simply as an international treaty. This view was rudely upset by the intervention of Raymond Crotty and the subsequent Supreme Court ruling that a constitutional referendum was indeed necessary because, in the view of a majority of judges on that bench, the implications of codifying European Political Co-operation by treaty changed the terms of Ireland's EC membership. The resulting 1987 referendum campaign was conducted at an extremely low level of debate and attracted less than 45 per cent of the electorate to the polling stations. Those who turned out approved the treaty changes, but the whole affair raised many questions on the depth of Irish commitment to European integration and the quality of information about, and understanding of, the many issues arising from it.

The enlargement of the European Community by the arrival of Spain and Portugal led in its turn to new debates on economic and social cohesion and on the political dimension of a growing international entity. The increasing likelihood of political change in the USSR and the Soviet Bloc as a whole and the beginnings of globalisation through world trade negotiations all added to the scope and scale of discussion of international matters. Inevitably, thoughts began to return to the fundamental arguments of Patrick Keatinge's 1973 book and to the idea of an institute.

The Institute of European Affairs

So it was that, in 1989, a small group of friends of Brendan Halligan, former MEP and general secretary of the Labour Party, began to meet to talk about setting up an institute to promote objective discussion of Ireland's policy options within an evolving European setting. It was agreed that this concentration on Ireland's European relationships was appropriate and reflected the correct priorities at the time. They quickly set about canvassing support for the idea in the belief that it might be one whose hour had finally arrived.

The early dynamics of this process were extraordinary. The group grew rapidly as individuals from the political parties, academia, business and media expressed interest and then commitment. An organising committee was swiftly established, with Brendan Halligan as chairman, and a regular schedule of meetings developed. Approaches to leaders in different fields drew immediate expressions of support, building up a remarkable 'autograph book' of endorsements. The early decision that funds should be sought from the private sector – to avoid the disastrous pitfall of the 1973-1974 pioneers – led to a fund-raising campaign in which the first major executive contacted responded by saying 'Come in. I have been waiting for you, and your idea to arrive for a long time!' Enough financial support was pledged in the initial drive to ensure an early start-up. And, critically, approaches to senior civil service figures, produced a mould-breaking decision by the Taoiseach of the day, Charles Haughey, to permit public servants to participate in the new Institute's study groups and deliberations.

Planning proceeded throughout 1990 with the production of the necessary legal documentation for the establishment of the Institute of European Affairs (IEA) and the preparation of budgets. Initial staffing was arranged and, crucially, premises were obtained through a generous arrangement whereby two of the founding members purchased what is today Europe House in Dublin's North Great Georges Street to be rented to the IEA with the option to purchase at the lesser of cost or market price at an agreed future date (this option has since been taken up, at cost!). The IEA set out its objectives very clearly from the outset:

> The Institute of European Affairs is an independent self-governing body which promotes the advancement and spread of knowledge on the process of European integration and, in particular, on the role and contribution of Ireland within Europe.

> The Institute provides a permanent forum for the identification and development of Irish strategic policy responses to the continuing process of European integration and to the wider international issues which impact on Europe. The main aim is to provide objective analysis of the key political, economic, social and cultural issues for those charged with representing Irish views within the European policy-making structures. This is done by facilitating policy discussion with inputs from all relevant sectors, assembling information on key topics and disseminating research results.

> As an independent forum, the Institute does not express an opinion of its own. The views expressed in publications are solely the responsibility of the authors.

> The legal form of the Institute is that of a company limited by guarantee and not having share capital. It is funded by annual membership subscriptions from companies,

> organisations, institutions and individuals. A number of
> foundation members enable the Institute to operate on a
> financially secure basis. (IEA, 1991)

Attention was directed at an early stage to the subject matter of
the Institute's policy research. The key to success in this
endeavour was the twin resource of civil service involvement –
helping to define and refine the agenda – and quality academic
contribution. The IEA enjoyed the input of senior personnel
from every government department involved in EU matters,
including the most sensitive such as Justice and Defence. On the
academic front the main players from all third-level institutions
were on board from the outset. In particular, the involvement in
the initial organising committee of Patrick Keatinge, Brigid
Laffan and Rory O'Donnell set standards which have since been
maintained.

The organising committee met for a celebratory lunch at a
Baggot Street restaurant during the 1990 Christmas season.
Over the festive table decisions were taken about the subjects
and shape of the IEA's first two publications. These were to deal
with the range of issues covered by the Intergovernmental
Conferences which were to lead to the Treaty on European
Union (Maastricht) and to the single currency project. A study of
'Political Union' was to be edited by Patrick Keatinge and an
analysis of the prospects for 'Economic and Monetary Union'
by Rory O'Donnell. These volumes, published in 1991,
contained contributions by the authors and Brigid Laffan,
Patrick Honohan, Edward Moxon-Browne and myself. They
were the first publications in a series that by now numbers
twenty-seven books and more than thirty reports together with
many newsletters, commentaries and updates and a periodical
documentary archive.

Speaking at the official opening of the IEA at its North
Great Georges Street premises on 23 April 1991, the Minister
for Foreign Affairs, Gerard Collins TD, referring to the
Intergovernmental Conferences then underway stressed the
need to 'examine all the complex issues involved and assess their
implication for Ireland and for the future development of the
European Community'. He went on to identify four basic
ingredients of a successful public debate on issues such as those
which arise in respect of Ireland's periodic European
referendums. First 'a clear understanding of all the issues
involved and of their implication for Ireland and for the

European Community whose destiny is inextricably linked to our own'. Secondly 'an awareness by the general public that the subject is of fundamental importance to their future prosperity and well-being'. Thirdly 'we require a body of articulate and lucid communicators capable of making even the most complicated issue seem straightforward'. Finally 'we need a well informed and objective media willing to devote time and space to a proper interpretation of what is being spoken and written …' (Collins, 1991).

A most important element in the development of the IEA was the input of Patrick Keatinge. Not alone was he a major player in the organising committee from the outset but much of the last ten years of his academic career were centred on the Institute for which he worked in a full-time capacity from 1993 to 1996 as senior research fellow. In that capacity he set up and chaired the Institute's Research Programmes Committee which sets the agenda for research activities and monitors progress from concept through to publication. The latest annual report of the Institute lists as many as twenty-three active projects. He also led the IEA's substantial analysis of the development and implications of the EU's Common Foreign and Security Policy. This led to the publication, in 1996, of his comprehensive study, *European Security: Ireland's Choices*, and to a series of detailed studies and summaries on the general subject area.

Concluding thoughts

The IEA has just celebrated its tenth anniversary. It is for others to assess its performance but it is worth quoting the view of the Taoiseach, Bertie Ahern, that its 'research is always oriented towards the real world concerns of policy-makers … the coming period will be important for Ireland and for Europe, and it is good that the IEA is here to take part in the debate. At a time of transition we need voices like the IEA's – voices which are clear and well-informed, sympathetic but honest' (Ahern, 2001).

The IEA project, with its emphasis on research and dialogue directed to the practical goal of national policy formation, fits with Patrick Keatinge's often-expressed views on the study of international relations in Ireland. The first words of the Preface to *The Formulation of Irish Foreign Policy* lament the fact that 'relatively little has been written about the substance of Irish foreign policy, and even less about the political and administrative setting in which it is made'. The IEA, although with a specific focus on Ireland's relationship with the European Union, can be seen to address both elements of that statement and, from the outset, every effort was made to ensure that both were on the agenda of the new institute.

The first effort to establish an institute failed to a considerable extent because of the concentration on government funding. The initial RIA effort was diverted by the need to obtain funding from the Department of Education. Therefore, the promoters of the IEA turned to the private sector to provide a stable organisational foundation. Nearly thirty years after the first meeting of the IIIA promoters there is an institute, although with a particular focus on EU matters. The third-level sector has expanded its activities and networks in important fields of research and policy debate. The government departments have strengthened their capacity. And, there is a growing capacity to utilise international know-how through structures such as the Trans European Policy Studies Association.

However, there remains a lack of comprehensive coverage of the many areas of policy studies arising in a complex international setting. Globalisation, environmental concerns, migration, water resources, regional crises across the world - the agenda is broad and challenging. It must be recognised and it must have a positive response in both the public and private sectors. There are two prerequisites: leadership and, as always, resources. It remains to be seen how an existing body such as the IEA may develop and what parallel institutions may emerge.

The resources question must be confronted by all relevant interests but in particular, by government. Ireland remains unique in its almost total failure to provide significant funding for public policy research. This may be put in context by referring to one or two examples in other European countries.

In Denmark, the Institute of International Affairs (DUPI), established by an Act of the Folketing in 1995, is devoted to 'the execution, promotion and co-ordination of independent research on international politics and Danish foreign policy ... (and) as an important link between Danish and foreign research in these fields'. DUPI has statutory independence in its professional work and receives an annual government grant of £1.13 million.

In Austria, the Renner Institute was established in 1973 under the 'Act for the Promotion of Civil Education' which provided that each political party represented in parliament should have a policy research capability. The Renner Institute is the institute of the Social Democratic Party, with annual funding of more than £15 million for a programme which includes extensive educational provision. Similar provisions exist in Germany with major state funding of renowned institutes such as the Konrad Adenauer Stiftung and the Friedrich Ebert Stiftung.

In the UK, the Economic and Social Research Council has a budget of £4 million for its extensive three-year research programme 'One Europe or Several?' which 'examines the contemporary processes of political, security, economic, social and cultural change across the European continent ...'. It comprises twenty-four research projects, ranging from 'Germany and the Reshaping of Europe' to 'National and Supranational Economic Policy to Correct Internal Disequilibrium Under EMU'.

Some form of public funding – on an inclusive basis – is needed to support and further develop efforts that can only go so far on the basis of membership contributions from private sources. The quest for an institute of international affairs has been a long and frustrating one with constructive and rewarding results, in the shape of the RIA National Committee and IEA. However, as the world beyond our shores becomes ever more complex and challenging there is even greater demand for incisive, objective and informed analysis of global issues and their implications for Ireland, its policymakers and its citizens. That remains an unfinished agenda item and one which will require the input of persons with the qualities and perseverance of Patrick Keatinge.

References

Clarke, Brendan (1973), Unpublished draft memorandum on IIIA project.

Collins, Gerard (1991), Address at the official opening of the Institute of European Affairs.

FitzGerald, Garret (1975), 'Irish Foreign Policy Within the Context of the EEC', Address to the Royal Irish Academy.

IEA (1991), Mission Statement of the Institute of European Affairs.

Keatinge, Patrick (1973), *The Formulation of Irish Foreign Policy*, Dublin, Institute of Public Administration

Royal Irish Academy (1977), Statement in connection with the establishment of the National Committee for the Study of International Affairs.

Royal Irish Academy (1995) Statement on Agreement to publish *Documents on Irish Foreign Policy*.

Ahern, Bertie (2001), Address to the Founders' Dinner, Institute of European Affairs.

Contributors

Ronald J Hill

Professor Hill is Professor of Comparative Government at Trinity College Dublin. His research and teaching interests centre upon Russian, Soviet, East and Central European politics and he has held previous posts as Senior Associate Member, St Antony's College, Oxford (1979), Visiting Fullbright Professor, Lafayette College, Easton, PA (1981-1982), Associate of Institute for Soviet and East European Studies, University of Glasgow (1988) and Fellow-in-Residence, Netherlands Institute of Advanced Studies. Professor Hill is General Editor of *Studies of Communism in Transition*, Edward Elgar Publishers, Style and Managing Editor, *Journal of Communist Studies and Transition Politics* and Editor of *Irish Slavonic Studies*.

Ben Tonra

Dr Ben Tonra is Deputy Director of the Dublin European Institute based at University College Dublin (UCD) where he is also Associate Director of the Institute for the Study of Social Change. Previously he was a lecturer with the Centre for European Studies at the Department of International Politics, University of Wales, Aberystwyth and from 1993 to 1996 he was a lecturer at the Department of Political Science, Trinity College Dublin (TCD). Dr Tonra's published work includes *Europeanisation of National Foreign Policies*, Ashgate, 2001; and *Amsterdam: What the Treaty Means* (ed), Institute of European Affairs, Dublin, 1997.

213

Eilís Ward

Dr Eilís Ward is a graduate of University College Galway, Northeastern University (Boston) and TCD. She is a former university lecturer, and currently is an independent consultant with Irish and international organisations in the areas of civic education, human rights and democratisation. She has worked in Central Asia, East Timor and Central America. She is contributing co-editor of *Contesting Politics: Women in Ireland North and South*, Westview Press, 1998 and has published on the areas of Irish refugee policy, women and political participation in Ireland and international dimensions of the conflict in East Timor

Ray Murphy

Dr Ray Murphy is member of the Irish Centre for Human Rights, Faculty of Law, NUI Galway. He is a graduate of NUI Galway, Kings Inns, Dublin University (Trinity College) and the University of Nottingham. He is a former practising barrister and captain in the Defence Forces. In the latter capacity he served with UN forces in Lebanon (UNIFIL) in 1981-1982 and again in 1989. He has worked for the OSCE, the EU, Amnesty International and the Irish government in human rights and election monitoring in Africa and in Europe. His main research interests include international peace operations and international humanitarian law.

Brigid Laffan

Professor Brigid Laffan is Director of the Dublin European Institute based at University College Dublin (UCD) and Jean Monnet Professor of European Integration within the Department of Politics at UCD. Her academic qualifications include a BCS (Limerick), PhD (Dublin) and a Diplôme de Hautes Etudes Européennes (Bruges) where she is also Visiting Professor. Professor Laffan is also a Council Member at the Institute of European Affairs (IEA), Dublin and an advisor on EU enlargement to the Oireachtas (Irish Parliament) Foreign Affairs Committee. Her publications include: *Integration and co-operation in Europe*, Routledge, 1992; 'The politics of identity and political order in Europe', *Journal of Common Market Studies* (1996); *The finances of the European Union*, Macmillan, 1996; *Constitution-building in the European Union* (contributing editor; Institute of European Affairs, 1996).

Helen O'Neill

Professor Helen O'Neill is Director of the Centre for Development Studies at University College Dublin. She obtained her BCom degree at UCD and her Masters and PhD in Economics at McGill University, Canada. She was President of the European Association of Development Research and Training Institutes (EADI) for two terms and was a founding member and Council Member of the Development Studies Association of Britain and Ireland for many years. Professor O'Neill is also a member of the Irish government's Irish Aid Advisory Committee and a member of the development correspondents group of the Development Directorat General in the European Commission. She has carried out assignments for a number of international organisations in more than one dozen countries in Africa and in the Trans-Caucasus region. Her most recent book (jointly edited with Professor John Toye) was *A World Without Famine*, Macmillan/St Martin's Press, 1998.

Martin Mansergh

Dr Martin Mansergh is Special Advisor to the Taoiseach. A graduate of Oxford University he subsequently joined the Department of Foreign Affairs. Since 1981 he has been the political adviser to three Taoisigh – Charles Haughey, Albert Reynolds and Bertie Ahern. In 1994 he was co-winner of the Tipperary Peace Prize (with Fr Alex Reid and Rev Roy Magee) for the part he played in brokering the first IRA ceasefire. Dr Mansergh was also part of the Irish delegation that negotiated the Belfast (Good Friday) Agreement.

Noel Dorr

Noel Dorr is a retired Irish diplomat. He served as Permanent Representative of Ireland to the United Nations in the period 1980-1983 (representative on the UN Security Council 1981-1982), Ambassador to London 1983-1987, Secretary (General) of the Department of Foreign Affairs 1987 to his formal retirement in 1995. Subsequently he has served as the Irish representative at official level for negotiation of the Treaties of Amsterdam 1997 and Nice 2001.

Bill McSweeney

Dr Bill McSweeney is a former Director of International Peace Studies at the Irish School of Ecumenics and Trinity College

Dublin. He was educated at Essex (BA), York (BPhil) and Trinity College Dublin (PhD). His teaching and research areas include International Politics, Irish Foreign Policy, Ethics in International Affairs, Politics of the European Union, International Relations Theory, Security and the European Union and Security Theory. His publications include *Security, Identity, and Interests: A Sociology of International Relations*, Cambridge University Press, Cambridge, 1999; *Moral Issues in International Affairs: Problems of European Integration*, Macmillan, London, 1998 (ed); *Ireland and the Threat of Nuclear War*, Dominican, Dublin, 1985 (ed); and *Roman Catholicism: The Search for Relevance*, Blackwells, Oxford, 1980. Further articles have appeared in the *European Journal of Sociology,* the *Journal of Peace Research and the Review of International Studies.*

Declan Kiberd

Professor Kiberd is Professor of Anglo-Irish Literature and Drama at University College Dublin with an MA and DPhil (Oxon). His research interests centre upon Synge, Yeats, Joyce, Beckett, post-colonial writing, Anglo-Irish culture and children's literature. His most recent book, *Inventing Ireland,* Harvard UP, 1996), has won three major literary awards.

Michael D Higgins

Michael D. Higgins is a sitting TD for the constituency of Galway East. He is Labour Party spokesperson on Arts, Heritage, Gaeltacht and the Islands and was previously Minister for Arts, Culture and the Gaeltacht during the period 1993-1997. He is formerly a statutory lecturer in Political Science and Sociology at University College, Galway, and Visiting Professor at the University of Southern Illinois. His second book of poems, *Season of Fire,* was published in 1993. He is currently preparing a new academic work on political theory and practice, emphasising the necessity for an integrated approach and stressing the hegemony of values. His educational background includes University College, Galway, Indiana University and Manchester University.

Miriam Hederman-O'Brien

Dr Miriam Hederman-O'Brien is Chancellor of the University of Limerick. She is Chairman of the Foundation for Fiscal Studies and the Irish Council for the European Movement. She is also a Director of the Irish Centre for European Law and the Advertising Standards Authority. Dr O'Brien completed her PhD at Trinity College Dublin and is a Director of Allied Irish Banks plc. Her publications include *The Road to Europe: Irish Attitudes 1948-1961* IPA, 1983; *The Clash of ideas: essays in honour of Patrick Lynch* (ed), Gill and Macmillan, 1988 and *Eastern exchanges: interchange of education, training and professional formation*, Institute of European Affairs, 1992.

Robert Fisk

Dr Fisk was born and educated in England and is currently living in Beirut. He is the Middle East correspondent for the London *Independent*. He completed his PhD in Political Science at Trinity College Dublin in 1985 and has received an honorary degree in journalism from the University of Lancaster. He was the Irish correspondent of the London *Times* based in Belfast between 1971 and 1975. From 1976 to the present he has been reporting from the Middle East. He has covered the Israeli invasions of Lebanon (1978 and 1982), the Iranian Revolution (1979), the Iran-Iraq war (1980-1988), The Soviet invasion of Afghanistan (1980), The Gulf War (1991), the war in Bosnia (1992-1996) and the Algerian conflict (1992- onward). He has been the recipient of the Amnesty International Overall Media Award, 1998, the British International Journalist of the Year Award (seven times, most recently in 1995 and 1996), the United Nations Press Award, 1986 and the Johns Hopkins SIAS-CIBA prize for international journalism, 1996.

Tony Brown

Tony Brown is an economic consultant and lecturer. From 1997-2000 he was Alternate Director at the European Bank for Reconstruction and Development (EBRD) for Ireland, Denmark, Macedonia and Lithuania. He was previously a lecturer in European Social Policy at the National University of Ireland, Maynooth (1991-1997), Special Advisor to the Minister for Tourism and Trade (1995-1997) and he served as Vice-Chairman of the Combat Poverty Agency (1984-1989). He was a member of the Royal Irish Academy's National Committee for the Study of International Relations (1979-1984 and 1992-1997) and was the International Secretary of the Irish Labour Party (1977-1997). His publications include *Report on EU Enlargement*, IEA, 1994 and 'Defence, Peacekeeping and Arms Control' in

Barrington and Dooge (eds), *A Vital National Interest: Ireland in Europe 1973-1998*, IPA, 1999.